THE WORK OF CHARLES AND RAY EAMES : A LEGACY OF INVENTION

Essays by

Donald Albrecht

Beatriz Colomina

Joseph Giovannini

Alan Lightman

Hélène Lipstadt

Philip and Phylis Morrison

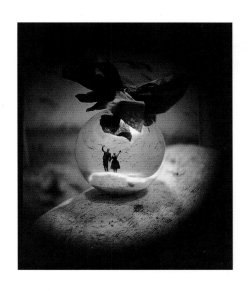

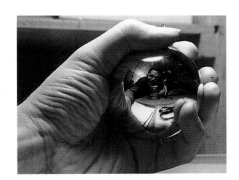

HARRY N. ABRAMS, INC., PUBLISHERS

IN ASSOCIATION WITH THE LIBRARY OF CONGRESS

AND THE VITRA DESIGN MUSEUM

THIS PUBLICATION ACCOMPANIED AN INTERNATIONAL TRAVELING EXHIBITION
ORGANIZED BY THE LIBRARY OF CONGRESS IN PARTNERSHIP WITH THE VITRA DESIGN MUSEUM.

FOR HARRY N. ABRAMS, INC.

Project Manager: **Margaret Rennolds Chace**
Editor: **Diana Murphy**

FOR THE LIBRARY OF CONGRESS AND THE VITRA DESIGN MUSEUM

Irene Chambers
Head, Interpretive Programs Office
Library of Congress

Alexander von Vegesack
Director, Vitra Design Museum

Rolf Fehlbaum
CEO, Vitra AG

Donald Albrecht
Exhibition Director and Catalogue Editor
Interpretive Programs Office, Library of Congress

Craig Hodgetts and Hsin-Ming Fung
Hodgetts & Fung Design Associates
Exhibition Designers

C. Ford Peatross
Curator, Center for American Architecture, Design,
and Engineering Project, Prints and Photographs Division
Library of Congress

Giulia Adelfio
Traveling Exhibits Coordinator
Interpretive Programs Office, Library of Congress

Eames Demetrios
Head, Eames Office, Exhibition Media Producer

Ralph Eubanks
Director of Publishing, Library of Congress

Blaine Marshall
Editor, Publishing Office, Library of Congress

Serge Mauduit
Chief of Collections, Vitra Design Museum

Phyllis Ross
Research Assistant
Interpretive Programs Office, Library of Congress

Mathias Schwartz-Clauss
Curator, Vitra Design Museum

Responsibility for concept development was shared by
Donald Albrecht and Hodgetts & Fung Design Associates,
in collaboration with the organizing institutions.

BOOK DESIGN

J. Abbott Miller, Scott Devendorf, Paul Carlos
Design/Writing/Research

On pages 2–3: Photographic sequence showing the process
by which the Eameses made their 1946 Christmas card

Library of Congress Cataloging-in-Publication Data
The work of Charles and Ray Eames : a legacy of invention
edited by Donald Albrecht; essays by Donald Albrecht [et al].
p. cm. Includes bibliographical references and index.
ISBN 0–8109–1799–8 (hardcover)
ISBN 0–8109–2752–7 (museum pbk.)
ISBN 0–8109–9232–9 (trade pbk.)
1. Eames, Charles—Criticism and interpretation.
2. Eames, Ray—Criticism and interpretation.
3. Design—United States—History—20th century.
I. Albrecht, Donald.

NK1535.E25W67 1997
745.4'4922—dc21
97–4086

Printed and bound in China
10 9 8 7 6 5 4 3 2 1

Harry N. Abrams, Inc.
100 Fifth Avenue
New York, N.Y. 10011
www.abramsbooks.com

Abrams is a subsidiary of
LA MARTINIÈRE
GROUPE

CONTENTS

One great American inventor and innovator, in the grandest sense of
the terms, was Thomas Jefferson—lawyer, architect, musician, political
thinker, linguist, and practical scientist. As the chief founder of the
Library of Congress, Jefferson believed that there was no subject "to
which a member of Congress may not have occasion to refer." This
principle, endorsed by the Congress, has guided the Library ever since.
It has assembled collections of matchless breadth and depth in all
formats, which now total more than 111 million items.

The wide range of the Library's holdings makes the Library of Congress
the ideal home for the collection of Charles and Ray Eames, which is
housed in three Library of Congress divisions: Manuscript; Prints and
Photographs; and Motion Picture, Broadcasting and Recorded Sound.
The collection reveals the Eameses as important American innovators,
thinkers, and entrepreneurs who operated beyond the traditional
boundaries of design.

Holding the world's premier collection of words, drawings, and images
by Charles and Ray Eames, the Library is pleased to join the Vitra Design
Museum, the repository for the premier collection of Eames furniture,
prototypes, and experiments, in presenting this retrospective exhibition,
The Work of Charles and Ray Eames: A Legacy of Invention. Drawing upon
the holdings of both institutions, this exhibition captures the essence
of the Eameses' creativity: the way they saw the world, the design
process they used, and the qualities they valued.

Charles and Ray Eames's notion was that modern industry should
get "the most of the best to the greatest number of people for the least,"
a philosophy that places them firmly in the tradition of American
innovation. It is entirely appropriate that the Eames archive should join
the collections of Alexander Graham Bell and Wilbur and Orville Wright,
among others, at the Library of Congress. As the Library preserves
the collection for future generations, may it inspire others to match the
Eameses in their creativity and imagination.

James H. Billington
The Librarian of Congress

When, in the early 1980s, I visited the Eames Office, at 901 Washington Boulevard in Venice, California, I had the feeling that I was meeting people who had succeeded in putting the ideals of the student revolution into functioning, everyday practice. Ray Eames, clothed almost like a Bavarian, with her hair in a bun, a radiant smile, and her gaily burbling voice, guided me through the labyrinth of rooms. From the lobby we crossed through the library into the studio, which was subdivided into various departments, and in passing, it seemed that I was being whisked into a world full of images from India, and at times into a circus. I walked by bulletin boards at which an exhibition was being prepared and entered a large, open-plan kitchen, where an old Asian woman greeted us with marvelous salads, vegetables, and tea. While we ate and Ray explained her projects, staff members or friends kept joining us at the table, said their hellos, and took part in the conversation or disappeared again in the direction of the film screening room, the workshops, or the archive.

That day, the variety of images, objects, people, and sounds in the Eames Office drew my attention incessantly and almost naturally from one event to another, and I remember well how surprised I was to find that the usual borderlines between work, relaxation, and leisure seemed to have been blurred there. When, late in the afternoon, I left the building with Billy Wilder and we drove with Ray through Venice in her black Jaguar, in my mind I was trying to find the key to this paradise.

In the years that followed, I met or visited Ray on various occasions. She advised me on the conceptual aspects of my exhibitions and brought about my relationship with Rolf Fehlbaum, CEO of Vitra International. At his request, immediately after Ray's death in August of 1988 I returned to the Eames Office and spent a few months there endeavoring to gain an overview of the oeuvre of Charles and Ray Eames, to assess it, and to acquire it for the Vitra Design Museum. I invited former staff members to meetings in the Eames Office and worked my way through the furniture storeroom and the endless pile of boxes and crates. Back then I realized that the paradisiacal setting I had sensed during my first visit was not simply the product of a choice community of the like-minded. Instead, a congenial driving force such as Charles Eames was needed in order to attract people from all the different areas of the world of work and integrate them into the overall project in keeping with their abilities. The main coordinates of the office were Charles's charisma, his curiosity, his enthusiasm, and his ability to develop and implement new ideas by trial and error, as well as Ray's artistically trained ability to elaborate the design and setting of objects in a completely harmonious manner. These qualities were the source of the energy that informed the atmosphere in the Eames Office, motivating everyone to give their absolute all in their work.

The Eames collection in the Vitra Design Museum comprises almost all their three-dimensional experiments and projects for series production, and it forms the core of the Museum's holdings. In their furniture Charles and Ray combined an innovative use of specific materials and technologies with the timeless shape of a perfect industrial product. But our collection can simply not do justice to the true scope of their work, which was far richer and more wide-ranging. Charles and Ray Eames were unique communicators. They created links between everything they worked on, be it furniture, films, toys, architecture, lectures, or exhibitions. It was thus fitting that they called the retrospective exhibition they and Marilyn and John Neuhart created toward the end of their lives *Connections*. The show embodied the spirit and the vision of Charles and Ray Eames, and these are examples for us to follow in many, many ways.

During the months I spent at the office at 901 drawing up a list of the Eames estate, I came into contact with C. Ford Peatross, the first person I would know at the Library of Congress. Ford, who organized the transfer of the two-dimensional section of the estate to Washington, and I soon became friends. Moreover, without the assistance of Don Albinson and Richard Donges I would have been lost when it came to technical questions. And the ongoing collaboration with Marilyn and John Neuhart has been a constant source of inspiration in my historical research. In the course of countless chats Billy Wilder has given me insight into his friendship with the Eameses, a friendship that stimulated the work of all three. Last but by no means least, Deborah Sussman, Elaine Sewell Jones, Johnny Johnson, and Parke Meek rounded out my impressions of the work of the Eames Office.

Lucia Eames wished for the estate of her father to be kept together in one institution to the furthest extent possible, thus ensuring that it could be processed by scholars over the long term. And this wish played a decisive part in enabling the Vitra Design Museum to acquire part of the estate. At the time I was happy to commit myself to involving American institutions in our work on the Eames collection and immediately after the acquisition visited the Library of Congress, the Henry Ford Museum & Greenfield Village, outside Detroit, and Herman Miller, the furniture manufacturer, in order to lay the foundations for a joint Eames exhibition. On a return trip to the United States I met with Irene Chambers, head of the Library's Interpretive Programs Office, who enthusiastically supported the project. Together with the Ford Museum and with the support of IBM, Herman Miller, and Vitra, we began to work out the conceptual and practical sides of the exhibition. After a national search Craig Hodgetts and Hsin-Ming Fung were selected as the designers. The team was completed with the hiring of Donald Albrecht as the exhibition's director. After two more years the Henry Ford Museum unfortunately had to leave the team owing to changes in its priorities. Despite the great distances, the numerous institutions, and the large number of people involved—not to mention the fact that communications predominantly took the form of phone calls and faxes—we have repeatedly managed to have truly animated discussions and reach a common consensus. The way that Irene Chambers has led the Library's end of the project has been an enormous help in this regard. Rolf Fehlbaum, the only member of the team to have been a longtime friend of Charles and Ray's, has been strongly committed to assisting us in our work. With his personal experience and familiarity concerning the issues involved, he has frequently made sure we headed in the right direction. We were also able to rely on the wisdom of an outside expert, namely, Christopher Wilk of the Victoria and Albert Museum, London. At a later date Charles's grandson Eames Demetrios also joined in, enriching the exhibition with an exciting media concept of his own. In this respect the whole project has evolved in a truly Eamesian fashion. For whenever Charles and Ray encountered something that triggered their interest, it led to a new project. Working, learning, and the joy of discovery were always part and parcel of their lives, and each product opened up a wealth of new perspectives.

Alexander von Vegesack
Director, Vitra Design Museum

ACKNOWLEDGMENTS

Great collections are the backbone of great exhibitions, and the Library of Congress's collection of Charles and Ray Eames's work is no exception. Donated by the Eameses at the request of Daniel J. Boorstin, then the Librarian of Congress, the collection comprises nearly one million items, including photographs, drawings, films, slides, and manuscript material—a dazzling representation of twentieth-century American ingenuity and its intellectual underpinnings.

This legacy of invention was the impetus for presenting an exhibition about the Eameses when, in 1990, Harold K. Skramstad, former president of the Henry Ford Museum & Greenfield Village, first mentioned the idea to me. But the concept moved toward realization only when Alexander von Vegesack, director of the Vitra Design Museum, visited the Library to discuss mounting an international exhibition on the Eameses. Their interest was energetically supported by C. Ford Peatross, curator of the Library's collections of architecture, design, and engineering, who had been instrumental in acquiring this remarkable body of work, and Alan Fern, head of the Library's Prints and Photographs Division. The Library agreed to collaborate, and the real work began. It has been an exciting, unnerving, stimulating, and remarkably complex process. I have loved the doing of it and especially all that I have learned.

Such a project cannot be achieved without the efforts of many people. At the Library, we wish to thank Maricia Battle, Katherine Blood, Christina Carbone, Rikki Condon, Jane Kogi, Madeline Matz, Sharon Ann McCarthy, Stephen Ostrow, Bernard Reilly, Peter Richey, Maria Santiago, Robert Vitrogowski, and Helena Zinkham. Margaret McAleer was particularly valuable in every aspect of the research.

The staff of the Library's Interpretive Programs Office is to be especially thanked. Ileen Sheppard-Gallagher helped launch the project, which was ably completed by Giulia Adelfio as well as Denise Agee, Jennifer Chisholm, Deborah Durbeck, Tambra Johnson, and Gwynn Wilhelm. Phyllis Ross provided excellent research assistance and much, much more. Donald Albrecht superbly directed the creative and administrative aspects of the whole project. His sense of humor saved the day many times.

At the Vitra Design Museum, in addition to Alexander von Vegesack's unfailing efforts and major contributions, we greatly appreciate the work of Mathias Schwartz-Clauss, who managed the project there, and Serge Mauduit, who contributed valuable insights into the Eameses' furniture. Rolf Fehlbaum has been a guiding force. His mind and his eye have led us to understand important aspects of the Eameses' legacy.

Herman Miller, Inc., has been a staunch supporter of the project, both financially and conceptually, and we wish specifically to acknowledge John Berry, Linda Folland, Mark Schurman, and Robert Viol.

In the creation of the book, we greatly appreciate the work of Ralph Eubanks, director of the Library's Publishing Office; Martha Kaplan, the Library's literary agent; Blaine Marshall, Nawal Kawar, and Margaret Wagner, who helped coordinate the publication. Natalie Shivers provided editorial assistance. Diana Murphy of Harry N. Abrams, Inc., sensitively edited the manuscript and completed the book, and we thank Margaret Rennolds Chace, Abrams's managing editor. The book's authors are to be congratulated for their scholarship and insight. We wish also to acknowledge the efforts of Janet Abrams, Paola Antonelli, and Peter Plagens. The contributors who provided appreciations collectively underscore the Eameses' enormous legacy. The book's thoughtful design is the work of J. Abbott Miller of Design/Writing/Research.

We also thank the following individuals who added their experiences and perspectives to the work: Robert Blaich, Barbara Charles, Mark Coir, William Davis, Judith Endelman, Andy Feighey, William Gartner, Mary Lynn Heininger, Elaine Sewell Jones, Pat Kirkham, Martin Manning, Parke Meek, David Paul, Robert Staples, Deborah Sussman, Judy Throm, Charles Vetter, and John Whitney.

Funding for the exhibition and book was provided by IBM, Herman Miller, Inc., Vitra AG, and CCI, Inc. Norma Baker, the Library's director of development, assisted in all fundraising efforts.

As is true of all exhibitions, the concepts, goals, and objects amount to little until they become one in a display format. Craig Hodgetts and Hsin-Ming Fung created this exhibition, capturing the spirit of the Eameses. Their staff, notably Doug Pierson and Yanan Par, provided excellent support.

Finally, we wish to thank the Eames family, especially Charles's daughter, Lucia Eames. We are also extremely grateful to his grandchildren Eames and Llisa Demetrios, and Lucia's daughter-in-law, Shelley Mills. They provided constant support, insight, and understanding. Eames Demetrios shared not only his talent as a film director but also his knowledge and documentation gathered over many years. Genevieve Fong and Russell Smith of the Eames Office are to be thanked as well.

Now that we know Charles and Ray Eames better than we once did, we trust that this exhibition and publication are the beginning of a growing, deserved interest in them and their work.

Irene Chambers
Head, Interpretive Programs Office
Library of Congress

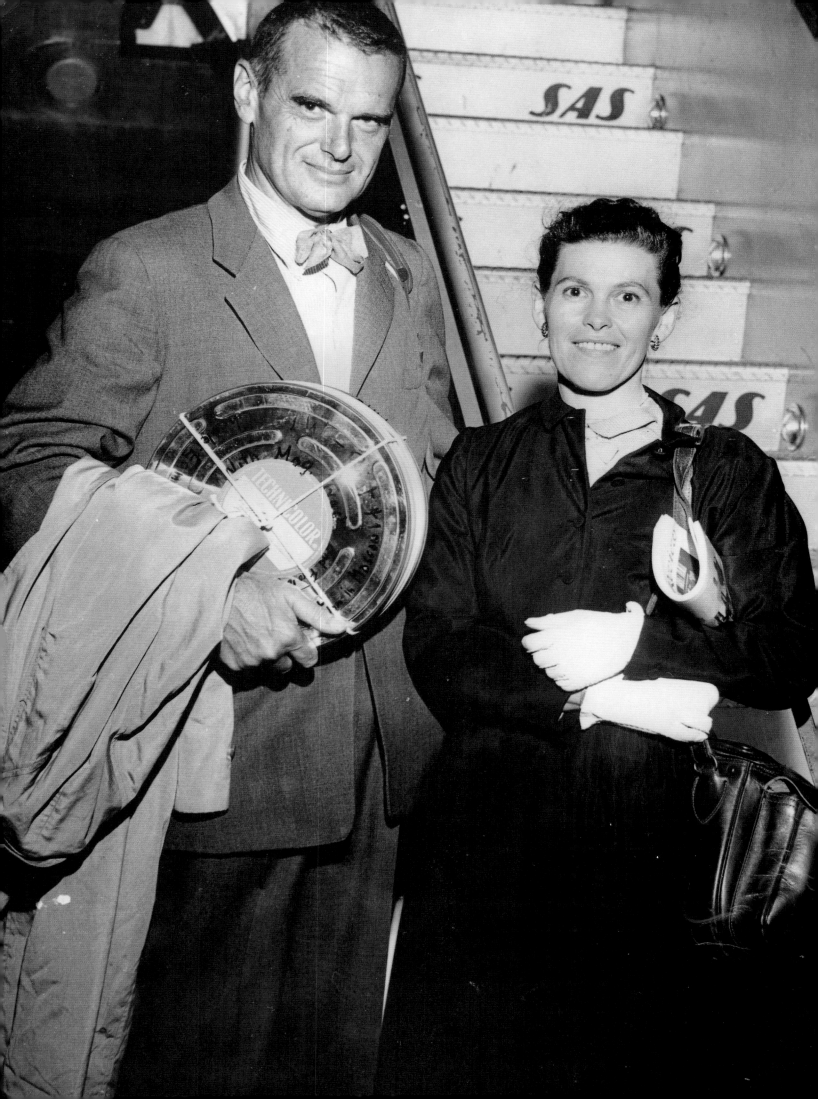

Introduction

Donald Albrecht

Charles and Ray Eames leaving Los Angeles for Moscow with the film to be shown at the 1959 American National Exhibition

Charles and Ray Eames gave shape to America's twentieth century. They witnessed firsthand many of its momentous historic events—such as the Depression and World War II—and in their lives and work they represented its defining social movements—the shift of the nation's attention from the East Coast to the West Coast, the rise of corporate and industrial America, the global expansion of American culture. In a rare era of shared objectives, the Eameses partnered with the federal government and the country's top businesses to lead the charge to modernize postwar America.

Charles and Ray Eames practiced design at its most virtuous and its most expansive: their furniture, toys, buildings, films, exhibitions, and books all aimed to improve society—not only functionally but culturally and intellectually as well. While designers with a social mission are now regarded with some skepticism, in the Eameses' time it was plausible that designers, businessmen, and government leaders had common goals, and their mutual aims were considered in their country's best interest. Designers like the Eameses had the ability to imagine America's future, and their major clients—the nation's government and corporations—had the political, financial, and technological capabilities to realize their vision.

The Eameses' success at interpreting contemporary America derived from their autobiographies. For their own histories were firmly entwined with the country's—formative events of their careers coincided with formative events of twentieth-century America. The Eameses in fact grew

up with the twentieth century. Both were born before World War I—
Charles Eames in 1907 in St. Louis and Ray Kaiser in 1912 in Sacramento.
Charles was raised in America's industrial heartland. As a young man he
worked for engineers and manufacturers, anticipating his lifelong interest
in mechanics and the complex workings of things. The Great Depression
was equally important in shaping his outlook. Charles's struggles to
develop his architectural practice were alleviated by a stint with the
Works Progress Administration, a New Deal model of the activist,
culturally beneficent government that the Eameses would advocate and
that would support their postwar projects.

While the Depression-era focus on art in the service of industry
enticed Charles, the modern art movements of the time prepared
Ray for their dynamic partnership. Ray's artistic leanings were fostered
by the theater, dance, and art programs of the college she attended,
the prestigious May Friend Bennett School, near Poughkeepsie,
New York. Upon graduating in 1933 Ray moved to Manhattan, as it was
poised to become the world's postwar capital of modern art. She
participated in the first great wave of American-born abstract artists,
exhibiting her paintings and studying with Hans Hofmann, one of
the decade's most important studio teachers and a vital link to postwar
Abstract Expressionism.

In New York Ray was introduced to the visionary concept of modern
design as an agent for social change. This philosophy also infused the
Cranbrook Academy of Art, outside Detroit, where both Ray and Charles
would gravitate in the late 1930s. Cranbrook forged a holistic view of
design, offering studios in architecture, art, urban planning, and craft
production. When Charles and Ray met, he was instructor of design,
and she was studying weaving, ceramics, and metalwork. Cranbrook's
message of better living through better design would imbue the Eameses'
sensibility for the remainder of their careers.

World War II provided new opportunities for the collaboration of art
and industry. Six months before the bombing of Pearl Harbor, Charles and
Ray married and moved to Los Angeles, at that time considered
America's final frontier. There they sought to start anew, away from the
social and professional distractions of Detroit, St. Louis, or New York.
Los Angeles proved an ideal arena in which to test the role of design in
a society forced to meet the war's unprecedented functional demands.
Within the circumstances of a global conflict dependent on airpower,
Los Angeles solidified its position as the aviation capital of the United
States. Major aircraft companies such as Douglas, Lockheed, and Vultee
employed many of those who emigrated to the Los Angeles region
in search of high-paying defense work. In the eyes of designers like the
Eameses, these companies also projected a compelling vision of the
future through the industrial architecture of their new aircraft factories
and the advanced materials and technologies of their flying machines.
"In the airplane," Charles Eames wrote shortly after arriving in Los
Angeles, "one feels strongly the appropriateness of its streamed lines
and they seem healthy and good."[1]

Within a short time, the Eameses and a group of inventive
collaborators found opportunities to put these words into practice,
designing and manufacturing molded-plywood aircraft parts, leg splints,
and litters for the federal government and the city's aviation industry.

These partnerships gave the Eameses access to funding and materials that would otherwise not have been available for civilian pursuits. Experiments with new molded-plywood techniques ultimately led to the design and manufacture of a line of chairs, tables, and screens that answered America's postwar demands for more flexible and casual ways of living. The most technologically and aesthetically advanced designs of their day, the Eameses' furniture proved to be revolutionary. Charles Eames, wrote the *Washington Post*, changed the way the twentieth century sat down.

The Eameses also sought to change the way the twentieth century lived. Responding to the pressing housing needs of returning veterans, they participated in the Case Study House Program, which sponsored the design and construction of a series of modern homes as prototypes for postwar housing. Established in 1945 by the avant-garde magazine *Arts & Architecture*, the program drew upon Los Angeles's progressive architectural traditions established by prewar modernists such as Richard Neutra and Rudolph Schindler. The Eameses' steel and glass house used standardized construction elements out of trade catalogues—some adapted from wartime use—and was intended to serve as a model for low-cost, do-it-yourself modern design. Instead it became a model of another sort. The house's kit-of-parts aesthetic prefigured the "high-tech" architecture of the 1970s, and its interior assemblages of handmade objects and folk artifacts successfully personalized modern architecture, offering a model of contemporary decoration and "organized clutter" for a younger generation of architects, such as the postmodernists Charles Moore and Robert Venturi.

The Eameses' career in the 1950s mirrored America's postwar shift from an industrial economy of goods and products to a postindustrial society of information and knowledge. Rather than furnishings and buildings, the Eames Office began generating communication systems in the form of exhibitions, books, and films. A series of media projects for the federal government signaled shifts in postwar America. The Eameses' majestic film project for the United States Information Agency, *Glimpses of the U.S.A.*, shown in Moscow in 1959, marked a thaw in the cold war. Their late-1960s proposal for a National Fisheries Center and Aquarium in Washington, D.C., presaged the rise of America's environmental movement. The office's last major project, *The World of Franklin and Jefferson*, celebrated the nation's Bicentennial with a book, three films, and an exhibition that traveled internationally. Projects such as these elevated the Eameses to the status of U.S. ambassadors overseas and cultural interpreters of the meaning of America at home.

Charles and Ray Eames practiced in the era when "what was good for General Motors was good for the country." They worked for such corporate giants as Westinghouse, Boeing, and Polaroid. For IBM— the "information machine" for whom they created more than fifty exhibitions, films, and books—they sought to demystify concepts of science and mathematics and familiarize the public with computers. As the Eameses were commissioned to convey larger and more complex amounts of information in short periods of time, they developed new media techniques. Their multiscreen presentations and slide shows fulfilled their belief that learning should be a sensory and pleasurable experience and that ordinary objects could convey lessons about major social and cultural issues. Devised for corporate and institutional clients, these presentations dazzled spectators at world's fairs. The Eameses' twenty-two-screen *Think*, shown at IBM's pavilion at the 1964 New York World's Fair, was their most ambitious and extravagant of these. Through all their efforts the Eameses advocated a humane modernism focused on man's ability to control the machine for society's benefit. "With the computer, as with any tool," Eames wrote in his script for the 1957 film *The Information Machine: Creative Man and the Data Processor*, "the concept and direction must come from the man."

The postwar era that nurtured the Eameses also witnessed a shift in the nation's center of gravity from the East Coast to the West Coast. The Eameses' move to Los Angeles was part of a wartime migration of more than fifteen million Americans in search of well-paid defense work. California, Oregon, and Washington, with their vast aircraft and shipbuilding industries, witnessed the most remarkable change: more than five hundred thousand people moved to the Los Angeles area alone. This migration resulted in economic and demographic shifts that permanently altered the nation's regional balance, giving the West Coast newfound status and independence. After the war Americans continued to be lured by the rich economy and mild climate of Southern California, and the region's population doubled between 1949 and 1965.

During those years Los Angeles and Southern California came to represent the American Dream to the world, proposing radical new ways of living, from patio homes to decentralized freeway cities. As captured in magazines from *Life* to *Vogue*, the Eameses enjoyed the fruits of postwar American life, combining living and working, indoors and outdoors, high style and accessibility, the best of contemporary technology with traditional handicraft. The Eameses and their work seemed free of historical precedent, feeding the notions of self-invention and self-reliance that have characterized both Los Angeles and America. And while they were never overt boosters of the city, the Eameses became emblems of postwar Los Angeles, a mythic place where mankind tamed the machine, nature, and history.

Today that era is regarded with ambivalence. In the days before Rachel Carson's environmental manifesto *Silent Spring*, an aura of progress and optimism surrounded most new materials and technologies. A booming economy seemed to offer the middle class unlimited horizons and a redistribution of wealth to the less fortunate. Inequalities certainly persisted, however, and books such as Vance Packard's *The Hidden Persuaders* and Sloan Wilson's *The Man in the Gray Flannel Suit* critiqued the nation's rampant consumerism. And if the era's emerging civil rights and sexual liberation movements helped realize America's egalitarian values, so too did they point toward the tumult and divisiveness of the 1960s. "The scary fact is that many of our dreams have come true," Eames said in 1971. "We wanted a more efficient technology and we got pesticides in the soil. We wanted cars and television sets and appliances and each of us thought he was the only one wanting that. Our dreams have come true at the expense of Lake Michigan. That doesn't mean that the dreams were all wrong. It means that there was an error somewhere in the wish and we have to fix it."[2] The Eameses' wholehearted belief that design could "fix it" and improve people's lives remains their greatest lesson. What is all the more remarkable about them—especially in light of our more cynical times—is how they achieved their ambitious seriousness of purpose with elegance, wit, and beauty.

Charles and Ray Eames were both of their time and ahead of it. Their marriage was one of creative talents as well as traditional domesticity. Their house exemplified the era's home-and-hearth focus, yet it was also a studio where they made many of their early films. They worked for corporate clients, but with their own agenda. And although they were often called upon by the American government to produce designs that represented the nation abroad, their impact went beyond national boundaries. Charles and Ray Eames belong to the twentieth century, yet their legacy will endure long into the future.

This publication was conceived as a multifaceted approach to the multifaceted careers of Charles and Ray Eames. Rather than focus on separate aspects of their work, the book takes a synthetic approach to the Eameses' projects, viewing them in the contexts of business, aesthetics, science, politics, and culture. The first essay, "Design Is a Method of Action," explores the Eameses' design agenda and its achievement in collaboration with major corporate clients. Joseph Giovannini's text, "The Office of Charles Eames and Ray Kaiser: The Material Trail," offers a provocative interpretation of their respective early careers. The Eameses' furniture designs are examined in two photo essays: one of newly commissioned photographs of pieces in the Vitra Design Museum collection and one of ephemera from the Library of Congress. "A Happy Octopus: Charles and Ray Learn Science and Teach It with Images" by Philip and Phylis Morrison and Alan Lightman's "A Sense of the Mysterious" examine the Eameses' fascination with science, especially their ability to communicate its history and principles to the general public through exhibitions, books, and films. Beatriz Colomina's text, "Reflections on the Eames House," situates the Eameses' own house within the context of the American and European architectural avant-garde after World War II. The final essay, by Hélène Lipstadt, "'Natural Overlap': Charles and Ray Eames and the Federal Government," looks at four projects for the American government, placing the Eameses' work in international as well as broad political contexts. Together, the essays present the Eameses' wide-ranging sensibilities and thus their immense contributions to the visual language of the twentieth century.

1. Charles Eames, "Design Today," *California Arts & Architecture* (Sept. 1941), 18.
2. This quotation appears in an article by Associated Press writer Saul Pett and was published on July 18, 1971, in the *Washington Star*, the *Los Angeles Times*, the *Grand Rapids Press*, the *Riverside Press–Enterprise*, and the magazine of the *San Juan Star*.

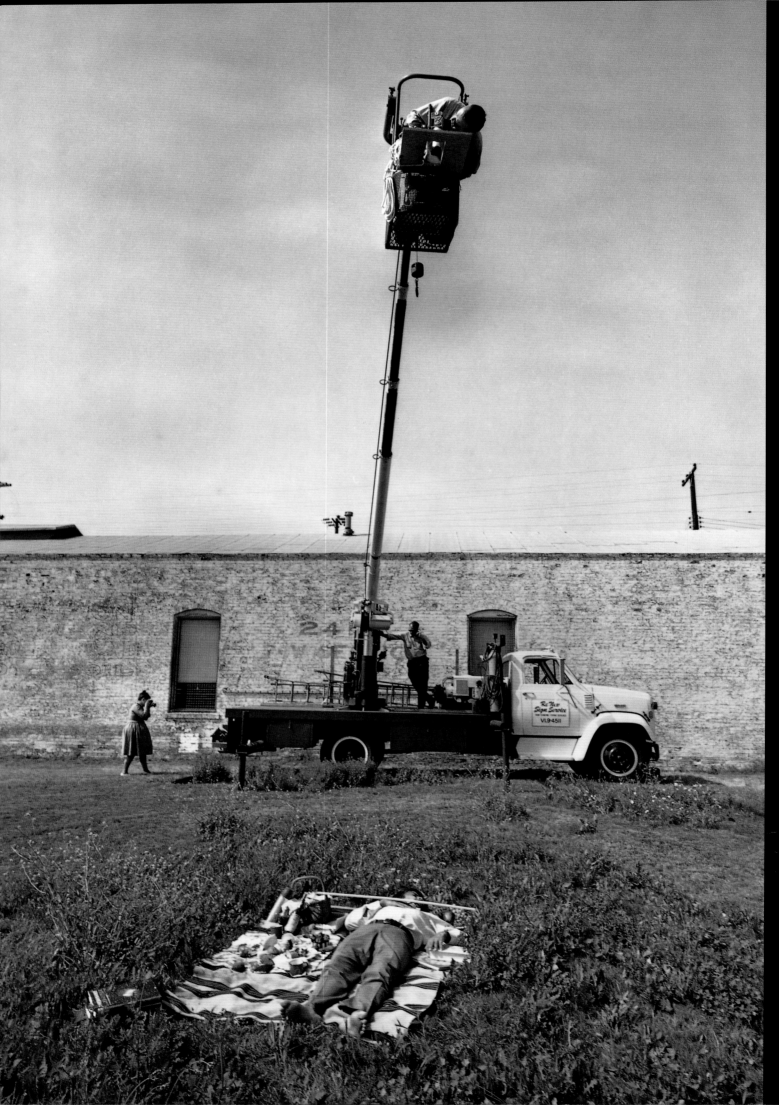

Design Is a Method of Action[1]

Donald Albrecht

Charles (in lift), Ray, and staff
outside their office filming the
picnic scene for the first version
of *Powers of Ten*, 1968

In the summer of 1954 Charles and Ray Eames needed a new car. Charles
had driven Fords since 1929. Together they had owned Ford convertibles
since 1941, the year they married and moved to Los Angeles from Detroit.
But wanting to buy a car in 1954 — when wartime austerity was only a
memory for many Americans — was difficult for the Eameses, who
considered the automotive industry's new two-toned models garish.
"We believe in the use of standard production models," Charles wrote
Henry Ford II, asking the company's president to help meet his need for
an "anonymous" black convertible with a natural top, an interior of tan
leather or good synthetic material, and a minimum of advertising logos.
In conclusion Charles thanked the corporate titan "for the many positive
things that bear the name of Ford."[2]

This simple one-page letter offers a key to understanding the many
positive things that bear the name of Eames. Like Ford's Model T, virtually
everything Charles and Ray designed solved a problem. Ford satisfied
America's desire for cheap and easy mobility. The Eameses[3] solved more
basic human problems, whether posed to them by clients or — as with
most creative geniuses — posed by themselves. Bill Lacy, their friend and
colleague,[4] summed up the couple's work: "There is no Eames style, only
a legacy of problems beautifully and intelligently solved."[5]

With the design of their own house the Eameses sought to solve the
postwar veteran's need for affordable shelter. Their mass-produced
chairs, tables, sofas, and storage units were beautiful yet inexpensive
ways to furnish the modern interior and meet the increased demand for
flexible, informal living. Their films, exhibitions, and books helped people

understand the complex workings of the world around them. As expressed by Charles, the Eameses' design credo—to bring "the most of the best to the greatest number of people for the least"[6]— resounded in their optimistic faith in modern industry and mass production. And in writing directly to Ford, Charles demonstrated his confidence that industry and designers could join forces and accomplish this uplifting mission.

Over the years the Eameses would infiltrate corporate America as few designers before or since have done. Starting as furniture designers, they became communicators who helped high-technology giants such as International Business Machines (IBM), Westinghouse, Boeing, and Polaroid explain themselves and their products. The Eameses only took on projects they were in sympathy with and only worked with companies whose objectives they shared—objectives that were often in tune with a booming American economy hungry for new consumer goods. The Eameses' range of corporate work was extraordinary: they received commissions from Herman Miller to design furniture, films, graphics, and showrooms; from Boeing to make a film promoting a proposed supersonic transport plane; from CBS for a series of short films for broadcast about popular culture; from Westinghouse for a film to illustrate the diversity of its product lines; and from Time Inc. to design lobbies for the new Time & Life Building in New York City's Rockefeller Center. The Eameses' protechnology stance also ensured a vaunted position developing dozens of exhibitions, films, and books for IBM over the course of two decades.

Charles and Ray Eames were especially well suited partners for America's progressive industries. When they tackled a project, they did so in a modern, "corporate" way, seeing their products and those of their clients through the multiple lenses of design, manufacturing, distribution, promotion, and use by the customer. Their relationship with their clients was often both personal and professional. Young and successful, the Eameses embodied a forward-looking perspective that fit well within the nation's expanding capitalist economy.

In order to understand the Eameses' achievements, one must understand the challenges they set for themselves and the processes— both conceptual and technical—they developed in their search for solutions. The Eameses' work can be viewed as a series of questions they posed to themselves: how to produce affordable, high-quality furniture; how to build economical, well-designed space for living and working; how to help Americans and people from other cultures understand each other; and how to make fundamental scientific principles accessible to a lay audience. Representative projects from the Eameses' vast body of work illustrate their solutions to these problems, which were often developed in collaboration with clients who shared key goals and provided the means to realize them.[7] This work reveals the ambition and scope of the Eameses' agenda—from the utilitarian chair to more complex issues of human perception, understanding, and knowledge—as well as the overlap of that agenda with corporate America's.[8]

Production Models for Modern Living

Recognizing the need, Charles Eames once said, was the primary condition for the practice of design.[9] At the outset of their careers together, Charles and Ray Eames identified the need for affordable, high-

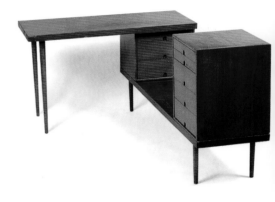

Storage cabinet and desk designed by Charles Eames and Eero Saarinen for the 1940 "Organic Design in Home Furnishings" competition at The Museum of Modern Art, New York

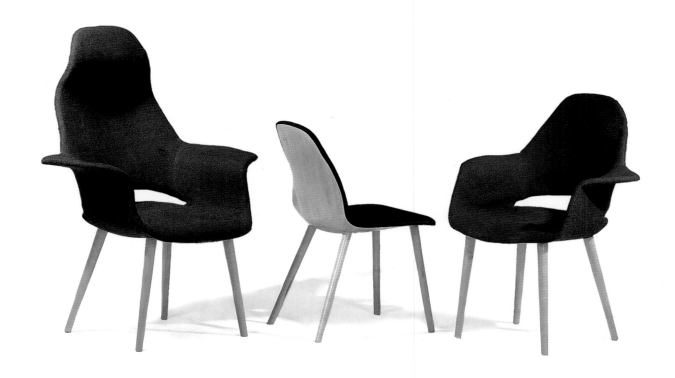

Chairs designed by Charles Eames
and Eero Saarinen for the 1940 "Organic
Design in Home Furnishings"
competition at MoMA

quality furniture for the average consumer—furniture that could serve a variety of everyday uses. For the next forty years, they continued to experiment with ways to meet this challenge, designing versatility and flexibility into their compact storage units and collapsible sofas for the home; seating for stadiums, airports, and schools; multipurpose furniture for dormitories; and stackable chairs for virtually anywhere. An ethos of functionalism informed all their furniture. "You usually find," Ray once said, "that what...works is better than what looks good. You know, the looks good can change, but what works, works."[10]

The Eameses' interest in creating functional furniture grew out of the egalitarianism of the Great Depression, when socially committed architects devised "new deals" to alleviate economic hardship through design. New York's Museum of Modern Art was especially active, promoting new ideas in housing for the poor and middle class and domestic products that were well designed and affordable. When Eames and architect Eero Saarinen won first prize in the museum's 1940 "Organic Design in Home Furnishings" competition, they and their colleagues advocated collaborations between designers, manufacturers, and merchants to create mass-produced furniture for the American family of moderate income. Edgar J. Kaufmann, jr., a representative of his father's trendsetting department store in Pittsburgh,[11] had proposed the idea for the competition, and twelve department stores planned to market the winning pieces. (Three companies, including the Haywood Wakefield Company, were set to manufacture the furniture, but the outbreak of war canceled the program.) Eames and Saarinen's winning entry included a sectional sofa, molded-wood chairs, and modular units that formed benches, cabinets, desks, and tables. The chairs were produced by a manufacturing method new to furniture: a light structural shell consisting of layers of plastic glue and wood veneer molded into softly curving three-dimensional forms. In their technical innovation, aesthetic brilliance, and social purpose, these chairs prefigured the Eameses' future furniture designs.

The organic design competition also propelled Charles and Ray into full-fledged membership in a coterie of architects, designers, curators, and other tastemakers who would become influential after World War II. The war had democratized modern architecture and design, as thousands of new armament factories and mass-produced houses for defense workers were built across the country. Their functionalist aesthetic came to embody the architecture of an optimistic Pax Americana. Military victory brought power and prosperity, thrusting Americans, their government, and their business corporations into an international spotlight. For many, modern design symbolized the country's new political and technological prowess. The machine-made gridiron of the steel and glass office facade—free of nationalist symbols and prewar traditions— became the established emblem of a new world order based on international business and finance.

A leading generation of postwar architects and designers—such as Saarinen, Eliot Noyes, Alexander Girard, George Nelson, and the Eameses—merged this postwar aesthetic with their own sophisticated sensibilities. The result was a humane, mass-produced modernism that appealed to America's corporate and institutional elite. The design equivalent of the suave and elegant Gregory Peck in Hollywood's *The Man in the Gray Flannel Suit*, the style struck a middleground between dollars-and-cents propriety and material luxury. Objects and fabrics made by hand tempered the machine-made. Buildings and interiors were colorful without being garish, progressive without being radical or threatening.

To this mix the Eameses added their own effervescent whimsy and playfulness, a "look" that was visible as early as their demonstration room for the Detroit Institute of Arts's exhibition *For Modern Living*, one of many postwar efforts that sought to convince middle-class homeowners to buy products of contemporary design. The Eameses' room featured an artfully random arrangement of a kite, a Mexican mask, and a pot of paper flowers, all hung from a rectangular grid of pegs. Such grids were one way contemporary designers positioned "natural" or handmade objects within the framework of man-made modernity. The "ESU" (Eames Storage Unit) made its public debut here as well. Its off-the-shelf materials and modular design contrasted dramatically with displays of straw baskets, clay pots, stones, and starfish. This collagist aesthetic of organized clutter—the studied contrast between old and new, rich and humble, foreign and familiar, mass-produced and handcrafted—became the Eameses' signature.

The Eameses had designed the ESU for the Herman Miller Furniture Company in Zeeland, Michigan, which began marketing the unit in 1950. By the time of the Detroit exhibition, they had already enjoyed a four-year relationship with the company. Herman Miller had entered the then-untried market for modern furniture in the early years of the Depression

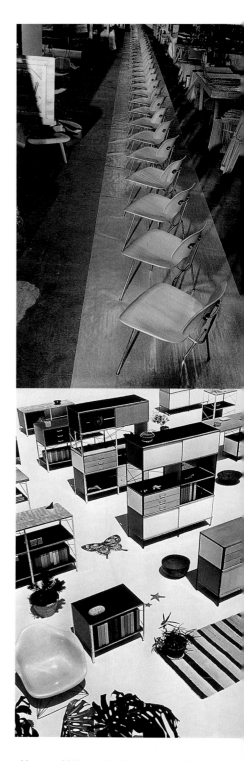

Herman Miller publicity photograph for the Eames Storage Unit, 1951

for "moral" reasons. George Nelson, later director of design for the company, remembered that "Gilbert Rohde, a pioneer New York industrial designer [and Nelson's predecessor], convinced D. J. De Pree, head of Herman Miller, that it was dishonest to manufacture period reproductions. De Pree, a deeply religious man committed to carrying his beliefs into everything he did, accepted Rohde's argument and in the mid-1930s switched production to pieces representing what he and Rohde considered 'honest' design."[12] Rohde also taught De Pree a lesson that would later mesh with the Eameses' philosophy: "You're not making furniture anymore," Rohde predicted, "you're making a way of life—a life style."[13]

Rohde and De Pree's decision to manufacture modern furniture proved prophetic. After the war, when Americans had money in their pockets and were looking for new ideas for a new America, modern furniture became an essential component of stylish offices and institutions. In 1945 De Pree hired Nelson as design director—Rohde had died in 1944—and one of his first acts was to take De Pree to The Museum of Modern Art's exhibition *New Furniture Designed by Charles Eames*. Eames furniture suited De Pree's criteria for good and truthful design: "durability, unity, integrity, and inevitability."[14] The furniture was also visually striking, fulfilling Nelson's recommendation that Miller adopt unusual designs that would attract free editorial coverage in print.

Within a few years the collaboration was formed between Herman Miller and the Eameses, who enjoyed wide latitude in developing new furniture ideas. D. J. De Pree's son Hugh recalled that the company never did any market studies of what they should produce. Charles Eames "had a good sense of what was needed...of what people ought to have. This was particularly true in chairs. I don't think that we have ever successfully given Charles a charge and said that we want such and such a product. When we've done it and he tried to respond, we've gotten something different than we started with."[15] The Eameses' initiative and inventiveness would set a pattern throughout their careers: they created what they found interesting, followed their instincts, and believed their good ideas would ultimately find a market.

Which at Herman Miller they certainly did. At the core of the Eameses' furniture ideas for Miller were four groups of chairs, distinguished by their unique aesthetic expression of materials and methods of manufacture: molded plywood, fiberglass-reinforced plastic, bent and welded wire-mesh, and cast aluminum. Each was conceived in response to functional and technical challenges. The first three groups were an attempt to create a chair that was a single, body-fitting shell that would be comfortable without expensive upholstery, could be quickly mass-produced, and could be shipped cheaply by nesting the shells together. The cast-aluminum chair was conceived as an indoor-outdoor seat—an all-weather, all-purpose chair that would be both beautiful and durable.

The great commercial success of the Eameses' furniture was in large part due to the pieces' adaptability to myriad markets—domestic, office, and institutional—as well as their multiple uses within different rooms of the home. In fact, many of the Eameses' furniture designs grew out of concepts and technical processes developed for the core group of chairs. A molded-plywood table and a screen to be used as a room divider were designed as companion pieces to the molded-plywood chairs. Wire-base

Molded-plywood chairs in factory, 1947

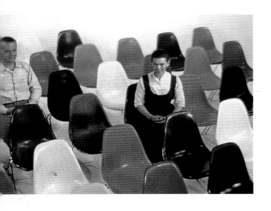

Charles and Ray in a scene at the end of *Kaleidoscope Jazz Chair* (1960)

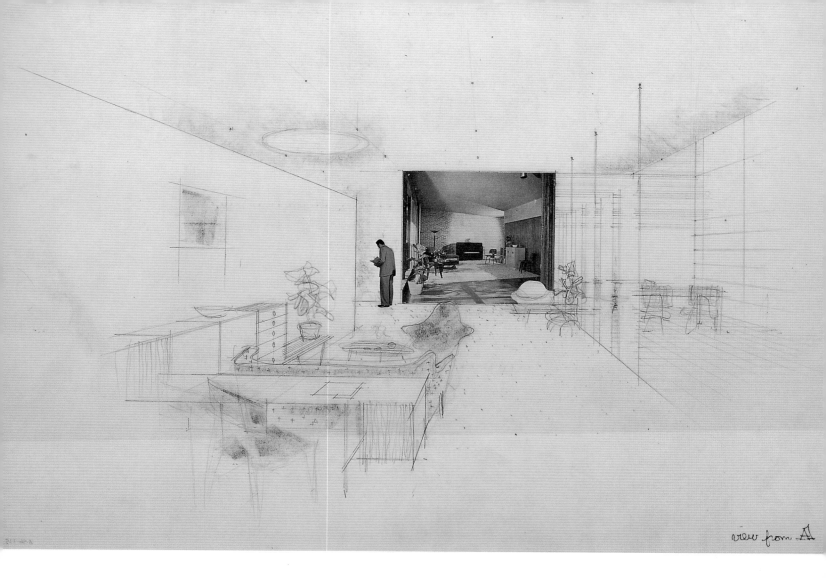

view from A

tables, designed in the early 1950s, were offshoots of the wire-mesh chairs. The fiberglass chair spawned the 1954 stadium seating and the 1961 La Fonda del Sol restaurant chair. The aluminum group's sling-seat concept reappeared in the interlocking seating, designed for Chicago's O'Hare and Washington's Dulles airports.

This adaptability was possible because much of the Eameses' furniture was made of standardized parts that could be combined into different arrangements, offering customers the flexibility to mix and match different pieces to suit their needs. The fiberglass chair, for example, was available in a broad range of colors, upholstery, and leg configurations—from a constructivist assemblage of wire struts to traditional wood rockers. The buyer actively engaged in the processes of assembling, arranging, and disassembling the Eameses' furniture, customizing the products for his or her own use.

Throughout their relationship with Herman Miller, Charles and Ray worked closely with the company to position their furniture as modern and progressive. Where advertising was concerned, the Eameses often art directed their own photo shoots and graphic layouts. They developed the settings for retail furniture displays and Herman Miller showrooms. These advertisements and schemes for merchandising decor represented the furniture as lively, colorful, and fun to own. The graphics were witty and often didactic, instructing potential buyers about the furniture's manufacturing process, its lineage from industrial

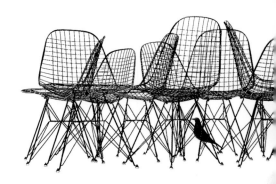

Photograph used in Herman Miller advertisement for Eames wire chairs, ca. 1951

Wire dress form photographed by the Eames Office, 1950

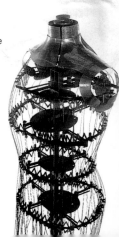

Interior perspective of Herman
Miller's 1949 Los Angeles
showroom, pencil on paper
with photocollage

technologies, and its diverse uses. While the Eameses' art direction
would certainly have appealed to architects and designers—who were
the first to purchase the furniture (Herman Miller initially sold the
plywood chairs for as little as $14.25)—institutions would later become
the leading buyers, making the furniture practically ubiquitous. This new
market opened in the early 1950s. Robert Blaich, then a young Herman
Miller sales representative, remembers contacting the purchasing officer
of his alma mater, Syracuse University, to try to sell the Eameses'
fiberglass chairs for dormitory and dining hall use (in 1952 the price of the
fiberglass chairs started at $30). The G.I. Bill of Rights for veterans'
college tuition had expanded the university market dramatically, and the
Eames chairs' reputation for durability (and Herman Miller's for
reliability) soon made the chairs institutional best-sellers.[16]

Beyond its successful sales record, the Eameses' furniture was—and
continues to be—beautiful. This quality, according to D. J. De Pree, was
the final criterion of good design. "It's part of that last 10%," he once
noted, "that Charles Eames always talked about being so hard to get."[17]

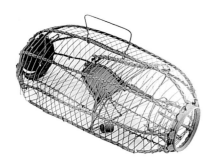

Wire rat trap photographed by
the Eames Office, 1950

What Is a House?[18]

Like the Eameses' furniture, their architecture promised good design for
minimal cost, as well as maximum flexibility through the use of
prefabricated, standardized parts. At the end of World War II the Eameses
were part of a larger movement of architects and builders seeking to
supply the veteran with affordable housing. In January 1945 the avant-
garde magazine *Arts & Architecture* announced the Case Study House
Program, which would sponsor the design and construction of low-cost,
single-family homes for the middle class as models of postwar living. The
houses were designed, and the majority constructed, between 1945 and
1966. The program was a conscious crusade to bring "the good life" to the
general public, integrating high and low art forms, modern materials and
construction technologies, craft and design. The program emphasized
mass-produced architectural components, furnishings, and accessories
as the ideal way to spread low-cost, high-quality modern design
throughout America.

Eames and Eero Saarinen collaborated on two Case Study houses,
one (#8) for the Eameses themselves and one (#9) for John Entenza,
editor and publisher of *Arts & Architecture*. The Eameses' house, created
for a meadow overlooking the Pacific Ocean, offered a model for
customizing standardized building parts to suit the couple's particular
needs—a home that would function as a "center of productive activities"
and a "background for life in work."[19] The Eameses ordered parts for one
house, a steel and glass box elevated on columns, but redesigned it when
the parts arrived in order to create a more spacious dwelling for about the
same amount of money. In its final iteration, the house comprised two
volumes—one for living and one for working—separated by an outdoor
courtyard and nestled into a hillside. The house used ordinary, mass-
produced materials that virtually anyone could buy. The Eameses said the
exterior steel framing took a mere one and a half days to complete. With
its kit-of-parts, Erector set aesthetic, the Eames House symbolized the
liberating possibilities of technology.

The Eameses' dream of the truly do-it-yourself house was almost
realized in the early 1950s, when they were commissioned to design a

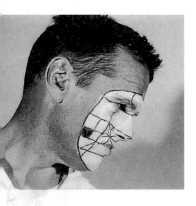

Charles wearing grid face makeup
for Halloween, 1953

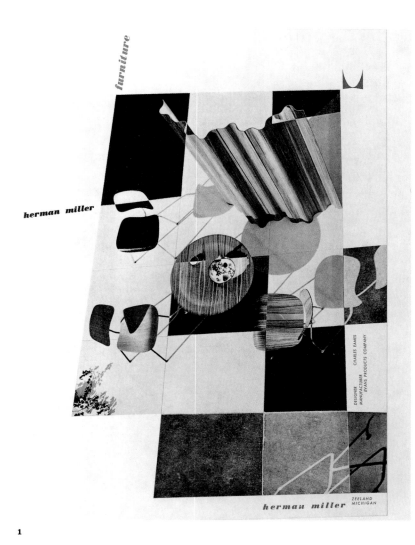

1

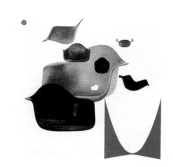

2

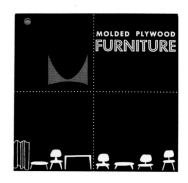

3

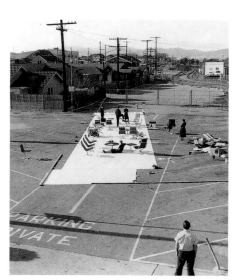

4

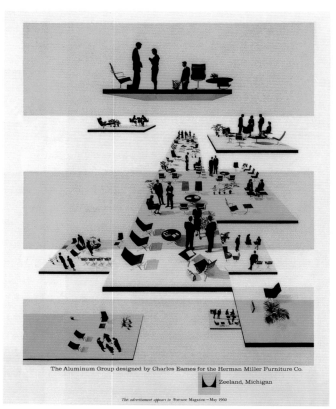

5

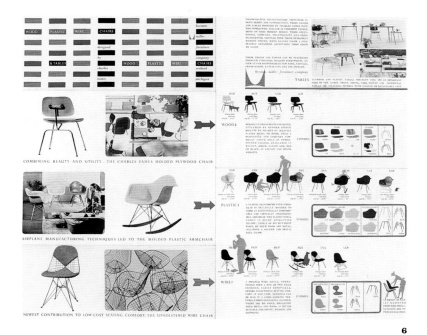

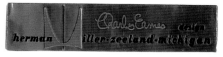

6

7

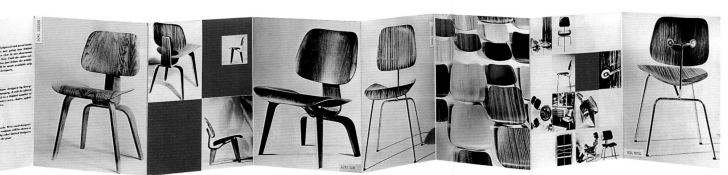

8

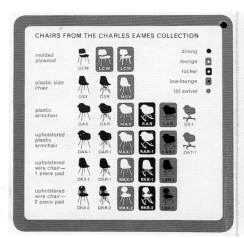

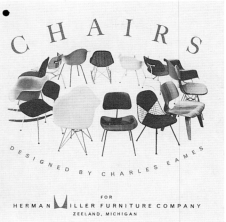

9

**Promotional material
designed by the Eames Office
for Herman Miller Furniture:**

1 Advertisement for plywood
furniture, 1948

2 Hang-tag for plywood furniture

3 Hang-tag for fiberglass chairs

4 Aluminum furniture advertisement,
Fortune, May 1960

5 Photo shoot for aluminum
furniture advertisement near
the Eames Office, 1959

6 Brochure designed to promote
plywood, fiberglass, and wire chairs,
ca. 1954

7 Aluminum label for furniture

8 Mock-up of furniture brochure,
ca. 1948

9 Hang-tag for Eames chairs,
ca. 1954

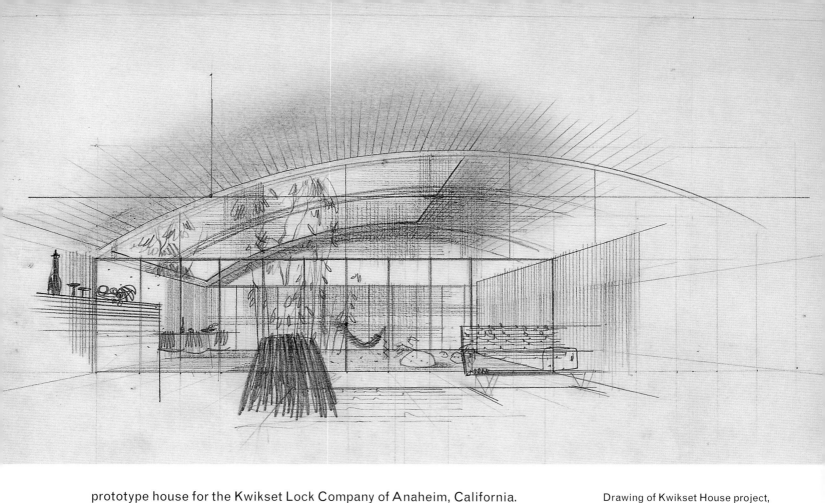

prototype house for the Kwikset Lock Company of Anaheim, California. (The house was never built.) Kwikset had already demonstrated an interest in modern design: the company's hardware was used in the Case Study houses, and it advertised in *Arts & Architecture* magazine. When it became interested in expanding into the booming Southern California housing market, the company turned to the Eameses to develop its prototypical house. Kwikset may have chosen them because of all the Case Study houses theirs was the one that most clearly advanced the off-the-shelf approach to architecture that Kwikset wanted to sell. A postwar wooden variant of the metal wartime Quonset hut, the Kwikset House was intended to be sold as a package of modular parts. The one-story building featured a curved roof made of sections of exposed plywood supported by curved, laminated plywood beams and wood columns. Like the Eameses' own house, the front facade was a gridded metal framework into which doors and windows were inserted. The open-plan interior used free-standing walls and cabinets to create a large living room, dining room, kitchen, and two bedrooms. Similar to the Eameses' own house and their furniture, the Kwikset House was an interactive product that encouraged owners to engage directly in the process of its construction and to customize the design for their own needs—a fundamental premise of the Eameses' philosophy.

Both the Kwikset and the Eames homes remained prototypes—neither was developed into mass-produced housing.[20] Their failure coincided with Charles's disenchantment with conventional modes of architectural practice.[21] "I guess I'm a cop-out," he said in retrospect. "Designing a whole building is just too demanding of attention to keep the basic concept from disintegrating. Builders, prices, materials, so many things work toward lousing it up. I've chosen to do things which one can attack

Drawing of Kwikset House project, interior with experimental wire sofa, detail, pencil and colored pencil on paper, ca. 1951

and better control as an individual. Furniture design or a film, for example, is a small piece of architecture one man can handle."[22]

While the Eameses moved away from standard architectural practice, they continued to develop basic tenets of their architecture in their toys and, especially, furniture. Their designs for storage units, for example, were fundamentally architectural, providing standardized modules that could be arranged to form room dividers, as well as to accommodate varied storage, residential, and work functions.

The Eameses' treatment of their own house prefigured other interests that came to dominate their practice—the architecture of display and information, with everyday objects as source material. The artfulness of the Eames House, in fact, lies in its use of ordinary things to humanize its cool, mass-produced modernism. Initially, Japanese tatami mats and pillows decorated the interior, but over time—certainly by the late 1950s—stark austerity evolved into elaborately staged domestic tableaux: a Thonet bentwood chair among Eames furniture, a Piero Fornasetti plate in a cluster of seashells, dime-store trinkets with Indian kites and Mexican pots, and other exotic objects.

For the Eameses, the objects in their home provided valuable lessons in eternal design truths. Simple objects from the past, such as toys, were for them historical artifacts that revealed the same quiet elegance, truthfulness to materials, and expert craftsmanship that they sought in their own modern, mass-produced work. "We were not *collectors* of toys," Ray told design historian Pat Kirkham. "We found things and kept them as examples of principles or aspects of design. We kept it to show it, to *use* it, to share it, to give insight to others and to ourselves."[23]

In the Service of Mankind

"This is a story of a technique in the service of mankind," Charles Eames concluded his 1957 script for the film *The Information Machine: Creative Man and the Data Processor*. Promoting data processing as the best technique with which to solve contemporary society's most complex problems, *The Information Machine* also solved another problem set by the Eameses: how to help one culture understand another. The film was commissioned by the Eameses' colleague and friend, Eliot Noyes, then director of design for IBM, and presented at the company's pavilion at the 1958 Brussels World's Fair. Launching the Eameses' career as cultural ambassadors and interpreters of American society, *The Information Machine* was explicitly about IBM computers, but its implicit message to foreign audiences was about America, a land of beneficent corporations and advanced technologies working "in the service of mankind."[24]

In this regard the Eameses served their country as well as IBM, expressing political ideas covertly through design. (In addition to their film's being shown in the IBM pavilion, their furniture was featured throughout the American pavilion.[25]) According to the United States Information Agency (USIA), the fair was intended to present informality, flexibility, and a sense of humor as the defining characteristics of American culture. The Eameses' film and furniture did just this; they were fresh, lively, and seemingly nonideological. The flexibility of their furniture embodied a notion of individual freedom suggestive of American democracy, in contrast to the authoritarian nature of Soviet communism. The film and the furniture advanced the idea that in America's market-

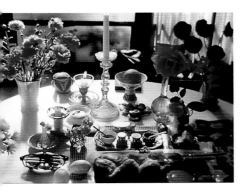

on this and the following page: Images of the Eames House from the office's slide collection

on page 31: Eames House, living room, 1993

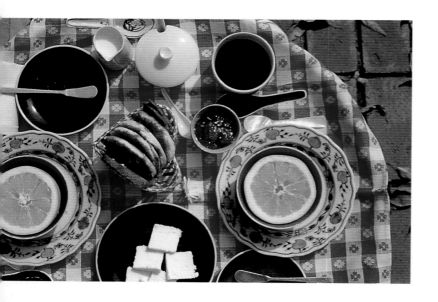

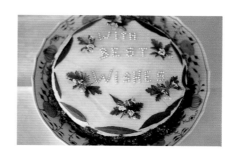

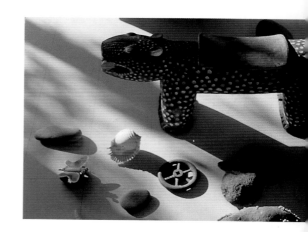

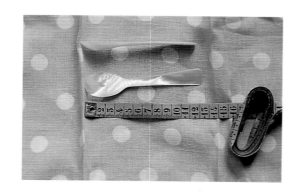

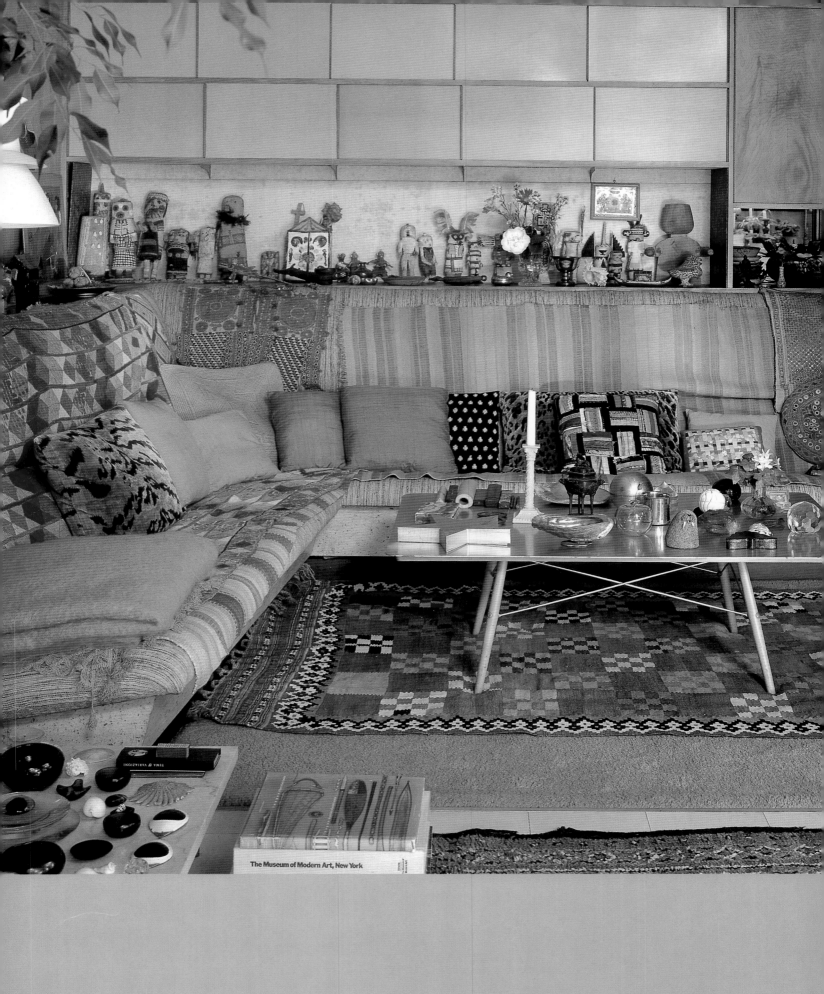

The Museum of Modern Art, New York

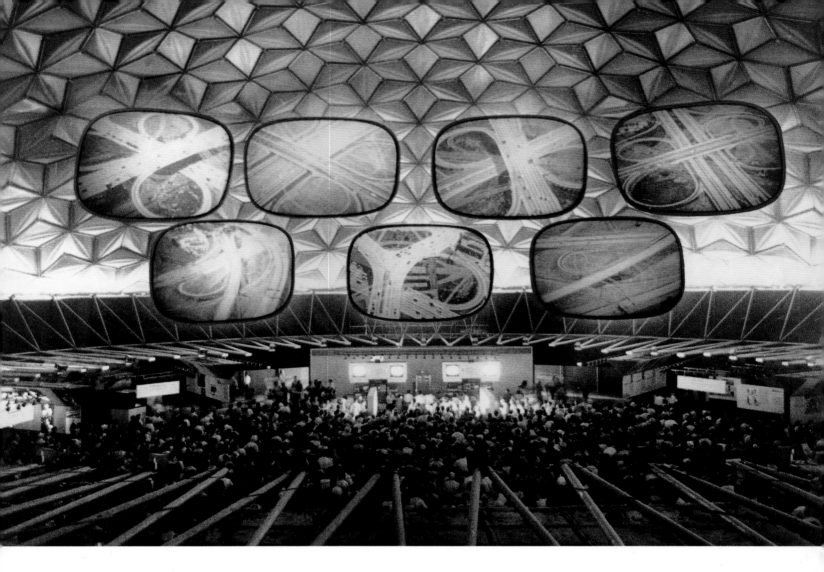

driven system, government and industry collaborated to spread the nation's material wealth.

The year after the Brussels World's Fair, the Eameses became involved in their most ambitious attempt to teach one culture about another: the 1959 American National Exhibition in Moscow—the first cultural exchange between the two countries since the Bolshevik Revolution. The Eameses received this commission at the request of George Nelson, who was hired by the American government to oversee the design of the entire project. Seeking to present a positive portrait of American life, the Eames Office created a seven-screen film, later entitled *Glimpses of the U.S.A.* Projected onto seven twenty-by-thirty-foot screens, *Glimpses of the U.S.A.* provided a dazzling portrait of postwar American values— egalitarian and consumerist— as twenty-two hundred images of supermarkets, freeways, skyscrapers, factories, and suburban housing communities sped by the viewer. (An IBM RAMAC computer sat beneath the screens and answered selected questions about the United States.) Like virtually all the Eameses' films, exhibitions, and books on cultural themes, imagery of daily rituals, vernacular architecture and landscapes, and ordinary objects promoted popular culture as the currency of exchange between nations. Eames later noted that the "multiple projection of images [in *Glimpses*]...was not simply a trick; it was a method to employ all the viewer's senses. The reinforcement by multiple images made the American Story seem credible."[26]

Glimpses of the U.S.A. projected at the American National Exhibition, Moscow, 1959

No country offered the Eameses such opportunities for cross-cultural lessons as India. Alexander Girard's exhibition *Textiles and Ornamental Arts of India*, presented at The Museum of Modern Art in 1955, inspired their fascination with the country.[27] Charles decided to film Girard's installation—an imaginary bazaar of brightly colored and fantastically patterned fabrics, dolls, pillows, and other decorative objects—in order to reach a wider audience than that able to attend the exhibition itself. This film was an example of the overlap of culture and politics that would increasingly characterize the Eameses' work.

According to Edgar Kaufmann, jr., the exhibition's director, who also worked with Girard to gather material for the show, the purpose of the exhibition was to improve Indian-American relations by arousing enthusiasm in the U.S. for the splendor of Indian achievements. This goal, Kaufmann reported, "was part and parcel of the Museum's program of international artistic exchange...and took its point from the urgency with which India today, independent and industrially burdgeoning [sic], was being courted by both parties in the cold war contest of world influence—the United States and Russia."[28] The Eameses' film served the needs of this goodwill program through its foreign distribution by the USIA and the philanthropic Ford Foundation.[29]

As a result of the film,[30] the Eameses were commissioned to research and write the "India Report" for the Indian government. According to the commission, they were to look for ways to prevent modern Western design and technology from overwhelming and destroying their country's traditional design culture. The purpose of the report, submitted in 1958, was to guide India into the future and recommend how the country could industrialize and make mass-produced goods without losing the quality of its traditional handicrafts. Funded by the Ford Foundation, the Eameses spent three months traveling throughout India, immersing themselves in its culture; photographing people, artifacts, architecture, and landscapes; and meeting with government officials, philosophers, sociologists, industrialists, artists, and teachers.

Among the Eameses' recommendations was the establishment of a kind of Indian WPA, a design institute that would be an arm of the government and that would study and assist the country as it underwent revolutionary changes. At the same time, it would help small industries produce quality consumer goods. The prototype for India's mass-produced goods, according to the Eameses, was the traditional Indian lota, or water jug. The design of the lota had followed an evolutionary process and was the product of "many men over many generations" responding to a complex set of considerations. In typical Eames analysis, these ranged from the functional to the sensual, the local to the global: the optimum amount of liquid the lota could carry; how it would be handled, transported, and cleaned; and how it felt and sounded "when it strikes another vessel, is set down on the ground or stone, empty or full—or being poured into." Thus, like the Eameses' vintage toys, the lota exemplified fundamental principles of design that should be maintained as the country's manufacturing structure moved from handicraft to mass-production. "The hope for and the reason for such an institute [of design] as we describe," the Eameses wrote in the report, "is that it will hasten the production of the 'Lotas' of our time."[31] The National Institute of Design was established in 1961 in Ahmedabad.

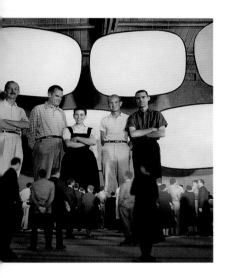

Staff members John Whitney, Charles and Ray, Parke Meek, and John Neuhart in model of the dome for the American National Exhibition in Moscow

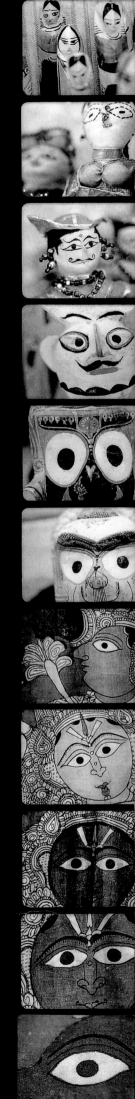

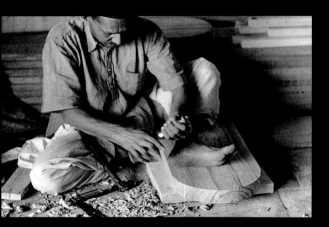

Woodworker photographed during
the Eameses' trip to India, 1964

Images of objects in the 1955
exhibition *Textiles and Ornamental
Arts of India* at The Museum of
Modern Art, New York, from the
office's slide collection

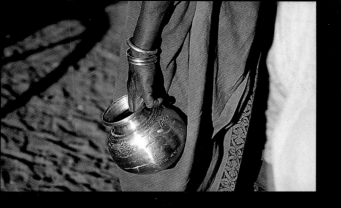

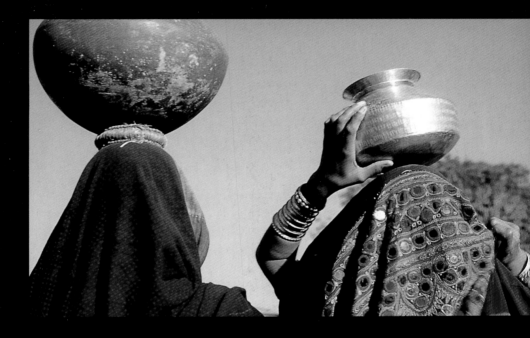

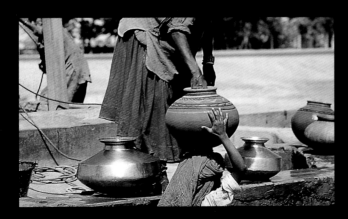

Images of Indian lotas from the
office's slide collection

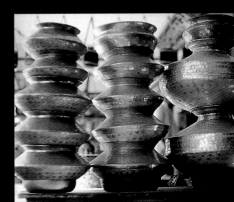

But the story of the lota was also relevant for Westerners. Some years later it was the subject of a slide show Charles presented as part of his Charles Eliot Norton Lectures at Harvard. As he told his audience: "Now, we can't bring the method of making a lota back with us, but there's one thing—kind of that [we]...did bring back from India—and when you make a trip like this, in a sense, the great virtue of it is that you get to see your own problems here a little bit."[32] To the Eameses, the evolutionary design of the lota was a credible story on a cross-cultural scale, proving the value of connections between past and present, handcrafted and machine-made, foreign and native. Not unlike Ford's Model T or an Eames chair, the lota was a standard production model for the service of mankind.

Information Machines

Fostering the universal understanding of what the Eameses considered socially beneficial science was another challenge they addressed in their work. In this effort, they produced approximately sixty films, exhibitions, and books, many of which were commissioned by corporations in need of the Eameses' expertise in helping people understand new technologies and their potential.

The Eameses' films for the Polaroid Corporation represented the near-perfect marriage of their interests with those of their client. Charles and Ray's philosophy of the educational role of everyday things led them to develop projects that would help people find beauty in the ordinary. "They really loved the world and how it looked," recalled MIT physicist Philip Morrison and author Phylis Morrison, his wife, "and they tried

Charles and Ray at the office, 1968

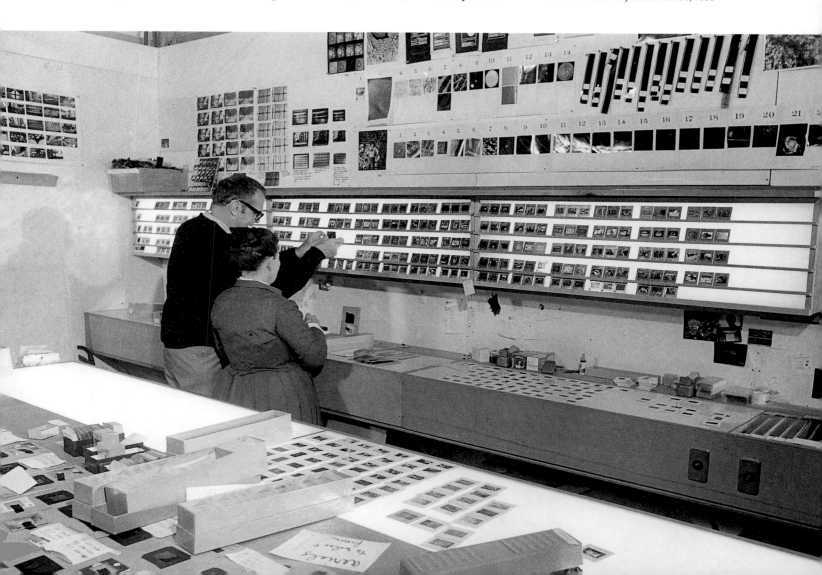

to understand why it looked that way and what it meant for people and what it meant to see beauty and to see form and to see the absence of those things and everything else and they just went around the world doing that for people—in buildings, and in text, and in film....That is what Charles and Ray did, they were always extending experience by bringing things together, by looking at them closely and all....And to some extent they bridged the gap between science and art."[33]

Multiscreen slide shows were perhaps their most effective method for presenting everyday things in new ways and relationships. Often using cinematic juxtapositions of close-ups, medium shots, and long views, these shows gave the spectator, in Eames's words, a "new depth of vision."[34] Encompassing an enormous breadth of subject matter—railroads, seascapes, road races, German pastry shops, movie sets, historic and contemporary architecture, marine life, and foreign cultures—the slide shows were assembled for school courses and lectures as well as for their clients' corporate events. For these elaborate presentations, the Eameses drew upon their meticulously catalogued collection of approximately 350,000 slides, their very own "cabinet of curiosity," which were gathered largely from photo jaunts around Los Angeles, trips, and research. Like objects themselves, the Eameses' slides and photographs were valuable media of information, essential connections to distant times, other places, and foreign cultures.

The ability to recognize the abstract beauty in everyday occurrences—and to convey that beauty to a wide audience—made the Eameses ideal partners in Polaroid's campaign to market its new instant cameras in the 1970s. Extending to everyone the pleasures of instant photography and instant motion pictures—immediate and relatively inexpensive ways to record the beauty of the everyday world—was the primary message of four films commissioned by Polaroid.[35] The first film, *SX-70* (1972), was a sales tool that functioned as part of the company's yearlong $20-million advertising blitz to introduce the technical functions and potential uses of the revolutionary SX-70 camera. The intended audience included Polaroid shareholders, dealers, photographic product manufacturers, and customers.[36]

With technology clients such as Polaroid, Charles set the office's creative path and functioned as its spokesperson and liaison to the world at large. To create *SX-70*, he and the office worked closely with Polaroid's technical and marketing personnel, as well as with close friend Philip Morrison. He also consulted with the inventor Edwin H. Land, Polaroid's founder and president, with whom he shared many philosophical affinities. Like Eames, Land never regarded his inventions as mere commercial products made in the pursuit of corporate profitability. He believed new technologies must be developed to benefit mankind and was convinced that industry "must have an insight into what are the deep needs of people that they don't know they have."[37] Both men began each project by defining problems to be solved, and they shared a desire to create products that could help average people gain significant aesthetic rewards. The SX-70 camera, Land told investors at Polaroid's 1972 annual meeting, "engenders a system that will be a partner in perception enabling us to see the objects around us more vividly than we can see them without it, a system to be an aid to memory and a tool for exploration."[38]

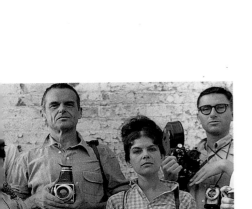

Eli Noyes (Eliot's son), Ray and Charles, and staff members Deborah Sussman and Glen Fleck outside the office with cameras, 1963

SX-70 combines simple, animated diagrams that explain and demystify the complex optical and chemical workings of the camera with close-ups of the camera's mechanical parts. From Land's standpoint—and perhaps from the Eameses'—the most powerful scenes were those of people photographing and sharing their images. These were visual embodiments of his extravagant but humanistic claims for the camera. "A new kind of relationship between people in groups," Land wrote in *The SX-70 Experience*, "is brought into being by the SX-70 when the members of a group are photographing and being photographed and sharing the photographs: it turns out that buried within us—God knows beneath how many pregenital and Freudian and Calvinistic strata—there is latent interest in each other; there is tenderness, curiosity, excitement, affection, companionability, and humor."[39]

Charles Eames's interest in science and technology can be traced to his youth, when he taught himself the principles of photography, and to his and Ray's experiences during World War II, when scientists were major players in efforts to win the war. Out of that conflict came the Eameses' plywood chairs—elegant and forthright applications of new techniques and technologies. The war also fostered networks of scientists working in concert with universities, corporations, and the government to meet society's urgent needs. Inventions and phenomena as diverse as radar, jet propulsion, and the atomic bomb quickened the pace of technology and permanently altered American life. After the war the Eameses remained committed to this scientific community and their positive notion of progress. They counted many scientists as colleagues and friends and joined their community—their "house of science," as the Eameses' 1962 film was entitled—as visual communicators.[40]

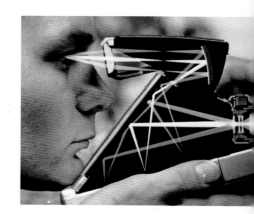

Frames from the film *SX-70* (1972), commissioned by the Polaroid Corporation

The Eameses focused many of their postwar scientific endeavors on the computer, the information machine that for them epitomized human efforts to solve problems by processing increasingly complex information. By the mid-1950s "computer"—or "that marvelous electronic brain," as Walter Cronkite famously dubbed it in 1952—was fast becoming a magical word as well as a somewhat frightening one.[41] Business executives rightly believed that the companies of the future would be run by electronic computers, while a segment of the public feared a world controlled by faceless machines.

Allaying these fears and helping promote computers to an international business community were the goals of IBM, then emerging as the world's leading computer manufacturer. The Eameses' involvement with IBM was part of a corporate design program, officially established in 1956 and guided by Eliot Noyes and graphic designer Paul Rand. Inspired by a similar effort at Olivetti, Italy's leading business machine manufacturer, IBM's new design strategy was the brainchild of chief executive officer Thomas J. Watson, Jr. With the program Watson sought to use vanguard design as a way to visually identify IBM's transformation into an international corporation. At the time the company was experiencing unprecedented growth as it moved from punch cards into new electronic calculating technologies. Also, in 1956, the younger Watson had finally taken over the company's reins from his father, and he wanted to define his regime as forward-looking in contrast to Watson Sr.'s more conservative business strategy and design taste. Watson hoped to provide a cohesive design identity for IBM's activities that embraced the company's products, architecture, interiors, graphics, exhibitions, and films.[42]

Benefiting from IBM's unique philanthropic-cum-promotional largesse, the Eameses enjoyed a two-decade relationship with the company, for which they created more than fifty films, exhibitions, and books. Their relationship with IBM officially began with such commissioned projects as the film *The Information Machine* for the 1958 Brussels World's Fair, and, with Eero Saarinen, the company's pavilion for the 1964 New York World's Fair. Here, their most significant contribution was a twenty-two-screen presentation extolling the problem-solving capacity of the computer. By the late 1960s the company developed an ongoing collaboration with the Eames Office, which designed a museum for IBM's headquarters in Armonk, New York (which was never built), and several exhibitions for its Corporate Exhibit Center in New York City. Accompanied by related books and films, these shows, installed on the ground level of one of Manhattan's most trafficked intersections, gave the Eames-IBM partnership tremendous publicity. Throughout this period IBM communications personnel made many visits to the Eames Office, which had its own direct phone line to the company. (As with so many of the Eameses' clients, their relationship with IBM reveals the stagecraft underlying the office's workings. Their voluminous files are filled with inter-office notes and correspondence tracking meetings held, food served, films shown, annotated and saved for posterity.) Certainly by the early 1970s IBM was a large and essential revenue source for the wide-ranging activities of the Eameses' office.[43] Charles and Ray also enjoyed personal relationships with many IBM employees, and became "members of the IBM family," in the words of Watson, who praised "Charlie" for his "contributions to my success and the company's success over the years."[44]

IBM's soft-sell approach addressed "the need for science to be better understood by the American public."[45] Its sponsorship of films, exhibitions, and books was intended to foster a climate in which computers would be perceived as acceptable and benign. In its ongoing film program in the 1970s IBM directed the Eameses to convey three points: IBM is an international company; technology is a basic economic resource—like land or water—for a country; and computer technology is being applied to improve the quality of life for people around the world.[46] The need to convey these benevolent messages had become all the more important for IBM in the late 1960s, when the government brought an antitrust suit against the company and social critics such as Ralph Nader stepped up their attacks on computers as dehumanizing forces.[47]

No matter how vociferous the attacks became, IBM instructed the Eameses to present its message in a "low-key, entertaining, human manner."[48] In their films the Eameses employed bright colors, bouncy music, and simple—almost childlike—animation to evoke the playful spirit of cartoons. Imagery such as hearts and flowers appeared in the films to humanize the computer. Charles and Ray even designed a special edition of their House of Cards for IBM, which allied science with game playing.

A major theme in all of the Eameses' endeavors for IBM was the beauty and elegance of scientific principles and the tools used to study and

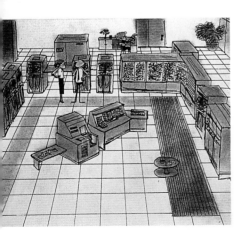

Frame from the film
The Information Machine (1957)

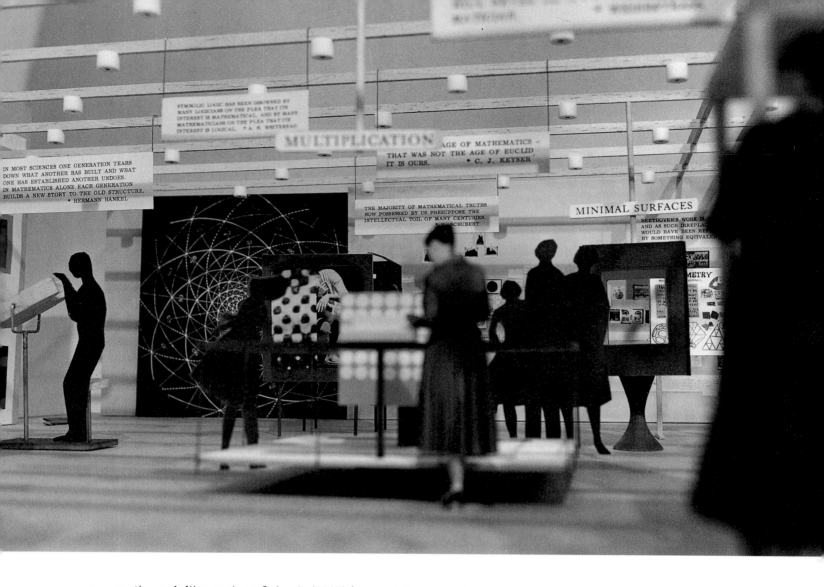

In most sciences one generation tears down what another has built and what one has established another undoes. In mathematics alone each generation builds a new story to the old structure. • Hermann Hankel

Symbolic logic has been disowned by many logicians on the plea that its interest is mathematical, and by many mathematicians on the plea that its interest is logical. • A. N. Whitehead

MULTIPLICATION

age of mathematics - that was not the age of Euclid. It is ours. • C. J. Keyser

The majority of mathematical truths now possessed by us presuppose the intellectual toil of many centuries. • H. Schubert

MINIMAL SURFACES

Beethoven's work is ... and as such irreplaceable ... would have been here ... by something equivalent ...

convey them. A film such as *Scheutz* (1967) focused the viewer's attention, through a series of intense close-ups, on the intricately designed workings of the hand-powered calculating machine—a kind of protocomputer—built by Georg and Edvard Scheutz in Sweden in 1853. The 1972 exhibition about the Polish astronomer Nicolaus Copernicus created for IBM's New York exhibit center was accompanied by a selection of beautiful objects used in Polish Christmas celebrations. Revealing science's complex integration of art, philosophy, and nature, these films and exhibitions successfully related the unfamiliar aspects of science with familiar and comfortable facets of everyday life.

IBM also underwrote the exhibition *Mathematica*, which the Eameses designed for the 1961 opening of a new wing at the California Museum of Science and Industry, in Los Angeles. The first major exhibition produced by the office, *Mathematica* translated complex ideas into simple images to make them understandable to the lay person. "Charles really had...this habit of abstract thinking," science historian I. B. Cohen said, "and it seems to me that was a very important quality....Charles did not really think in terms of words...he thought in terms of ideas, and ideas expressed themselves in images."[49]

Mathematica included two fifty-foot display walls and nine participatory displays dealing with topology, probability, the laws of minimal surfaces, projectile geometry, celestial mechanics, and multiplication. In one case the beauty of a set of geometric models

Conceptual model for the exhibition *Mathematica*, 1960

illustrates the jewellike precision of abstract mathematics: "Take a good look at these models," the sign above the case reads, "it can suggest the richness and variety within the discipline of geometry." The Eameses also brought to the exhibition a fun-house atmosphere with exhibits that made raucous noise. To present astronomer Johannes Kepler's theories of celestial mechanics, they devised an exhibit in which steel balls, activated by the visitor, revolve within the well of a plastic funnel, analogous to the movement of the planets around the sun. "One of the best kept secrets in science," Eames noted, "is how unpompous scientists are at their science, and the amount of honest fun that for them is part of it. In doing an exhibition, as in *Mathematica*, one deliberately tries to let the fun out of the bag."[50]

No exhibition, film, or book better conveys the Eameses' ability to make science come alive than *Powers of Ten: A Film Dealing with the Relative Size of Things in the Universe and the Effect of Adding Another Zero* (1977, first version 1968). The ultimate Eamesian expression of systems and connections, *Powers of Ten* explores the relative size of things from the cosmic to the microscopic. With the camera pulling back at the rate of 10^{10} meters per second, the film travels from an aerial view of a man in a Chicago park to the outer limits of the universe directly above him and back down into the microscopic world contained in the man's hand. *Powers of Ten* portrays the universe as an arena of both continuity and change, of everyday picnics and cosmic mystery. It also reveals the scope of the Eameses' ambition. Charles and Ray Eames started by designing a simple molded-plywood chair, and they ended by tackling the challenge of explaining the nature of the universe.

1. A set of questions asked by the Musée des Arts Décoratifs was the basis of the Eameses' section of the exhibition *Qu'est-ce que le <design>?* (*What Is Design?*), held at the Louvre in 1969. When asked if design is "a method of general expression," Charles Eames answered, "No—it is a method of action."
2. This Aug. 26, 1954, letter is in the possession of Lucia Eames, Charles's daughter; © 1997, Lucia Eames dba Eames Office. In 1975 *Fortune* magazine reported that Charles Eames drove a 1955 Ford convertible for eighteen years before he gave it away, and Ray drove a 1960 model for twelve years. Afterward he bought a small Mercedes and she a Jaguar sedan. Walter McQuade, "Charles Eames Isn't Resting on His Chair," *Fortune* (Feb. 1975), 99.
3. Throughout this essay I use the term "Eameses" in order to reinforce the collaborative nature of Charles and Ray Eames's design practice.
4. Bill Lacy is currently the president of Purchase College, State University of New York.
5. Bill Lacy, "The Eames Legacy," *Los Angeles* (June 1989), 77.
6. "A Designer's Home of His Own: Charles Eames Builds a House of Steel and Glass," *Life*, Sept. 11, 1950, 152.
7. These questions form the conceptual basis and organization of the exhibition that this book accompanies.
8. Certain quotations in this and other essays are from interviews conducted by Eames Demetrios, Charles and Ray Eames's grandson, with Eames staff, friends, and colleagues. They are part of the ongoing Eames Office Video Oral History Project, © 1995, Lucia Eames dba Eames Office.
9. Another question asked in conjunction with *What Is Design?* was "What do you feel is the primary condition for the practice of design and its propagation?" "Recognition of need," Charles answered.
10. Ray Eames, interview with Ralph Caplan, Feb. 24, 1981, Venice, Calif., Herman Miller archives, Zeeland, Mich.
11. Edgar Kaufmann's father had commissioned Frank Lloyd Wright to build him a house in Mill Run, Penn., in 1934; the result was Fallingwater. Kaufmann wrote to Barr in Jan. 1940, and the competition was inaugurated on Oct. 1, 1940. An exhibition related to the competition was held at the museum from Sept. 24 to Nov. 9, 1941.

12. George Nelson, "Introduction," in Mildred Friedman, ed., *Nelson, Eames, Girard, Propst: The Design Process at Herman Miller, Design Quarterly* 98/99 (Minneapolis: Walker Art Center, 1975), 7. Rohde's earliest modern designs for Herman Miller were featured at Chicago's 1932 Century of Progress exposition.

13. D. J. De Pree, interview with Ralph Caplan, Aug. 4, 1980, Herman Miller archives, Zeeland, Mich.

14. D. J. De Pree and Ralph Caplan.

15. Hugh De Pree, interview with Virginia Stith and Beryl Manne, Aug. 29, 1977, St. Louis County Dept. of Parks and Recreation.

16. Robert Blaich, telephone interview with Donald Albrecht, Sept. 16, 1995. Blaich graduated from Syracuse University in 1952 and was associated with Herman Miller from 1953 until 1979. From 1965 to 1979 he was vice president of corporate design and communications.

17. D. J. De Pree and Ralph Caplan.

18. "What Is a House?" is the title of an article by Charles Eames and John Entenza in the July 1944 issue of *Arts & Architecture* magazine. The issue was devoted to the subject of industrialized housing.

19. Charles Eames and John Entenza, "Case Study Houses 8 and 9 by Charles Eames and Eero Saarinen, Architects," *Arts & Architecture* (Dec. 1945), 44.

20. Solving the problem of the mass-produced postwar house was largely achieved by speculative developers such as Levitt and Sons, whose colonial-style tract houses most modern architects despised.

21. The Eames Office designed a house for film director Billy Wilder in 1950; it was never built. In 1954 the office designed a house for D. J. De Pree's son Max, which was constructed in Zeeland, Mich.

22. This quotation appears in an article by Associated Press writer Saul Pett and was published on July 18, 1971, in the *Washington Star*, the *Los Angeles Times*, the *Grand Rapids Press*, the *Riverside Press–Enterprise*, and the magazine of the *San Juan Star*.

23. Pat Kirkham, "Introducing Ray Eames (1912–1988)," *Furniture History* 26 (1990), 140–41.

24. The script is dated Dec. 16, 1957. Project Inventory, IBM/Office of Charles and Ray Eames, compiled by the Office of Neuhart Donges Neuhart Designers Inc., 1981. Project: *The Information Machine*, Narration—Part II, 5–7. The Work of Charles and Ray Eames (henceforth WCRE), Prints and Photographs Division, Library of Congress.

25. The Eameses visited the fair in 1958 and photographed people using Eames–Herman Miller furniture. They later converted these 35-mm slide images into a film, *Herman Miller at the Brussels World's Fair*, and presented it to the company. Herman Miller subsequently showed the film to customers and staff.

26. Charles Eames, panel discussion with Philip Morrison, "The Role of Films and Other Artistic Creations in the Teaching of Science," sponsored by the University of Colorado, July 20–29, 1964. In *The Proceedings of the Boulder Conference on Physics for Nonscience Majors* (Boulder, Col.: University of Colorado, 1965), 233–34.

27. Additional Eames projects about India include the 1965 exhibition *Nehru: His Life and His India*, which traveled to India, England, and the United States, and the unfinished 1972 film *Banana Leaf: Something about Transformations and Rediscovery*.

28. The Museum of Modern Art Archives, Record Citation ICE-D-5-54 (1/5): Preliminary Report on the Indian Voyage, from Edgar Kaufmann, jr., to Porter McCray, Nov. 30, 1954. The exhibition at The Museum of Modern Art was the basis for a smaller traveling show that the museum organized entitled *Modern Textiles and Ornamental Arts of India*. This show toured from Nov. 1955 through May 1958, going to Massachusetts, California, Rhode Island, Kentucky, Illinois, Michigan, upstate New York, Tennessee, Florida, Pennsylvania, Hawaii, and Texas.

29. The museum reported that by the end of 1956, the USIA and the Ford Foundation had purchased a total of twenty-five copies of the film for foreign distribution. The Museum of Modern Art Archives, Record Citation ICE-D-5-54 (4/5): Eames Film, Memo from Monroe Wheeler to Porter McCray, Dec. 7, 1956.

30. The connection was made largely through Mrs. Pupul Jayakar, who was India's representative for The Museum of Modern Art's exhibition and the narrator, with Edgar Kaufmann, jr., of the Eames film. The Eameses may also have been aided by Gira and Gautum Sarabhai, whom Kaufmann and Alexander Girard visited in India while researching the exhibition. The Sarabhai family were in the textile business and later involved in the National Institute of Design in Ahmedabad, where they lived.

31. Quotations are from "India Report—1958" (1979 reprint), Box 45, WCRE, Manuscript Division, Library of Congress.

32. The slide shows *India* and *Lota* were presented during the fifth lecture, on Mar. 29, 1971. The quotation is from transcribed excerpts of the lectures, dated Nov. 7, 1984, Folder 4, Box 96, WCRE, Manuscript Division, Library of Congress, © 1997, Lucia Eames dba Eames Office.

33. Eames Office Video Oral History Project with Eames Demetrios, Mar. 16, 1992, Cambridge, Mass., © 1995, Lucia Eames dba Eames Office.

34. Charles used this term in an interview with Digby Diehl, published in "*Charles Eames: Q & A*," *Los Angeles Times WEST Magazine*, Oct. 8, 1972.

35. The subsequent films are *Something about Photography* (1976), *Polavision* (1977), and *Sonar One-Step* (1978). Unfortunately, Charles's most democratic scheme for Polaroid was never realized. He proposed printing ideas of how to achieve better photography on the small card ejected when the user inserted a new package of still film into the SX-70 camera. These mini "sample lessons," free with the purchase of film, would enhance the user's enjoyment of photography and expand the new technology's aesthetic expression.

36. The camera was formally introduced to the public on the evening of Oct. 26, 1972, when the Eames film was shown to twelve hundred people assembled in the grand ballroom of Miami Beach's Fountainbleau Hotel. The film had its New York premiere on Oct. 30, 1972.

37. Mark Olshaker, *The Polaroid Story: Edwin Land and the Polaroid Experience* (New York: Stein and Day), 206.

38. Ibid., 254.

39. Quoted in ibid., 255.

40. *The House of Science* was commissioned by the Department of State to be shown in the U.S. Science Exhibit at the 1962 World's Fair, in Seattle. It was a multiscreen presentation on the history of science.

41. Walter Cronkite reportedly said this on CBS on election night, 1952.

42. Thomas Watson, Jr.'s ideas on the program are provided in his book, written with Peter Petre, *Father Son & Co.: My Life at IBM and Beyond* (New York: Bantam, 1990).

43. For example, *Fortune* magazine estimated that in 1974 the Eameses' office brought in gross revenues of approximately $750,000, of which $400,000 came from IBM and the American government toward the cost of the Bicentennial exhibition the office was preparing about Benjamin Franklin and Thomas Jefferson. McQuade, 99.

44. Thomas J. Watson, Jr., letter, to Charles Eames, Nov. 2, 1972, inviting "Charlie" and Ray to dinner at Watson's home in Greenwich, Conn., Folder 4, Box 48, WCRE, Manuscript Division, Library of Congress.

45. Jane P. Cahill, letter to Charles Eames, June 16, 1972, Folder 4, Box 48, WCRE, Manuscript Division, Library of Congress.

46. Charles G. Francis, letter to Charles Eames, Apr. 24, 1972, Folder 4, Box 48, WCRE, Manuscript Division, Library of Congress.

47. Eliot Noyes sent Charles an article from *The New York Times*, Sept. 2, 1970, describing a speech delivered by Ralph Nader, who claimed that without government regulation the computer would turn the U.S. into a "nation of slaves." In an attached memo Noyes commented that the article "relates to some of the things that we were talking about." Folder 3, Box 48, WCRE, Manuscript Division, Library of Congress.

48. Jane P. Cahill, letter to Charles Eames, June 16, 1972.

49. Eames Office Video Oral History Project with Eames Demetrios, Mar. 17, 1992, Belmont, Mass., © 1995, Lucia Eames dba Eames Office.

50. Charles Eames as quoted by John Neuhart, Marilyn Neuhart, and Ray Eames in *Eames Design: The Work of the Office of Charles and Ray Eames* (New York: Abrams, 1989), 255.

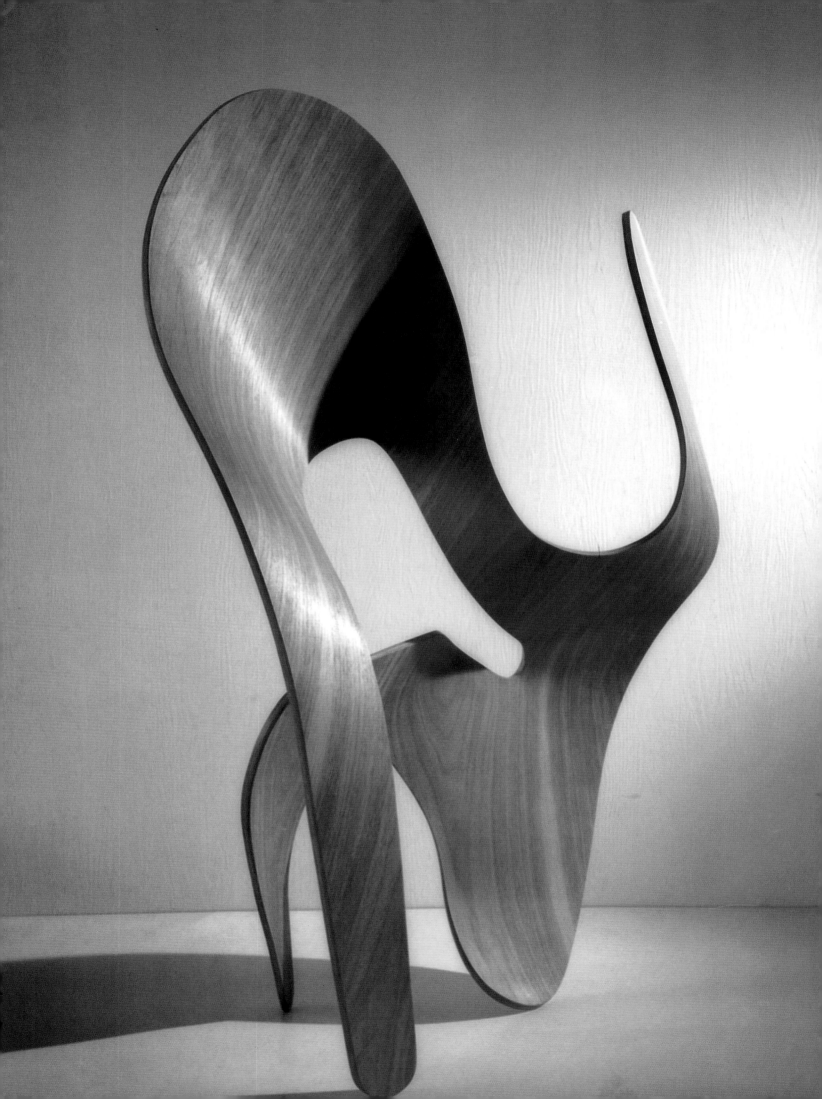

The Office of Charles Eames and Ray Kaiser

THE MATERIAL TRAIL

Joseph Giovannini

Molded-plywood sculpture
by Ray Eames, 1943

Ray Eames was, in the words of architectural historian Esther McCoy, "a sublime pack rat,"[1] and among the tens of thousands of objects, pictures, and documents she packed off to the Library of Congress from the office of Charles and Ray Eames is "Ray's Trunk," a collection of the things that passed through her life into her adhesive fingers until her momentous meeting with Charles in 1940. There are, of course, the juvenilia—the childhood sketch of a house with a sun blazing in the sky, papers neatly cut and folded like origami. But the accumulation gets especially dense, charged, and telling after she leaves her hometown, Sacramento, for the May Friend Bennett School, Millbrook, New York, in the fall of 1931, and continues as she settles in Manhattan after graduation in 1933. We find folder after folder of the playbills from scores of shows and concerts she attended in Manhattan, all the notes from several cycles of classes taken with Hans Hofmann, and flyers from many exhibitions—on Boccioni, Cézanne, Picasso, Matisse, Balthus, Miró, Léger, Lipchitz, Soutine, Calder, Vlaminck, Lehmbruck, Maillol, Archipenko. Dance was a passion pursued, with an emphasis not only on modern but also on classical Indian.

At an especially rich cultural moment in New York, when traditional and modern art confronted one another head-on through artists who were often effectively activists, Ray was not only a sponge, every pore open, but also a brilliantly placed player in the course of events for the rest of the decade. The paper trail in the trunk documents a material biography of how she voraciously fed her eye and mind the most stimulating material of her intense day, and how she developed her own work at the easel. Her formative decade coincided with the rooting and transformation of European abstraction in American artistic practice—Ray's firsthand, in-the-thick-of-it experience of that critical and pivotal moment in art history made her one of a privileged few.

Hundreds of letters to her mother, until her mother's death in 1940, confirm her pursuits and effectively constitute a diary. The trunk is a *Bildungsroman* of evidence that allows us to piece together her artistic development. Most important, it tells us what she knew and when she knew it by the time she met Charles at the Cranbrook Academy of Art in Michigan in 1940. Strangely, after that year, the trunk all but closes and little enters. Her life takes on his interests and direction, and as his career subsumes hers, its trajectory obscures her contribution to their partnership and the origins of her point of view.

Except for her obituaries and various biographical entries, very few—if any—articles have been written about Ray alone, while Charles magnetized the press and gathered almost all the accolades for decades. The misplaced attention unfortunately confuses analysis of their early work, throwing off the scent. Ray Kaiser, who enjoyed her own identity as an emerging artist in New York, nearly vanishes behind Charles. Inexplicably, The Museum of Modern Art's 1946 exhibition *New Furniture Designed by Charles Eames*, which unveiled their epochal furniture in Ray's home territory, omitted mention of her. Writing in *Arts & Architecture* magazine in September 1946, Eliot Noyes, then the director of the industrial design department at MoMA, unapologetically observed, "Charles Eames has designed and produced the most important group of furniture ever developed in this country." Arthur Drexler, a successor of Noyes's at MoMA, did not mention Ray when he called Charles "the most original American furniture designer since Duncan Phyfe."[2] Ray's transparency to Charles was so ingrained in the Eameses' career that by the time Esther McCoy wrote "Eames Perspective" for the well-fact-checked *New York Times Magazine* in 1973, the editors took Ray out of the profile of the firm altogether—after consultation with MoMA—over McCoy's loud and deeply embarrassed protests.[3]

Assumed to be only a nominal partner—the nurturing wife standing behind the great man—Ray Kaiser was marginalized in the perception of their work, a victim of common contemporary prejudices, which were perpetuated even through her obituaries in 1988. The prejudices were compounded by another major fault-line in the art world. Kaiser was a founding member of the American Abstract Artists group, an association that exhibited vociferously in New York from 1937 on and whose paintings and sculptures director Alfred H. Barr, Jr., refused to admit into The Museum of Modern Art. Barr's lack of interest in what he considered derivative work suggests that the museum harbored a blind spot for Kaiser's background and would therefore find it difficult to later correct its position by acknowledging the quality of her contribution to the Eames partnership. Her career as a designer belonged to Charles. And her career as a painter was overlooked, not only because of Charles's dominance in the firm but also because MoMA officially disparaged the movement to which she belonged.

Then there is the matter of the simple ignorance of an underappreciated period that is only now being reassessed. Until 1996,

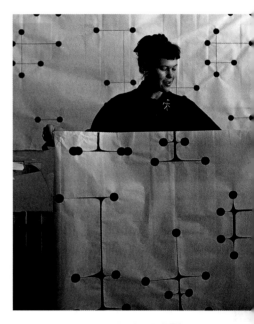

Ray holding Dot Pattern fabric design, ca. 1947

even the Whitney Museum of American Art did not know that a lithograph in their collection by Ray Kaiser was Ray Eames's—the museum had catalogued her as a man. Nor did the Snyder Fine Art gallery in New York, which specializes in art of the period, make the connection between Ray Eames and Ray Kaiser.

In his 1946 *Arts & Architecture* piece about the Eameses' furniture, Noyes wrote that Charles Eames's "achievement is a compound of aesthetic brilliance and technical achievement." He continued, "To this revealed structure, Eames has added sensitive seat and back forms which give each chair the quality of a brilliant piece of abstract sculpture." Had Noyes seen Ray's trunk, he would have been able to deduce that while Charles offered the technical achievement, Ray in large part provided the aesthetic brilliance in the great, early period of the office (through the 1950s). Digging more deeply into the trunk, he would have discovered that the brilliance had been nurtured under MoMA's very nose—first at the Art Students League, then in Hofmann's Manhattan teaching lofts, and, very publicly, in the annual *salons des refusés* held by the American Abstract Artists beginning in 1937. It did not occur to Noyes that the plywood chair represented the marriage of equal but different talents—that, insofar as one can separate such intertwined, collaborative work, the revealed structure and engineered connections were Eames's, and the abstract sculpture was Kaiser's.

"Ray knew what was art and Charles knew she knew it," says Deborah Sussman, the Los Angeles graphic artist whose decades-long association with the office began when she went to work there in 1953.[4] Even Eames—who was never swift to share credit—admitted Kaiser's talents. "She has a very good sense of what gives an idea, or form, or piece of sculpture its character, of how its relationships are formed. She can see when there is a wrong mix of ideas or materials, where the division between two ideas isn't clear. If this sounds like a structural or architectural idea, it is. But it comes to Ray through her painting... any student of Hans's [Hans Hofmann's] has a sense of this kind of structure."[5]

Whether he did so intentionally or not, Eames avoided specifics and effectively masked her contribution in generalities. He also allowed shows to be exhibited and articles written crediting him alone. "He was always talking about the group, how the group was so important, and in the end it was only he who took all the credit," remembers Mercedes Carles Matter, who attended the Bennett School and Hofmann's classes with Ray, and accompanied her husband, Herbert Matter, to California, where he worked with the Eameses from 1942 to 1946.[6]

Five years older than Kaiser, Eames "converted" to modernism some six years after she first enrolled in Hofmann's classes in 1933. She had bloomed to the occasion early, and he, late—and with her help (along with that of Eero Saarinen, Eames's primary modernist mentor at Cranbrook). At this point Eames had completed two years of undergraduate architecture school education at the Beaux-Arts-oriented Washington University in St. Louis; she had finished an equivalent two years of liberal arts, with a concentration in art, at the highly regarded Bennett, a school in New York's cultural orbit. Then, while he conducted a basically conservative architectural practice (no small feat during the

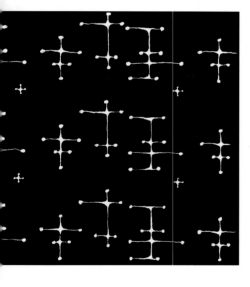

Design for Dot Pattern fabric, as reproduced in *Portfolio*, Summer 1950

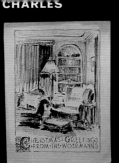

1 ca. 1928

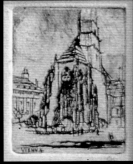

2 1929

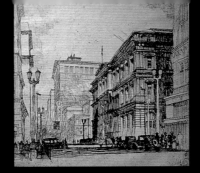

3 1931

RAY

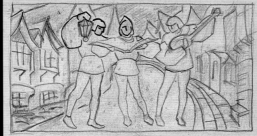

1 1932

2 ca. 1933

3 1933–34

Depression), she pursued for seven years a graduate education (albeit nonacademic) as an artist in what was fast becoming the most brilliant art capital of the world. Their respective Christmas cards, made within five years of each other, demonstrate that Kaiser was already well launched into much more ambitious artistic territory—free of the control of perspective—while Eames offered the charming but conventional verities of standard representation. As Eames was still building colonial revival houses in St. Louis, she was even contemplating modernism in his professional territory. On a postcard dated January 26, 1937, she observed, "Modern arch[itecture]—not a style. A philosophy of life. A waking up to the fact of living surrounded by forms because of industrial revolution."[7]

Though Eames had traveled to Europe in 1929 (where he saw the Weissenhof Siedlung, an early modernist housing development in Stuttgart, Germany), his training as a Beaux-Arts architect was not counterbalanced by another point of view. He later made much of the fact that he was expelled from the architecture school at Washington for siding with Frank Lloyd Wright—even though his designs never demonstrated a deep affinity for Wright's. What was unique about his development as a designer was that he worked during high school in a steel company and later in a printing plant and a lighting fixture concern. It was in these blue-collar jobs that he developed a practical sense for manufacturing. He was always interested in how a thing was made and how it worked so that he could not only produce an object but create and design the process as well.

But Eames's portfolio from the 1930s documents a conventional and conservative local practice that could fairly be called provincial. His sketches and renderings are deft academic efforts in perspectival

1 Christmas card, ca. 1928

2 Print of a European city based on 1929 travel sketches

3 Urban scene, etching on paper, 1931

4 Meyer House, Huntleigh Village, Missouri, designed with Robert Walsh, 1936–38

5 Card table and chairs designed for the Meyer House, Huntleigh Village, Missouri, 1937–38

6 Installation drawing for display of Herman Miller polyhedron and furniture, pencil on paper, ca. 1954

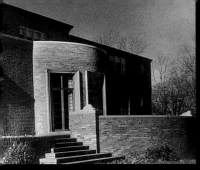

4 1936–38

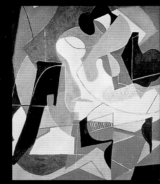

5 1937–38

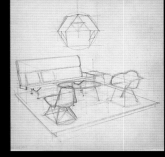

6 ca. 1954

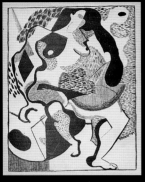

4 1937

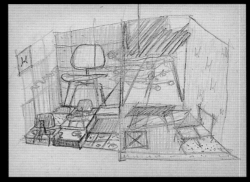

5 1939

6 1950

RAY

1 Drawing for May Friend Bennett School newsletter, pencil and ink on paper, 1932

2 Fashion drawing, ink on paper, ca. 1933

3 Christmas and New Years card design, pencil on paper, 1933–34

4 Lithograph included in American Abstract Artists exhibition, New York, 1937

5 Oil painting included in American Abstract Artists exhibition, New York, 1939

6 Drawing for 1950 window installation at Carson Pirie Scott department store, Chicago, pencil on paper

realism, akin to the semiromantic illustration work of the time. He seems at his most adventurous during a breakout year he spent in Mexico, when he did refreshing Impressionistic watercolors. There is no evidence that Charles was even tempted by abstraction before the late 1930s. He remained a representational artist doing equivalent traditional work in architecture. In the most prolific period of his practice, from 1933 to 1938, he produced houses modeled after or influenced by the colonial revival and Scandinavian modern styles, with traces of Wright. His St. Mary's Church in Helena, Arkansas (1935–36), with its steeple, buttresses, and arches, echoes Middle European traditions. By and large the work was competent and professional, with great care spent on such details as brick coursing. Occasional winks of wit lightened the work: hanging lamps in St. Mary's were designed as dark globes that would reveal their light as worshippers exited enlightened.

The building that brought Charles to the attention of Eliel Saarinen, then Cranbrook's president, was St. Mary's, when *Architectural Forum* published it in 1935. For the Meyer House (1936–38) in Huntleigh Village, Missouri, he consulted with the Finnish master, and the final design reflects Saarinen's influence. In *Charles and Ray Eames: Designers of the Twentieth Century*, Pat Kirkham[8] describes the interior of the Meyer House as "a combination of Georgian Revival, Scandinavian National Romanticism, Swedish modernism, Vienna Secession and Art Deco styles. The classical theme of the living room was emphasized by the use of coordinated motifs based on the acanthus leaf and clam shell."[9] Furniture designed by Eames included a veneered card table and four armchairs whose restrained classicism drew on a veneered table designed by Saarinen. The exterior also recalled the stripped-down, volumetric classicism of several Saarinen buildings.

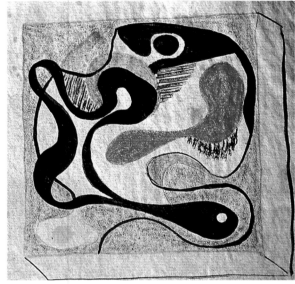

2

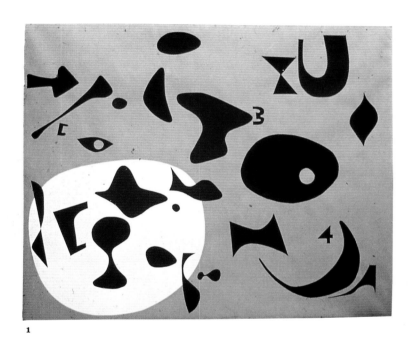

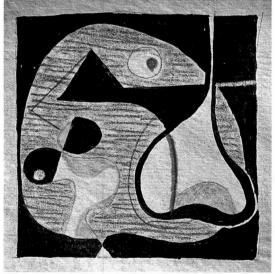

1

3

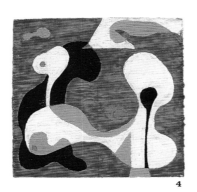

4

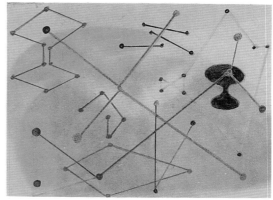

6

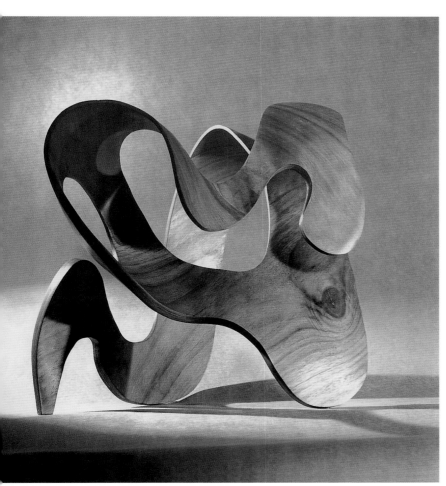

5

RAY

1   Paper collage, 1943

2/3 Studies for a mural project
    done in collaboration with
    designer Ben Baldwin, ink,
    colored pencil, and pastel
    on paper, 1940

4   Gouache painting on
    varnished plywood,
    before 1940 (?)

5   Plywood sculpture, before
    September 1942

6   Drawing, colored pencil
    on paper

If unadventurous, the Meyer House was refined, intelligent, and carefully crafted. Eames's work prompted Saarinen to offer the St. Louis architect a fellowship at Cranbrook. This, however, was not yet a full call to the modernism that Eames would eventually practice. Eames would be a fellow in a school headed by an architect whose work was still basically conservative and traditional.

Saarinen, however, knew the work of his friend Alvar Aalto, who was Finnish as well. The elder Saarinen was also influenced by his son, Eero, who had studied sculpture in Paris and traveled (after his Beaux-Arts education at Yale, from which he graduated in 1934) for two years on a fellowship in Europe, where he would have come into contact with Aalto's newest buildings.[10] After returning to the United States to work with Walter Gropius, Eero Saarinen held a job for a short time in the office of architect and industrial designer Norman Bel Geddes, who was doing streamlined designs at the time.

In 1937 the two Saarinens started collaborating as architects and soon thereafter formed an office. Though under the aegis of the father, the son pushed the firm in a modernist direction, introducing oval and curvilinear forms and other more abstract details. Eero directed the design of the Crow Island School project, introducing chairs with seats and backs made of integral molded plywood. In terms of planning and the design of the classrooms, the flat-roofed school with corner-glass windows and a semi-industrial vocabulary perhaps represented the first truly modern schoolhouse that translated the philosophy of John Dewey. The furniture—with molded-plywood backs and seats—was a bridge between Aalto's furniture and the chair designs Saarinen and Eames would submit to The Museum of Modern Art's 1940 "Organic Design in Home Furnishings" competition.[11]

Working with the Saarinens in their office in 1939–40, Eames was learning and, largely through Eero, became a modernist.[12] Eero Saarinen had seniority in the office, but beside his role as a delineator, Eames did acquire a design role, especially on the Tabernacle Church of Christ, which Eliel designed for a site in Columbus, Indiana (1940). Eames worked in particular on the furniture and parts of the altar area.[13] His background as a pragmatist able to make things dovetailed with modernism's concern for form resulting from the nature of materials and the industrial process.

Eames entered Cranbrook in 1938 "to make up what I had lost in the academic world" and "to live for a year in a library."[14] "The interesting thing," says Ralph Rapson, a Minneapolis architect who was studying at Cranbrook then, "was that Charlie spent no time in his architectural studio, absolutely none—he spent all of his time in the ceramics studio, in the photography studio, in the metal shop, in the weaving studio, obviously preparing himself for the things he would do later on....He did not do any architecture or planning....One of his major interests at the time was photography....Charlie spent lots of time with Carl Milles, the sculptor, and with Maija Grotell, who was in charge of ceramics and who influenced him. She did wonderful glazes on beautifully formed ceramics—reasonably traditional things. But I don't have any great memory of the things that Charlie was doing. I can't even picture any of the designs he did. He was learning the technology of all of these things."[15]

After a year Saarinen appointed Eames instructor of design in the Intermediate School of Design, and after another year he made him head of the industrial design department.[16] In his studio Eames taught the classic modernist subject—the strengths and properties of materials. Don Albinson, one of a half-dozen students in Eames's first design class, recalls, "What he was teaching was pretty basic—how to use tools, how to cut out of wood, how to find out how strong you could make sheets of paper by folding them. He wasn't trying to teach us artistic styles—no furniture design, just learning about materials and tools."[17]

Cranbrook, conceived as a kind of master's program, attracted people already embarked on careers, and many came with, or formed, their own ideas about furniture. "Just who was the real source of the idea of molded chairs would be kind of hard to say—it was in the air," says Rapson. "Harry Weese had been in Scandinavian countries studying before he came to Cranbrook and had seen the Aalto furniture and was making sketches of bent-wood furniture. He was very knowledgeable of Aalto. I think all of us were. Aalto visited Cranbrook while I was there in 1938–39 and gave talks during which he showed his furniture. But Aalto never got into molding and three dimensional things as much as he did lineal kinds of molds. A lot of us were thinking about it, and certainly Eero and Charlie and Harry Weese and Ben Baldwin and myself were talking and sketching and thinking about it....I did a number of molded-chair designs at that time."[18] Rapson also sent proposals for bentwood furniture to the 1940 MoMA competition.

Aalto, who had been a friend of Jean Arp's and was well versed in European abstract painting and sculpture, produced furniture whose rounded shapes were much warmer and more approachable than the famous tubular steel pieces coming out of the Bauhaus.[19]

After the Crow Island School project, work started for the "Organic Design in Home Furnishings" competition. Eero Saarinen and Charles Eames, who had become close friends, entered jointly, producing

Installation of furniture designed by Charles Eames and Eero Saarinen, displayed at The Museum of Modern Art's 1941 exhibition presented in conjunction with the "Organic Design in Home Furnishings" competition

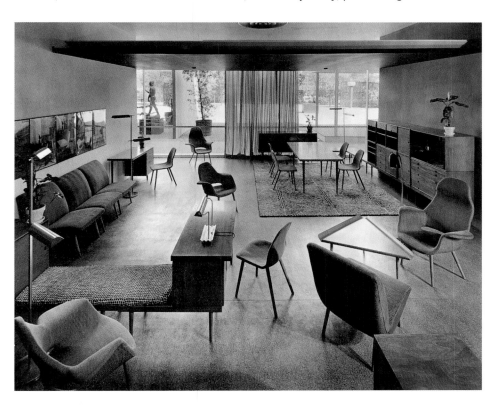

furniture for two categories—a line of highly rational and rectilinear case goods and tables, and seating that was, according to Albinson, "molded to fit people."[20]

Albinson notes that Saarinen and Eames worked, respectively, on the seating and the case goods. "I personally think Eero had more to do with the shell chairs, and Charles more to do with the case goods. The development of the shell chairs did not happen in the Eames classrooms. It happened in Eliel and Eero's space, which was in back of the main house where Eero was working. I was working on all the quarter-scale models for the case goods, and that took place in Eames's drafting room and the tool room. My feeling is that the sculptural shapes were coming more from Eero. I also have worked with him; he was a sculptor; he worked three-dimensionally."[21]

Florence Knoll Bassett, a Cranbrook student who was close to the Saarinens, was at the school during the competition. "Eero was far more interested in the shell furniture [than in the case goods] because Eero started out as a sculptor, which was his natural talent. Most of his architectural work is very sculptural, not all. His great contribution was always in the shell form; he was very involved in that."[22] And according to Kirkham, Rapson "recalled that Eero had plenty of ideas about how the chairs should look but knew very little about construction and technology, whereas Charles knew a great deal about the latter."[23]

"No, I don't think that's true at all," says Bassett, emphatically. "Eero was highly involved in all that sort of thing, the technological side, and with a sculptural point of view. I think he had a lot more experience in that than Charlie. I would say that Charlie actually had very little experience in the curvilinear world; his buildings in Missouri were very straight, simple, straightforward vertical sort of buildings. I think the strong sculptural influence is Eero's. I know that. I know that."[24]

The work Saarinen did on the shell chairs at this time—including the actual furniture shapes and types—would form the idea behind the furniture presented in the 1946 MoMA show *New Furniture Designed by Charles Eames* and the subsequent Eames Office entry for MoMA's 1948 "International Competition for Low-Cost Furniture Design."

In 1940, on her way to California to build a house, Kaiser stopped at Cranbrook and spent four months studying design there, presumably to acquire expertise for the house. "I hadn't had any practical training, and I thought that would be a very good thing to know—you know, to increase my knowledge of how things are done. At one time, just before finding Hofmann, I was going to go study engineering…somehow I've always been interested in structure, whatever form it was—interested in dance and music, and even my interest in literature had that base, I think…as structure in architecture. This seemed the perfect place because [I had heard] about Eero Saarinen, and [the] great potter, Maija Grotell."[25]

At Cranbrook, with Don Albinson and Harry Bertoia, Ray worked for Eames and Saarinen preparing the presentation drawings for the panels that were eventually submitted to the MoMA home furnishings competition. She was not involved in the design, but the shapes of the chairs shared an etymology with nearly a decade of work she had recently completed in New York. Directly and indirectly, both traced their lineage to European abstraction.

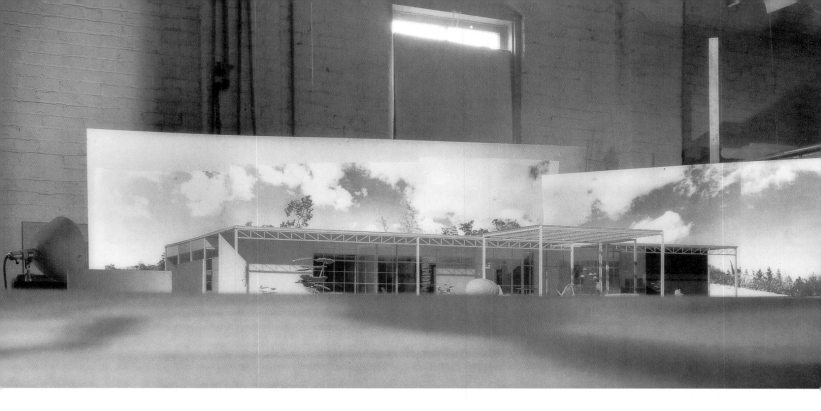

Model of proposed house for film
director Billy Wilder, 1950

Throughout his career as a designer, Eames maintained he always worked as an architect, which meant to him that he saw problems in terms of their basic structure. The architecture Eames produced after leaving Cranbrook perhaps best represents this reliance on structure to define a problem. He conceived the design of his own famous Case Study House #8 in Pacific Palisades as an issue of enclosing the maximum volume with the minimum amount of material. Within the structure of the idea, there was also the actual structure itself, and Eames chose to expose the supporting steel members as much as possible. The 1949 house represented a significant departure from the beautifully crafted, labor-intensive Meyer House of the previous decade. Eames's great insight in the house, of course, was to buy the material off the shelf, demonstrating that the house of the future and the solution to housing were already at hand in the catalogues. The concept was all the more powerful because Eames removed the house from the pedestal of the platonic Miesian ideal and made it everyday rather than heroic.

Except for this insight, its promise for mass housing, and the rectangles of color on the facade, the building is a rudimentary prism—just the kind of box Frank Lloyd Wright (and presumably Eames as a student) decried. This and other examples of Eames's architecture, both before and after his modernist epiphany, were planimetric, concerned primarily with plans and elevations rather than the spatial development of sections. Because he chose to work in steel, the structures were orthogonal rather than curved and behaved strictly within a rigid perspectival world he deftly constructed. By the 1940s, after Cranbrook and in the rich architectural climate of Southern California, Charles had become more familiar with the work of Walter Gropius, Ludwig Mies van der Rohe, Marcel Breuer, and other European modernists, and he knew Richard Neutra and Rudolph Schindler personally. But in none of his architectural designs did Eames indicate any interest in curvilinear abstraction and biomorphic shapes within the building itself. He seemed uncomfortable with curves.

While his drawings show that he had well absorbed lessons of industrial modernism, what was lacking in Eames's work was the spatial dimension—even in a project on which he collaborated with Eero Saarinen, Case Study House #9, for publisher and editor John Entenza (1950). In a commission for the house of Hollywood director Billy Wilder, the design is stiff, lacking richness in the third dimension. Color offered the only play. And it was this spatial dimension that, in the complementary fit of their relationship, Ray Kaiser brought to their early partnership.

While most observers say that Ray's talent was in developing forms, shapes, and color, the assessment is incomplete because it does not acknowledge her expertise in something more fundamental—space that is richly three-dimensional. If Eames absorbed structure as the great lesson of modernism, Kaiser brought to the collaboration another great foundation of modernism: the understanding that abstract art was spatial. She scribbled on an undated receipt found in her trunk, "Abstract Art. Based on pictorial spacial [sic] expression. Not based on representation." And it is in this marriage of his affinity for structure and hers for space that the quality of their early work resides. In their house, the structure was basically static: the dynamics of the space, achieved through the push-and-pull of color blocks on the facade, breathed life into the box.

Whatever Ray touched turned to beauty, whether a table setting of Chinese tea bowls, a tiny bouquet of violets wrapped in aluminum foil, or an arrangement of objects on a shelf. But her obvious gift for composition was not simply intuitive. It was cultivated by years of instruction in courses taught by Hans Hofmann, who had lived in Paris between 1904 and 1914, during the Fauvist and Cubist years, frequenting the haunts also visited by Braque, Delaunay, Picasso, Rouault, Pascin, Picabia, and Matisse. Kaiser's art teacher at Bennett, Lucinda Duble (who had studied with Hofmann in Munich in the 1920s), directed her to the Hofmann classes in New York City, held first at the Art Students League and later in his own studios. Kaiser was among his first students in New York. Others included Lillian Kiesler, Mercedes Carles Matter, Harry Holtzman, and George McNeil, and by 1937 Arshile Gorky, Jackson Pollock, Willem de Kooning, Clement Greenberg, and Harold Rosenberg attended. Besides teaching there, he conducted classes during summers in Gloucester and later Provincetown, both in Massachusetts. Hofmann was a key bridge between pre–World War I Paris and post–World War II New York. For Kaiser, the classes constituted an intense year-round professional training after her liberal-arts education. She came by her understanding of space through Hans Hofmann.

Ben Baldwin, an architect-designer who was a close friend of Kaiser's and studied with her under Hofmann, described his mode of instruction: "Well you know, he would come in and look at what we were doing and very often we were working in charcoal from a model and he would take a razor blade and slice the thing in lots of different pieces and move it all around, with thumbtacks, so that it had a much more spatial relationship....He was very fond of her [Ray] and very fond of her work. But it was very different from everybody else's in the class. There was nobody doing anything like what she was doing....her work was always very recognizable and not completely abstract. But still, it had the Hofmann stamp in that it had this spatial business that he was so adamant about."[26] After cutting open a drawing, Hofmann would rearrange the parts to establish tensions in compositions that were otherwise rigid and inert. Kaiser recalled, "He talked about plasticity."[27] Similarly, Hofmann advised students to test color tensions by moving and pinning small pieces of colored paper on their canvases.[28]

Synthesizing Cézanne and post-Cézanne concepts of the "new space," which most young Americans had seen only in publications, Hofmann taught his students to open up the spatial structure of the canvas by pushing and pulling planes into and from the depth of the picture plane to create dynamic volumes that activated the entire space in a three-dimensional field. The force and counterforce of the planes tense the composition and bring it to life. In Hofmann's spatial formulation, the planes that first composed the Cubist figure were now dispersed volumetrically throughout the canvas in a two-dimensional environment of omnidirectional plasticity. Hofmann taught that the function of color is to create volume, and that the void, or "negative" space, around the volumes created by the thrusting planes is also a "positive" space or volume. All the volumes exist in a compositional relationship in which the object is in movement, as is the space around it. Plasticity of a canvas comes from the tensions created by movement and countermovement, and the tensions produce its liveliness: "Life comes to expression through tensions," Ray noted at a Hofmann lecture.[29] In his studio, to give a figure the sense it belongs in an active three-dimensional space, he constructed backgrounds with sheets of colored paper set off by bright lights, which created deep shadows and a sense of compositional vitality.[30] "He didn't close anything, he opened everything and made it possible to see wholly, I think, as we do see," recalled Ray. "We don't see a line, we see a line and both sides of the line. It took his large view to make it possible for all of us to see and feel and know more."[31]

We know from Ray's meticulous—though sometimes elliptical—notes that she was repeatedly exposed to Hofmann's mantras about three-dimensional space: "Aim for plastic results—to make something full not flat. But [the] object is only part of experience. The object exists in something—it exists in space....Perspective [is] bad because [it is] all the time concerned with one movement in the depth, while plastic experience goes in and comes back to the observer....Perspective is scientistic—remains construction—may have value other places but not art."[32]

Foreshadowing Ray's future concerns, Hofmann even touched on the notions of architectural construction, whether in a building or in geometries on a canvas. "A great work of art must overcome this [constructivism]," she noted on July 25, 1936. Pictures are "dead without being vitalized through...the space experience. When [we] see a picture from Miró these are not geometrical forms—concerned not only with space in the object but space around the object. We experience depth through volume." And elsewhere, she recorded, "I experience the object never in itself—in relations through light, through color....In this way I experience something much greater than the object. What I really experience is space-forms."[33] Regrettably, most of Kaiser's paintings and drawings from this period were lost in storage.[34] "She had a character all her own in painting, a sort of arabesque quality," recalls Mercedes Matter,

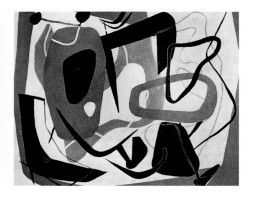

Ray's painting *Composition with Yellow*, exhibited at the Los Angeles Museum and published in *Arts & Architecture*, October 1944

"and studying with Hofmann, she was necessarily involved with 'push and pull.'"[35]

The lessons Kaiser learned through Hofmann were reinforced in courses she took in modern dance, which emphasized "plastic movement." In undated class notes (probably from Bennett), she wrote, "To make any given rhythm dance, the change of weight (fall and recovery) and dynamic pull must be used. The geometry consists of linking up fragments of space. Living plastic movement links up degrees of energy."[36] And elsewhere, "Rhythm is created through the pull of gravity and recovery. The recovery creates the rhythm."

Her observations recall the "push and pull" into and out of the depth of Hofmann's canvas, though for dance, the floor is the datum. Ray recalled in an interview that at Bennett "I knew there was a link someplace....I never thought of actually performing—I was studying to gain knowledge of movement and body and space, which is related to painting, which is related to Hofmann, which is related to music and architecture, actually. Which I feel was a preparation, in my way, for later work in terms of architectural design. They all seemed interwoven."[37]

Most of the painters and sculptors who founded the American Abstract Artists group in 1936 were Hofmann's students. They banded together because abstract art by American artists was being ignored by the Whitney Museum of American Art, The Museum of Modern Art, and prominent galleries. The most conceptually advanced artists in New York, called America's "first truly avant-garde artists," decided to take their own initiative, and—as they learned from the highly politicized, issue-charged decade—there was strength in union. At the studio of Piet Mondrian's leading proponent in America, Harry Holtzman, they gathered to organize a group show that would bypass an establishment that dismissed them. Kaiser sent work with Hofmann's blessings, and both she and Josef Albers were accepted as members at the same meeting.[38] Discussions at artists' meetings brought their goals and constituency into focus: the group would not represent realist or Surrealist tendencies, but a nonobjective ideal that included Expressionist, biomorphic, and geometric elements—often combined.[39] The association of artists was hardly unified as a movement and never promulgated a universal style or pronounced a manifesto. Though some kept an Expressionistic sensibility throughout their careers, others moved to Neoplasticism and geometry from free-form late synthetic Cubism and biomorphism.

Kaiser was one of thirty-nine artists who participated in the inaugural show of 1937 at the Squibb Galleries on 57th Street. She exhibited again in 1938, 1939, and 1941 (she did not exhibit in 1940, the year her mother died).[40] She was at the core of a movement that gathered momentum and would lead to the emergence of Abstract Expressionism: the 1941 show included Albers, Ilya Bolotowsky, Lenore Krasner, Fernand Léger, László Moholy-Nagy, A.D.F. Reinhardt, and Vaclav Vytlacil. For several years de Kooning and Gorky maintained a loose association with the group.

Balcomb Greene, the first chairman of the American Abstract Artists, wrote in the 1938 yearbook of how abstract art reached below consciousness through the immediacy of aesthetic experiences, perhaps a reference to the notion of primary forms constituting a universal language, but also perhaps suggesting the influences of Freud and Jung, then settling into the awareness of artists. Though long overshadowed in the histories by Abstract Expressionism and earlier American modernist painting, this exciting but overlooked period—the second generation in American abstraction—is being rediscovered by art historians and galleries. The research sheds light on the work of Eames and Kaiser, especially regarding curvilinear form, spatial movement, and color.

In his catalogue essay in the 1939 yearbook, George L. K. Morris, chief spokesperson for the group, commented on the character of the work in the American Abstract Artists exhibitions. He cited two major sources of influence: French Cubism and German abstraction, via the Bauhaus. The Bauhaus, he wrote, bifurcated into two traditions, "the open pictures of Klee and early Kandinsky on one hand, and on the other a movement toward closed integration that has influenced the art of today most strongly through Constructivism....Yet not many of the artists can be fitted into one specific category. The majority have learned from several of these tendencies which can be expanded indefinitely."[41]

Since many of the American artists had become familiar with European abstraction by the early 1930s, they had often transformed and personalized it, some very convincingly. Toward the end of the decade artists seem to have polarized between more geometric tendencies and freer, more lyrical shapes.[42] Kaiser's work was lyrical.

Reviews of the exhibitions were mixed at first, and then critics yielded grudgingly. In the February 15, 1938, issue of *The New York Times*, a cordial review by critic Edward Alden Jewell noted that the work was moving into its own. He cited Kaiser, among others: "Though palpably derivative, many of the abstractions might never be recognized at all by Picasso, Miró, Kandinsky, Mondrian, Rouault, Klee, Léger, and the rest. Yet it is for the note of greatest decorative freshness such as that frequently exemplified in the work of Josef Albers, Werner Drewes, Gertrude Greene, Frederick Kann, Ray Kaiser, Paul Kelpe, Rudolph Weisenborn and others."

Certain critics noted that the plasticity of some paintings was nearly sculptural, as in the works of John Ferren. Indeed, the search for three-dimensionality led sculptors in the group to seek it beyond the freestanding object. Ibram Lassaw, an Egyptian-born sculptor living in New York whom Kaiser knew, showed "open-space" sculpture philosophically akin to the space-forms mentioned by Hofmann and the mobiles and stabiles of Alexander Calder, who exhibited in New York during this time. Lassaw's work from the mid-1930s moved in and out of a "free space" contained within a stabilizing geometric frame.[43] Fluid and cursive, his wire sculptures, metal cutouts, and freely shaped plaster pieces opened the sculptural form to establish continuities between interior and exterior faces.[44]

After marrying in 1941 Charles and Ray headed out to California. There he designed sets for MGM under the direction of Cedric Gibbons. They settled in Neutra's Strathmore apartments, near UCLA, where they set out to develop techniques for molding plywood in the compound curves that had eluded the Cranbrook team. Remembering the experiments in their small apartment during the war years, Ray laughed about casting Eames's leg in plaster to develop their plywood leg splints, and as air raid sirens sounded, leaving his leg to bake as the plaster heated.[45]

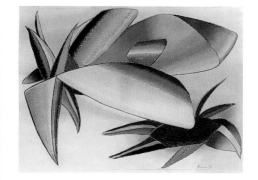

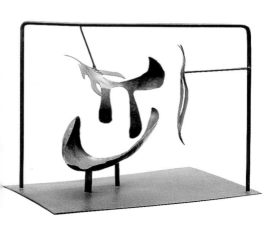

Untitled, No. 8, pastel on paper by John Ferren, 1938

Sculpture in Steel, by Ibram Lassaw, 1938

While he worked at MGM, she experimented with the capability of plywood in molds and produced two beautifully grained plywood pieces sculpted with molds made by Charles in 1942 and 1943 (see pages 44, 51). If Esther McCoy called their great "potato chip" chair the "chair of the century," it owes a considerable debt to what may well be among the most beautiful and least celebrated sculptures of the century. The two curviplanar pieces behave by all the rules of spatial plasticity and space-form that Hofmann outlined in his lectures. One sculpture, a kind of compounded Möbius strip with inside planes becoming exterior planes, graced the cover of *Arts & Architecture* in September 1942 and was meticulously described inside in a way that separates their respective contributions: "A piece of wood sculpture by Ray Eames designed in a complex form to take advantage of a system of molding laminated wood developed by Charles Eames. In its practical application in the defense and commercial fields an important feature of the system is its principle of mass production." Because of their plasticity, these sculptures must be considered as much a prototype for the eventual Eames chair as those from the organic design competition.

In these sculptures Ray succeeded in giving form to an aesthetic definition she had written in a pre-1940 note on a scrap of paper saved in her trunk. She defined a "Plastic Unit" as a "combination of positive and negative space." Especially in the turning forms of the sculptures, she fulfilled Hofmann's terms of plastic tension and vitality, as recorded in her lecture notes: "We have said the object expresses this force—this life—which comes to expression through the surface tensions, comes from experience of volumes—not enough just the experience [of] the volume planes....These planes are dependent upon the movement of the volumes—bound to the movement of the volume....Through the movement of the volumes are created other tensions, spacial [sic] tensions between the volumes."[46]

The pieces, which undulate in and out of the space they positively sculpt, also recall the principles of the open-space sculpture Lassaw pursued. In both, interiors and exteriors evolve from each other, are simultaneously revealed, though Ray's involuted forms catch and shape much more vital spaces than his. In what is basically an interpretation of volumetric Cubism, she also eschewed any geometric frame.

Ray Kaiser, however, was working with her husband and mentor Charles rather than her teacher and mentor Hofmann, and she took on Eames's persuasive intellectual coloring in clarifying why this was not art. Explaining the work in Eames's industrial design terms, and not the terms ingrained in her own eye by nearly a decade with Hofmann, she said to Ralph Caplan in an interview, "The sculpture was never done as sculpture. It was only as experiments on ways of using—what the wood could do...how could it be molded?...That's the way we made the first sculpture, which was a way of seeing how it could—how far the compound curve could be carried, and varying all those thicknesses, keeping the balance to keep it from warping." Caplan remarks, "You must have made a lot of conscious choices about how that was going to look," and Ray responds, "Certainly, it had to be a finite object, and within that...what are the limitations, how far they could go....That was always very strongly in everything. Charles was talking about, you know, if there were none, looking for them."[47]

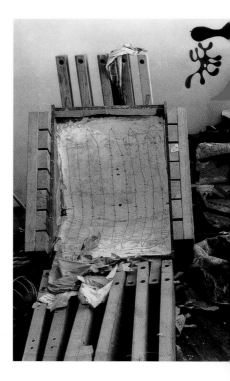

"Kazam! machine" in the Eameses' Los Angeles apartment, 1941

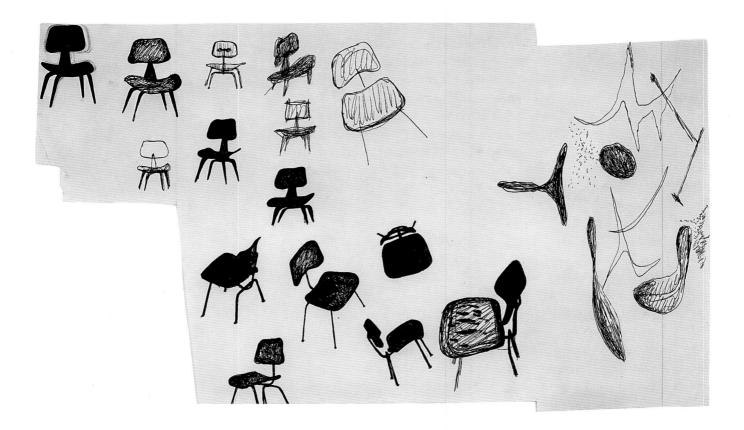

Drawing by Ray of plywood chairs, ink on paper

The lyrically beautiful plywood chairs that alighted in triumph on the floors of MoMA in *New Furniture Designed by Charles Eames* in 1946 grew out of the physical tests and aesthetic standards established by Ray and Charles's sculptural experiments. They were also predicated on the pieces submitted six years earlier by the Cranbrook team to the MoMA competition. "They developed from the other stuff," says Albinson.[48] Though the 1940 shell chairs were the point of departure and reference for the development of the new chairs, the original shapes were greatly transformed by Harry Bertoia, a Cranbrook teacher who headed the metal shop and went to California to work on the chairs in 1943.[49] According to Florence Knoll Bassett and Mercedes Carles Matter, whose husband worked in the same space as Bertoia at the time,[50] Bertoia reconceived the single-form shell chairs submitted to the MoMA competition as segments set on a skeletal frame.[51] (At Cranbrook, Bertoia had worked with Saarinen on the shell chairs and made metal models for them.)

But the breakthrough was not simply Bertoia's segmentation of the unified form into an independent seat and back, which avoided the difficult-to-manufacture compound curve where the seat bends up to form the back. The achievement was also in the shape of the chair itself, as subtle as the rim of a Panama hat falling and cresting through space—the "aesthetic brilliance" Noyes cites in his 1946 article. The 1940 chairs, though they introduced the concept of a shell shaped in compound curves, are stiff compared with their graceful descendants. Emphasizing their affinity to abstract, open-space biomorphic sculpture, one photograph, taken by Herbert Matter, shows an Eames chair and table next to a Calder stabile.

Commenting on the new chairs in the 1946 Eames show at MoMA, Edgar Kaufmann, jr., who was director of MoMA's industrial design department, refers to their visual sophistication: "And, therefore, we had already had some inkling of this kind of form in the joint efforts of Charles and Eero. And then when Charles's things came through on their own, that is his work with Ray, there was no question that the whole design approach had matured considerably from the earlier things and that these were more consistent and convincing visually...and there was too a fairly evident, but not exactly precise, echo of forms that one was familiar with from straight modern art—people like Arp and whatever—so it wasn't a great shock in the sense of something never before conceived of, but it certainly was a surprise to find it in that form." The conversation with interviewer Ralph Caplan continues:

> **Caplan**: Yeah—Do you suppose that was largely Ray's influence— I've seen pictures of pieces of sculptures that she's done that had that—the same sort of effect.
> **Kaufmann**: I would think it was.
> **Caplan**: Did you think of them as Charles' chair or Charles and Ray's chairs?
> **Kaufmann**: I guess I thought of them as Charles and Ray's chairs. I don't think I would have ever hesitated to say that it seemed to me Charles was the dominant individual of the two, but I still thought Ray played quite a role in it. But you know, I thought this without any specific knowledge to back it up at all, just what I gathered from visiting them and talking to them and so on.[52]

Gregory Ain, who worked in the Eameses' office during the war as the chairs were being developed, stated in an interview with Esther McCoy that Ray was able to "bring things into relation with one another" and to "find the inner order in whatever she touched." He went on to confirm that "the final form of the famous DCM chair owes a great deal to her interest in abstract art."[53] In this period Ray continued to think in Hofmann's terms. She wrote in the September 1943 issue of *Arts & Architecture*, "My interest in painting is the rediscovery of form through movement and balance and depth and light."

Did she apply Hofmann's ideas about space to a design situation, in real three-dimensional space? "There is no doubt about it—she was a true follower of that early form of modernism, cubism, [and] she had a sizable appreciation of just that, of volume against negative," says Lillian Kiesler, a classmate of Ray's who married the architect and theater designer Frederick Kiesler. "She spread the word about abstract art and cubist art, she was an educator, and in a way, she was militant, very militant. And she was born with a sense of design, which had nothing to do with Hans Hofmann."[54]

While there was little in Charles Eames's background to indicate that he would go on to sculpt these subtle pieces, there was everything in Ray's: after all, she was trained to forge three-dimensionality from a plane. For her a sheet of plywood and the canvas picture plane were merely different versions of the same problem. The forms wafted weightlessly, opening up the structure of the chair to the surrounding space. In her trunk she left a revealing sheet of plywood with abstract figures painted on the open grain (see page 51, no. 4)—an undated piece that either presages or documents her concern with finding space in

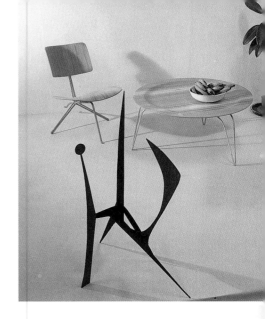

Publicity photograph by Herbert Matter for The Museum of Modern Art's 1946 exhibition *New Furniture Designed by Charles Eames*, with stabile by Alexander Calder

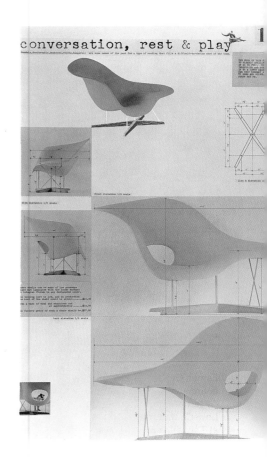

plywood by seeing it in the painterly terms she had learned with Hofmann.

In the chairs the forms are pushed and pulled both horizontally and vertically. She mischievously revealed her instincts to find and accentuate the space in objects by carving into free-form sculpture several of the molded plywood splints they had designed and which were manufactured by the tens of thousands for the navy during the war. Transformed, the useful objects reveal a source of their genesis.

For The Museum of Modern Art's 1948 "International Competition for Low-Cost Furniture Design," Charles Eames submitted a new series of chairs in molded plastic that again set new aesthetic and technological standards. The models grow more literally from those premiated in the 1940 competition than those in the 1946 show, but again the lilt of the chairs—the turn at the edges, the roll of the shoulder—bears Ray's fingerprints. Other designers in the same MoMA competition entered shell furniture with compound curves, but the aesthetic refinement of the Eames chairs distinguished them.

Most revealing is a voluptuous chaise that was submitted outside the main group. Named "La Chaise" after a Gaston Lachaise model the office imagined reclining in its undulating contours, it is a cloudlike fantasy piece separated from the more "serious" chairs submitted to the competition. According to Albinson and other sources, the design was attributed within the office to Ray Eames, though it was nonetheless submitted publicly under Charles's name. "Charles would say Ray did it," says Albinson, and indeed she was photographed working on the mold for the fiberglass. The chaise evolved from a similar shell developed in the Saarinen studio in 1940, but its attenuated, cloudlike form made it impracticable to manufacture at accessible prices. Only one prototype was made at the time.[55] As in a David Smith sculpture, the relationship of form and space denies any sense of mass.

"The business on the chaise is that, you know, Ray was the one that picked the color," says John Neuhart, commenting on its level of refinement. "She also started looking at the thinness of things and wanted things to be thinner, and then there would be arguments about whether that would hold up, you know. But she would come in sort of toward the end of all of these furniture things and look at the shape."[56]

Charles and Ray regularly discussed the development of a chair. Though Deborah Sussman calls Ray "the eye of the office,"[57] Albinson thinks she was "an eye" among several others, and that Charles and she would go back and forth in an equal discussion about the shapes of furniture (rarely did either make a drawing of a piece). Overlooked in credit, she was included in design meetings, where she played an integral part. Albinson reveals, "She sat in on all the presentations I made, and the two of them were very interested in forms and shapes. Then I would make the next prototype. Ray was there mainly in the capacity of discussing forms and shapes and color. He would make the final decision."[58]

Neuhart, who conceptualized mechanisms for the Solar Do-Nothing Machine, recalls that when Charles and he had agreed on its overall structure, Charles asked him to work with Ray on shapes: the result was a wondrous contraption, a miniature forest of shiny, spinning disks, typical of the magic her sensibility conferred on "structure." "Her eye. She had a

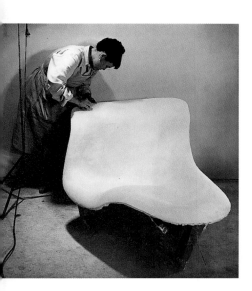

Ray preparing mold
for La Chaise, 1948

Eames Office presentation
board submitted to the 1948
"International Competition for
Low-Cost Furniture Design"
at The Museum of Modern Art,
New York

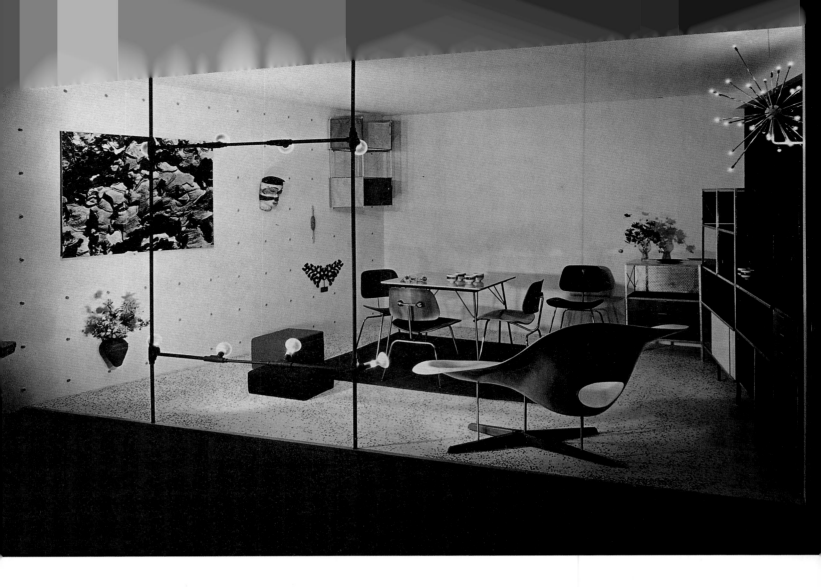

wonderful eye for detail. Color, form, shape," says Marilyn Neuhart, who
coauthored the book *Eames Design* with her husband and Ray. "She had a
kind of lyrical eye for color and form and shape...in putting things together
on this strictly aesthetic level. She was not a practical person at all."[59]
Mercedes Matter observes, "Charles was not a very original designer. Ray
was certainly the artist—her contributions were everywhere. She was the
most extremely talented painter, and she used that talent in whatever
they did."[60]

Crediting her eye with talent, however, does not acknowledge its
background and cultivation. Ray's occasional renderings of furniture
groupings give some idea of how she saw and understood the furniture,
as though a design film were run backwards, the pieces devolving to their
source ideas. Despite the logic expressed about industrial production, it
is clear that Ray viewed the chairs as active shapes moving through
space in all directions. In her rendering of the office display in *For Modern
Living*, an exhibition held at the Detroit Institute of Arts in 1949, the
chaise is a translucent cloud hovering in the foreground like a visual
whisper, while the seats and backs of other chairs, only nominally
attached to their frames, float in an antigravitational environment. Taking
abstraction into space, she posits it in the living rooms of everyday
houses, giving space framed by a box sophisticated visual life. In one
undated study (see page 63), the chair shells, viewed from all angles, drift

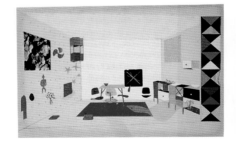

off into a loose, increasingly abstract formation, and the assortment seems to fall back into the start of a canvas in a Hofmann classroom. One of the most beautiful interpretations of the furniture is a photographic collage of the pieces and parts of Eames furniture done by Herbert Matter for a two-page spread in Noyes's 1946 *Arts & Architecture* article. The sum total of the topsy-turvy pieces, angled into and out of the picture plane, could easily be a work created according to Hofmann's spatial terms. The test of the furniture's abstraction is that the forms "read" whether right-side up or not. Bred in part from a two-dimensional art form, the shapes return to the "canvas" with natural ease.

In 1950 the Eames Office was invited to design a window for the Carson Pirie Scott department store in Chicago, and Ray sketched proposals; a few years later Charles designed another display, for a Herman Miller showroom (see page 49, no. 6). The two schemes allow a revealing his-and-her comparison of their respective design instincts. In Charles's version there is a controlled, matter-of-fact mise-en-scène, each piece sitting on its own feet occupying its own space in a calm room with a low horizon line defined by the furniture height. Ray, however, proposed a vitrine with larger-than-life shadows of the furniture projected and papered onto walls—a spectral display that activates all surfaces of the room in a composition as complex and spatial as any of her drawings for Hofmann. This way of seeing the furniture underlies its aesthetic formation, so that left on their own, the pieces evince a spatializing behavior. British architect Peter Smithson has noted, "Eames chairs can be put into any position in an empty room; they look as though they had alighted there. The chairs belong to the occupant, not the room."[61] McCoy made a comparable observation about the furniture: "It belonged not to the wall but the floor."[62]

Eames, an enchanting raconteur who spun yarns on design like a Will Rogers and humanized ideas in the telling, simply advocated what is commonsensical. His populist position hardly led him to dwell on the figures and ideas that formed Ray's decade in New York. Instead, Charles admonished designers to innovate only as a last resort. Marilyn Neuhart paraphrases Eames: "Don't try to be original, but build on something that really works."[63] In "Design Today," an article that appeared in the September 1941 issue of *California Arts & Architecture*, Charles revealed himself a design fundamentalist, lauding the "appropriateness" of the airfoil in airplane design but decrying efforts to streamline the vacuum cleaner and inkwell. He wrote for *Print* an article entitled "A Prediction: Less Self-Expression for the Designer."[64] For a designer the position seems unusual until one realizes Eames believed in functional rather than formal inventiveness—he had no interest in shapes invented for the sake of shape.

Despite his reputation, then, Charles was by his own admission a design conservative, and whether traditional or modern, his designs embody a cautionary formal reticence. Whether in the case goods he designed with Saarinen for MoMA's 1940 competition (and then later developed), or in his own house, he created a straightforward structure that defines a plain, simple volume. The structure is usually a conventional box and the innovation occurs in its manufacture, at the level of tools or systems assembly; what animates these boxes and their flat planes is color. "Charles might conceptualize about whether

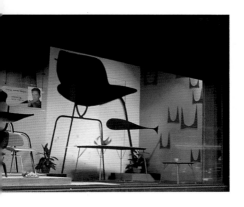

A 1950 window installation at Carson Pirie Scott department store, Chicago, based on a drawing by Ray

a color should be bright or subdued…Charles was brilliant at concept," says Sussman, "but color is basically one of Ray's contributions to their work. He was conservative about color."[65]

Ray's use of color is not merely rhetorical. When she chose colors for the planes on these boxes, it was, for her, more than "putting some shapes on." Some colors advance in space and some recede— a composition of colors, even in Mondrianesque squares, can start to achieve a complex spatiality akin to the plasticity advocated by Hofmann. She did not merely decorate the systems Charles built; she tried optically to spatialize them. Ray's colors for the facades of their house and the house Eames and Saarinen designed for John Entenza next door, the colors for the storage units in her plan of the office display for the Detroit show *For Modern Living,* and even the colors for their riotously patterned Houses of Cards (1952), all pulse with spatial tension due to her chromatic composition.

From the earliest days of their partnership, Charles Eames was the ringmaster. He organized the office, articulated the issues, and set the agenda. According to John Neuhart, Ray "had nothing to do with the inception [of a project]."[66] Though furniture dominated the office's defining decades—the 1940s and 1950s—Eames started turning his attention to information and communication theory in the early 1950s. The notion of being an artist, in Eames's view, was never sacrosanct, and it was devalued even more as the subjects he chose to address in the firm changed. Several markers, including their 1953 film *A Communications Primer* (based on Claude Shannon's 1949 book *The Mathematical Theory of Communication*), signaled a gradual paradigm shift in the office. Charles, who had always understood things through the lens of a camera, now explained things on screen to a captive (and usually captivated) audience. Like Charles, the films are at once sophisticated and homespun. The office also worked on corporate images and on exhibitions, the last of which, *The World of Franklin and Jefferson*, marked a change of emphasis from image to word.

Furniture design was no longer the sole concern, and tasks changed for everyone, including Ray. Film, of course, even film about information, is a visual medium, and her eye served not only in designing such sets as the picnic on the lawn in *Powers of Ten,* but also in visualizing information, as in the timelines —with streams of dates and facts—that the office produced so brilliantly. As the office focus moved from object to information, her talents in visual abstraction became less germane. Her eye may indeed seem most apparent in the films and exhibitions, but the media are not readily understood and conceived of as domains of plasticity. The shift, with an underlying change of emphasis from art to science, marginalized the significance of her contribution even as it required as much, if not more, of her visual input. The chairs were a medium for space; the films were a medium for transmitting ideas.

Though they eventually came to call their enterprise "The Office of Charles and Ray Eames," the billing was never as equal as their marquee implied. The issue of proper credit at least once precipitated sudden departures —Bertoia, Ain, Griswald Raetze, and Matter left in 1946 after the MoMA show and Noyes article. As John Neuhart observes, "And then the other thing was credit. Once Charles learned the information, you'd

Photocollage by Herbert Matter displayed in the 1946 exhibition *New Furniture Designed by Charles Eames* at The Museum of Modern Art, New York

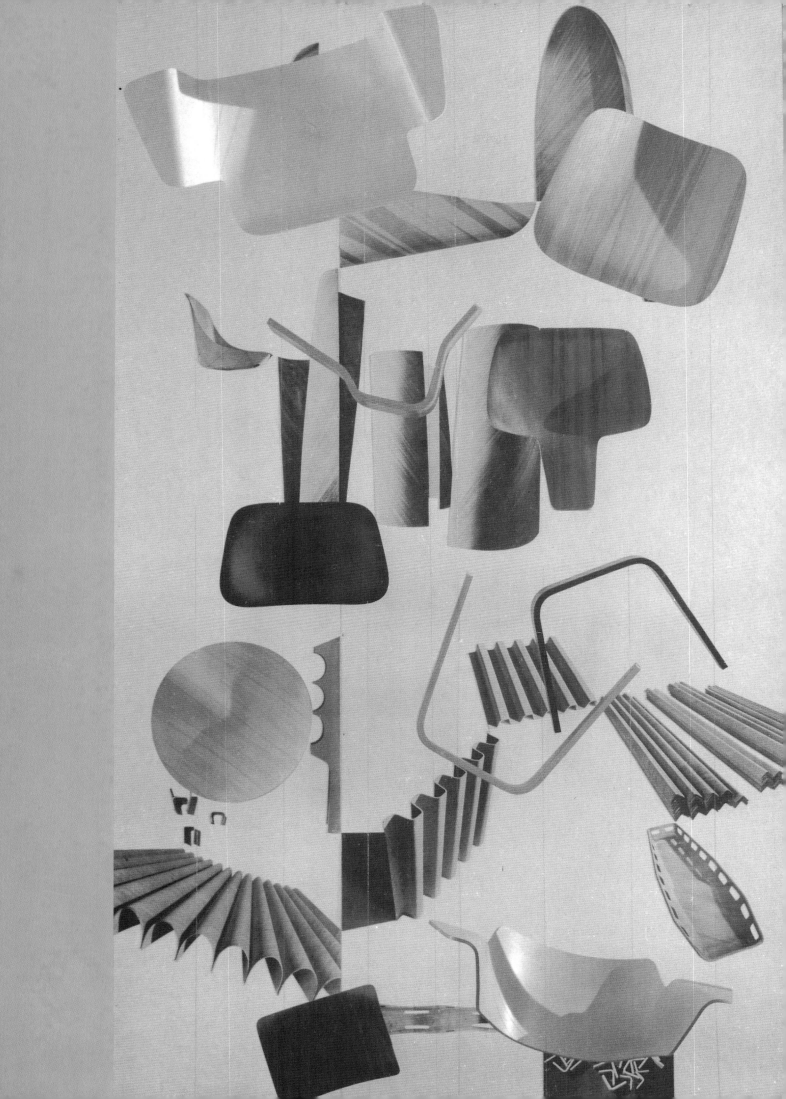

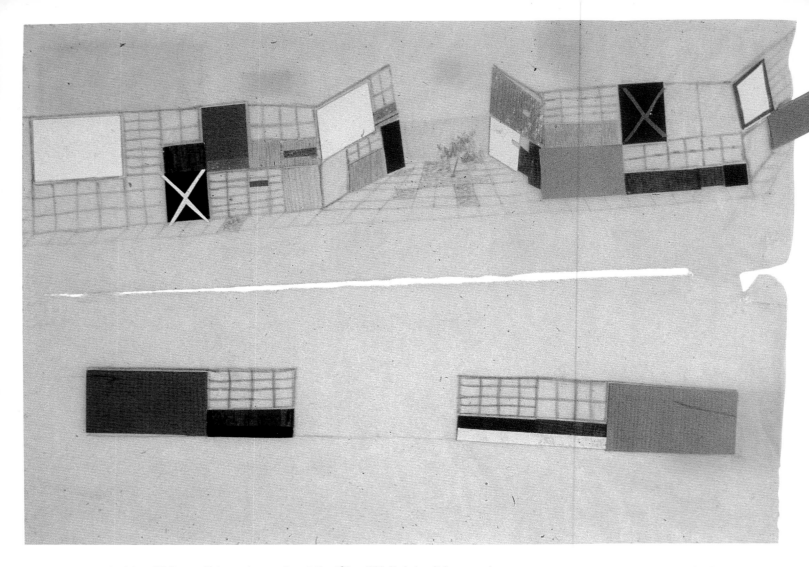

Ray's color studies for Eames House facades, 1949

say to him, 'Where did you hear about that?'—'Well, I don't know where that came from.' He never could remember....And the only person that he would give credit to was Eero Saarinen and Alexander Girard."[67]

"I saw this in action when he designed the house for John Entenza [Case Study House #9]," recounts Mercedes Matter. "He and Ray came here for dinner one night, and he was thinking about the design and asked what I would do if I were designing a house. I said I'd have a room, a studio without any windows, just a skylight, because I would want it to be a room that I would be completely private in, turned inward, so I wouldn't be distracted by looking at anything outside. And literally, three weeks later, he came over with a model of the house and said, 'Here is a room without any windows, it's a study, completely private, turned inward.' He used my words, and innocently: he didn't even *remember*. I was staggered. What Charles did was to organize the whole thing."[68]

But the question of what Charles knew and when versus what Ray knew and when amounts to more than an issue of simple fairness and attribution. Ray willingly played moon to Charles's sun, and he enjoyed his radiance. The problem with eclipsing Ray, however, is more than personal, for the shadow obscures an entire body of thought deeply indebted to a major artistic tradition that otherwise remains unacknowledged. The official explanation of the chairs—that is, Charles's version—is lucid, simple, and even noble in its social aspirations: "The idea was to do a piece of furniture that would be simple and yet comfortable. It would be a chair on which mass production would not have anything but a positive influence; it would have in its appearance the essence of the method that produced it. It would have an inherent rightness about it, and it would be produced by people working in a dignified way. That sounds a little pompous, but at the time it was a perfectly legitimate thing to strive for."[69]

The story overshadowed by this explanation is that the Eameses' furniture design is rooted in the American Abstract Artists movement and, beyond that, in overlapping traditions of European abstraction. The implicit subject of the chairs is not only structure but richly dimensionalized space. While Charles charmingly recounted how, using his father's chemicals, he coated emulsions on glass plates to take photographs before learning that George Eastman had already invented film, he failed to relate comparable stories of Kaiser and Hofmann knocking about Manhattan taking in Charlie Chaplin films, of Gorky storming out of the meetings of the abstract artists, and of Kaiser meeting Mondrian. Her contribution suffered passive neglect even at the level of lore. She herself refused to discuss her role and contributions apart from anyone else's: she felt the nature of the design process was collaborative (even though to the outside world the lion's share of the credit belonged to Charles).

What is remunerative about identifying Ray's contribution within what seems to be Charles's world is that the separation of strands reveals different idea genealogies. The complexity and ambiguity of the work lies partially in its hybrid character. The result is the intersection of their respective formations. Ray's modernism, rooted in artistic abstraction, crossed with Charles's, which was based in notions of industrial production. The cross-fertilization caused what biologists call vigor.

Although Ray never thought of the chairs as art—"no, no, no," she expostulated in an interview[70]—the argument could be made that their collaboration represented a fusion of disciplines. The chairs might even be considered an instance of art furniture *avant la lettre* (though they were conceived as multiples). As in the work of Frank Gehry, whose studio in the 1960s and 70s was only blocks away from the Eameses', the intersection of art and design sparked original work: the designs were produced outside the confined logic of a single discipline practiced purely. Hofmann admonished his charges to overcome construction, and Ray's eye, in an entirely unexpected application of his principles, transformed Charles's structure. The work of each was the stronger for the other's. Ben Baldwin remarked, "The combination was an extraordinary one, I don't know of any other one like it, of two designers who really contributed enormously to each other's work, and they both had very strong gifts in different directions and yet somehow the same direction."[71]

As their grandson Eames Demetrios has said, "Charles saw everything as an extension of architecture and Ray saw everything as an extension of painting."[72] He was interested in systems and structure, and while he structured the problem (and even the structure), she spatialized the structure, bringing it out of the coolness of reason into the space and tactility of the viewer.

Perhaps Ray did not set the agenda, but she was critical in the aesthetic matters without which the agenda would not have been nearly as significant. Pupul Jayakar, an authority on Indian crafts who knew both Eameses well, has observed, "Charles would not have been Charles without Ray."[73] There was power in the beauty and concepts at her fingertips, and the power resided in the levity her forms imparted to a room. If she painted from nature abstractly with Hofmann, with a change in medium she "painted" abstractly in architectural interiors with Eames. The character of her rooms, achieved with leaves of plywood carving space, along with colors doing the same, attains a plasticity equivalent to that in a Hofmann canvas. Sculpting space with form, she set the forms free in interiors, where they behave like flocks of mobiles, pushed and pulled by the people who use them. Rooms with this furniture come alive.

1. Esther McCoy, "A Love of Small Packages: A Friend Remembers Ray Eames," *California Magazine* (Dec. 1988), 22.
2. Arthur Drexler, quoted in John Neuhart, Marilyn Neuhart, and Ray Eames, *Eames Design: The Work of the Office of Charles and Ray Eames* (New York: Abrams, 1989), 10.
3. Esther McCoy, letter to Charles and Ray Eames, Apr. 23, 1973, Box 68, The Work of Charles and Ray Eames, Manuscript Division, Library of Congress, henceforth WCRE.
4. Deborah Sussman, interview with Joseph Giovannini, 1994.
5. Charles Eames, quoted in Pat Kirkham, *Charles and Ray Eames: Designers of the Twentieth Century* (Cambridge, Mass.: The MIT Press, 1995), 80. Originally published in Edward K. Carpenter, "Introduction: A Tribute to Charles Eames," *Industrial Design 25th Annual Design Review* (New York: Whitney Library of Design, 1979), 12.
6. Mercedes Carles Matter, interview with Joseph Giovannini, Aug. 25, 1996.
7. Ray Eames, notes on art, Box 276, WCRE.
8. Pat Kirkham, British design scholar now teaching at The Bard Graduate Center for Studies in the Decorative Arts, New York City.
9. Kirkham, 26.
10. Peter Papademetriou, interview with Joseph Giovannini, May 9, 1996.
11. Peter Papademetriou, interview with Joseph Giovannini, Sept. 8, 1996.
12. Kirkham, 49.
13. Papademetriou, Sept. 8, 1996.
14. Kirkham, 47, from interview between Charles Eames and Virginia Stith, 1977.
15. Ralph Rapson, interview with Joseph Giovannini, May 17, 1996.
16. Kirkham, 48.
17. Don Albinson, interview with Joseph Giovannini, 1996.
18. Rapson.
19. Papademetriou, May 9, 1996.
20. Albinson.
21. Ibid.
22. Florence Knoll Bassett, interview with Joseph Giovannini, May 18, 1996.
23. Kirkham, 211.
24. Bassett.
25. Ruth Bowman, interview with Ray Kaiser Eames, July 28, 1980, Archives of American Art, Smithsonian Institution.
26. Ongoing Eames Office Video Oral History Project with Eames Demetrios, Mar. 19, 1992, Sarasota, Fla., © 1997, Lucia Eames dba Eames Office.
27. Bowman.
28. Cynthia Goodman, "Hans Hofmann as a Teacher," *Arts Magazine* (Apr. 1979), 121.
29. Ray Eames, notes on Hofmann Lecture V, Aug. 21, 1936, Box 281, WCRE.
30. Goodman.
31. Bowman.
32. Ray Eames, notes on Hofmann Lecture II, Aug. 1, 1936, Box 281, WCRE.
33. Ray Eames, notes on Hofmann Lecture VI, Sept. 29, 1936, Box 281, WCRE.
34. Bowman.
35. Matter.
36. Ray Eames, WCRE.
37. Bowman.
38. Susan C. Larsen, "The American Abstract Artists Group: A History and Evaluation of Its Impact upon American Art" (Ph.D. Diss., Evanston, Ill., Northwestern University, 1975; reprinted in Ann Arbor, Michigan, University Microfilms International).
39. Carter Ratcliff, "1930s American Abstract Painting: An Overlooked Period of Dynamic Innovation," *Architectural Digest* (May 1996), 231.
40. Larsen, 458–59.

41. Ibid., 313–14.

42. Ibid., 312, 314.

43. Ibid., 588.

44. "I believe I'm exploring space: I want to go there. My concept is deep space. My predecessors were the Russian Constructivists, Gabo, and Pevsner, and in the 1930s, Julio González, a friend of Picasso." Ibram Lassaw, interview with Joseph Giovannini, Sept. 8, 1996.

45. Ray Eames, conversation with Joseph Giovannini, ca. 1982.

46. Ray Eames, notes on Hofmann Lecture IV, Summer 1937, Box 281, WCRE.

47. Ray Eames, interview with Ralph Caplan, Feb. 24, 1981, Venice, Calif., Herman Miller archive, Zeeland, Mich.

48. Don Albinson, interview with Alexander von Vegesack, Apr. 10, 1989, Allentown, Penn.

49. Matter; Bassett.

50. "Harry [Bertoia] was a sculptor, a painter, a silver maker, and he was very important in the development of the curvilinear chairs," says Florence Knoll Bassett, who later worked with Bertoia at Knoll. "And he was the one who finally persuaded Charlie to abandon the whole unified form [from the 1940 competition] in favor of the segmented form. Charlie's contribution to that chair was the rubber attachment [the round, rubber shock absorbers glued to the underside of the seat and the back and attached to the metal frame]." Bassett.

51. According to Bertoia, Charles Eames was "contending with the plywood by cutting, removing, and folding parts like a tailor" (Margaret Harris, a costume designer, had been consulting on the patterns), until Bertoia devised a tubular skeletal framework, which would support plywood seating segments. Bertoia recalled, "The tube I made was a little more flexible and more skeletal, just a skeleton was there. So Charlie kept an eye on this and already he was beginning to see that it really was away too far from what he had in mind and what had been done before, and that if anything was coming out of this it would have no real identity as the competition chair, and it seems that was the very beginning of a little bit of tension. . . .Finally a number of prototypes were brought to the point where we could actually sit on them and Charlie was still hesitant but it was Herbert Matter, you know, the photographer, who was then also in the same group, and he pointed out and became very blunt. He said Charlie, if you don't pick that one up there's nothing else around here. And it was Herbert and Mercedes I think that actually won Charlie Eames to at least give it a try. But once this was done very shortly after he got very enthusiastic and everything came his way." Harry Bertoia, interview with Paul Cummings, June 20, 1972, Archives of American Art, Smithsonian Institution.

52. Edgar Kaufmann, jr., interview with Ralph Caplan, Jan. 30, 1981.

53. Esther McCoy, "An Affection for Objects," *Progressive Architecture* (Aug. 1973), 66.

54. Lillian Kiesler, interview with Joseph Giovannini, May 9, 1996.

55. Vitra AG now produces La Chaise.

56. John Neuhart, Marilyn Neuhart, and Richard Donges, interview with Alexander von Vegesack, Oct. 13, 1988, Los Angeles.

57. Deborah Sussman, conversation with Joseph Giovannini, 1994.

58. Albinson.

59. Neuhart, Neuhart, and Donges.

60. Matter.

61. Peter Smithson, "Just a Few Chairs and a House: An Essay on the Eames-Aesthetic," *Architectural Design*, special issue, "Eames Celebration" (Sept. 1966), 447.

62. Esther McCoy, "Charles and Ray Eames," in Mildred Friedman, ed., *Nelson, Eames, Girard, Propst: The Design Process at Herman Miller, Design Quarterly* 98/99 (Minneapolis: Walker Art Center, 1975).

63. Neuhart, Neuhart, and Donges.

64. Charles Eames, "A Prediction: Less Self-Expression for the Designer," *Print* (Jan.–Feb. 1960), 77–78.

65. Sussman, 1994 interview and 1996 conversation.

66. Neuhart, Neuhart, and Donges.

67. Ibid.

68. Matter.

69. Neuhart, Neuhart, and Eames.

70. Ray Eames, interview with Ralph Caplan.

71. Baldwin.

72. Eames Demetrios, conversation with Joseph Giovannini, 1996.

73. Pupul Jayakar, conversation with Joseph Giovannini, Jan. 1997.

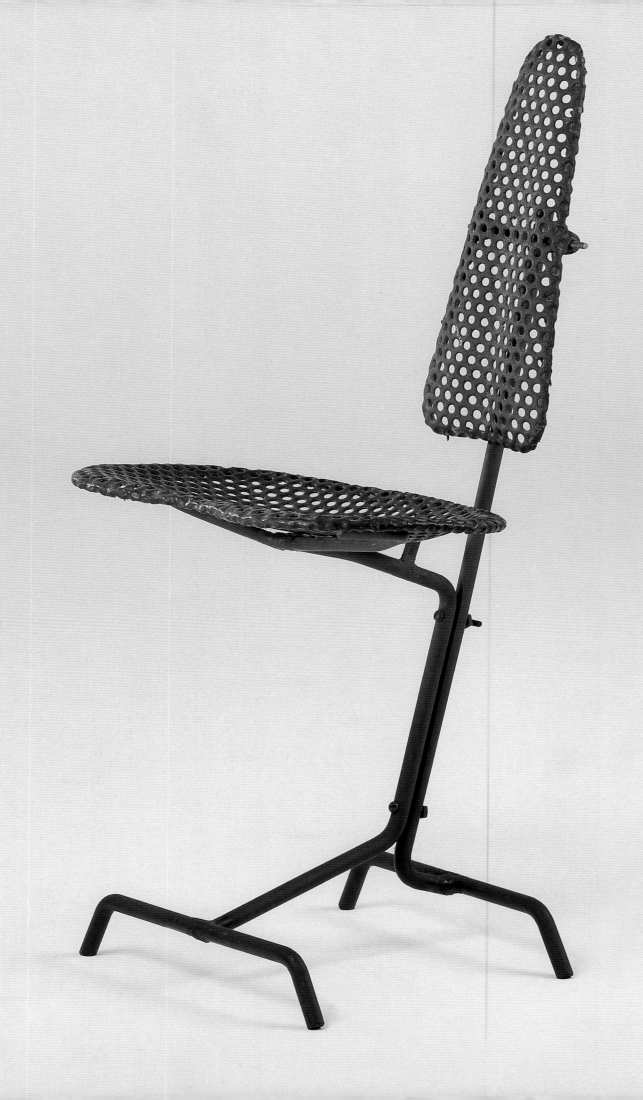

Evolving Forms

A PHOTOGRAPHIC ESSAY OF EAMES FURNITURE, PROTOTYPES, AND EXPERIMENTS

Experimental "minimum chair" with metal-mesh seat and back, produced by the Eames Office for The Museum of Modern Art's 1948 "International Competition for Low-Cost Furniture Design"

The Eameses' "minimum chair," a touchstone of their work in furniture design, is a testament to beauty in brevity. The Eames Office created this experimental piece in conjunction with their seating entries to The Museum of Modern Art's 1948 "International Competition for Low-Cost Furniture Design." The purpose of the experiment was to discover the least amount of material needed to produce a comfortable seat. Two versions were fabricated: one with a seat and back of sheet metal and another using metal mesh. The minimum chair achieved the formal purity of a Cycladic sculpture; however, it was never mass-produced.

The minimum chairs are two of roughly 350 pieces in the collection of the Vitra Design Museum, which documents the full range of the Eameses' work in furniture. The collection encompasses every type of their furniture: groups of chairs in four materials—molded plywood, fiberglass-reinforced plastic, bent and welded wire-mesh, and cast aluminum—as well as sofas, tables, storage cabinets, stools, and wall screens. There are also experimental pieces, prototypes, production models, and artifacts of the design process such as handmade molds and patterns. The conceptual backbone of this diverse work is an evolving search for seat and back forms that fit the human anatomy and distribute its weight without using traditional upholstery. Instead, each of the seating groups relies on a technical process in which a flexible material is formed into a distinctive body-fitting shape. As these photographs of the Museum's collection underscore, Charles and Ray Eames left a legacy of design excellence that is unparalleled in the twentieth century. *D.A.*

Plywood

The famous Eames molded-plywood chair of 1946 may be considered a brilliant failure, a partial solution to the challenge of making a chair out of a single, body-fitting shell. After moving to Los Angeles in 1941, Charles and Ray Eames set up an ad hoc workshop in their apartment. They experimented at night and on weekends, expanding on the molded-plywood chair ideas Charles and Eero Saarinen had developed at the Cranbrook Academy of Art and which won them first prize in The Museum of Modern Art's 1940 "Organic Design in Home Furnishings" competition. The Eameses made their own plywood-molding apparatus, a kind of curing oven dubbed the "Kazam! machine," from scraps of wood and spare bicycle parts. Using the machine they succeeded in creating a single-piece plywood shell, but the process was dangerous. "They had built this vast curing oven that required a lot more current than they could get from their house service," Eames Office member Alex Funke later recalled in an interview with Eames Demetrios. "So supposedly Charles climbed up the pole with a large piece of heavy insulated cable…so as to bypass the fuses to run this huge resistance oven they constructed. He has himself talked about doing this on occasion. He was scared to death."

The Eameses and their colleagues later received commissions from the U.S. Navy to develop molded-plywood leg splints for wounded World War II servicemen and from the aircraft industry for plane components, and they set up a shop in nearby Venice. (The Eames Office was located at 901 Washington Boulevard from 1943 until 1988.) Adapting wartime glues and techniques gave them hands-on experience that would later be applied to the furniture, and Ray's work with plywood sculptures helped refine their aesthetic sensibility. Returning to furniture development with a staff of sculptors, designers, and mechanics, the shop produced many single-shell experiments.

As hard as they tried, the team soon discovered that plywood did not easily withstand the stresses produced at the intersection of the chair's seat and back. As a result, they abandoned the single-shell idea in favor of a two-piece chair with one molded-plywood panel for the back and one for the seat. Innumerable experiments were studied: bases with three and four legs in metal and wood, a tilting base, and a base on sledlike rockers. The office applied rubber shock-mount and cycle-welding techniques from industry and produced special tools, prototypes, full-size plaster mock-ups, molds, and testing devices. The final chairs were unveiled to the public at The Museum of Modern Art's 1946 exhibition *New Furniture Designed by Charles Eames*. Variations are still in production.

opposite left: Molded-plywood leg splint, produced during World War II

opposite right: Sculpture by Ray Eames, carved from a molded-plywood leg splint, ca. 1943. Collection Eli Noyes and Augusta Talbot

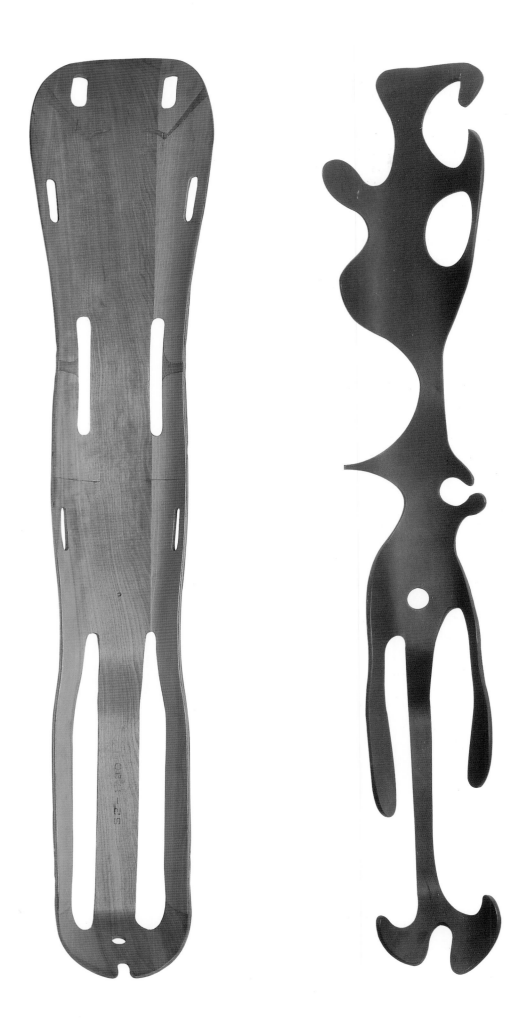

Single-shell variations

Because plywood tends to splinter when bent into acute angles, the Eameses and their colleagues cut slits and holes into these experimental molded-plywood chair shells. Eventually rejected in favor of the now-classic Eames chair with discrete seat and back panels, these wartime experiments explored aesthetic landscapes of solid and void, positive and negative space.

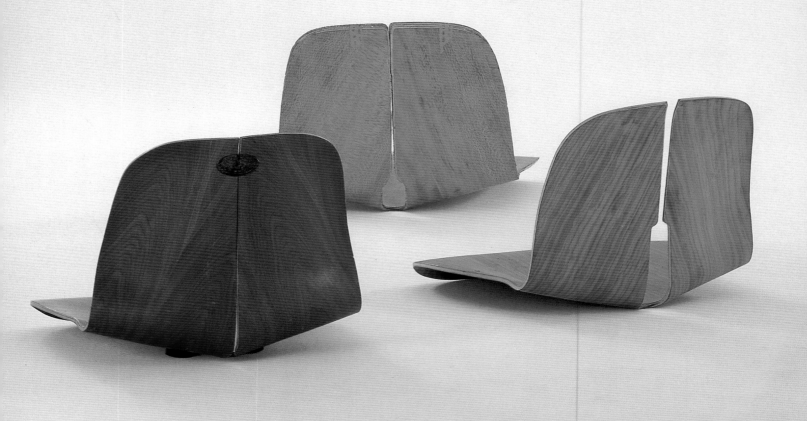

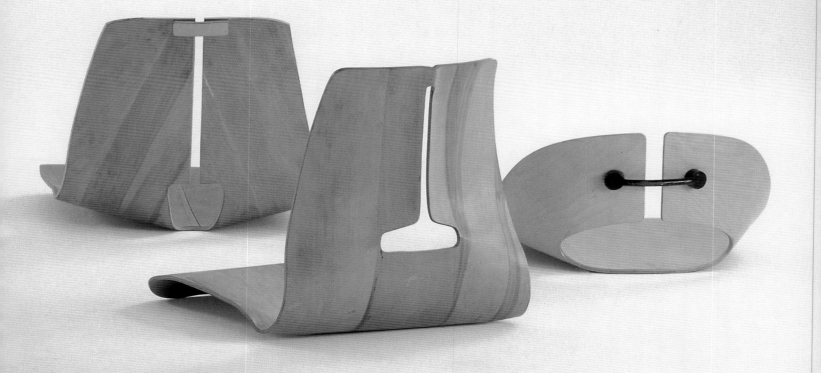

Leg variations

While the plywood parts of the Eameses' chairs functioned as a kind of "second skin," mirroring the body's own curves, the chairs' metal supports took skeletal form. These leg-and-spine experiments were welded assemblages of flat metal bars and tubes. From a minimum amount of material, maximum stability and resilience were gained.

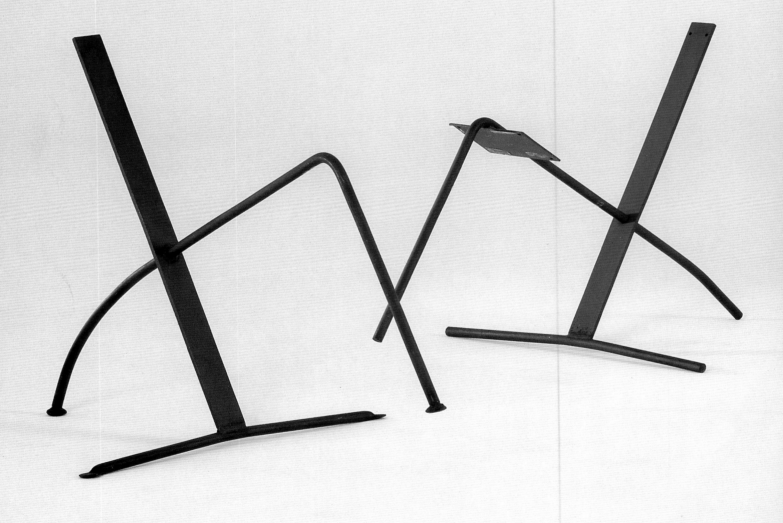

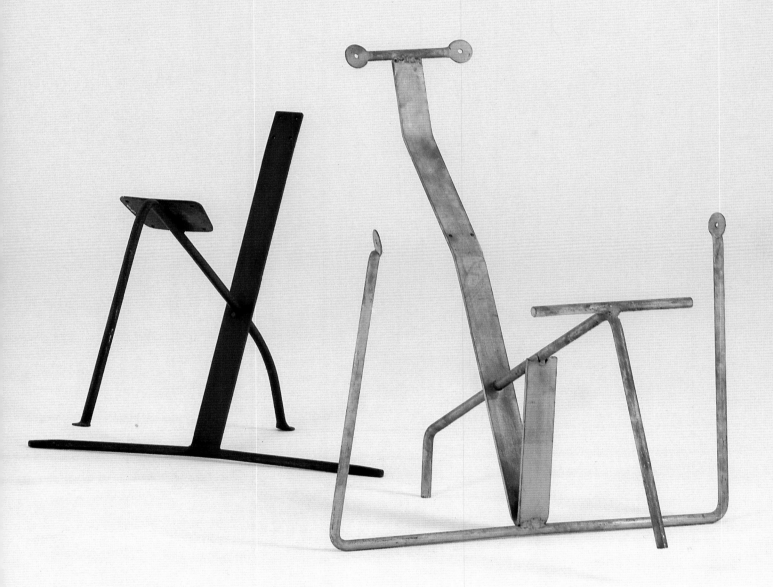

Experimental metal tilt-back chair bases, 1945
(far right, 1946)

Plywood variations

In its most ubiquitous form, the Eames plywood chair features legs of metal tubes. Although the office tried three-legged models, a more stable four-legged chair was selected for mass production in dining and lounge versions, which were dubbed in military fashion DCM and LCM, respectively. The Eames Office labored over the functional and aesthetic aspects of the chairs' plywood-to-metal connections. Screws attached the tubes to black rubber shock mounts, which were glued to the wood, adding graphic punctuation to the connections.

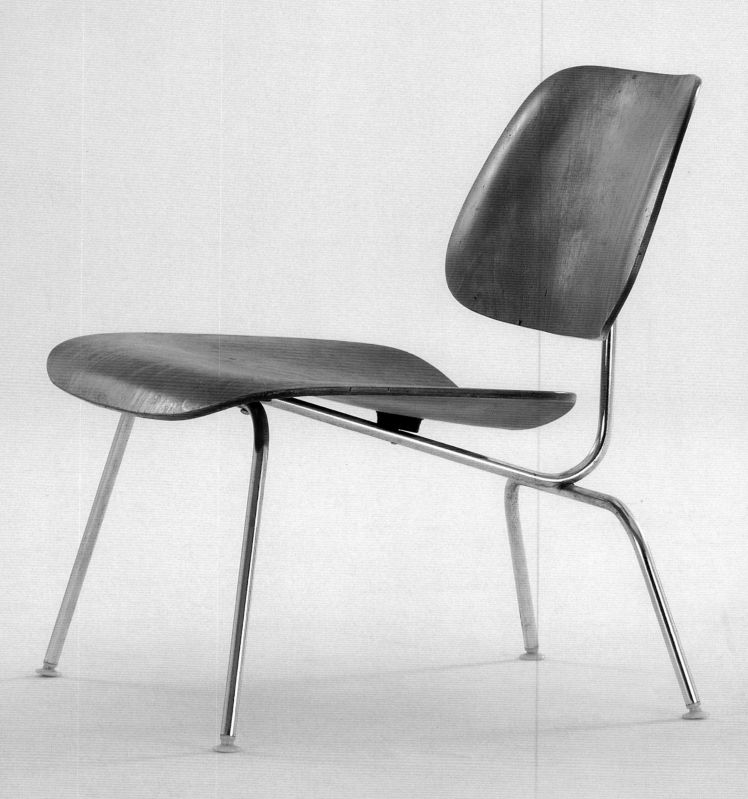

opposite: Molded-plywood lounge chair with metal legs (LCM), 1946

below: Dining chair with metal legs (DCM), 1945–46; two three-legged experimental chairs, 1945

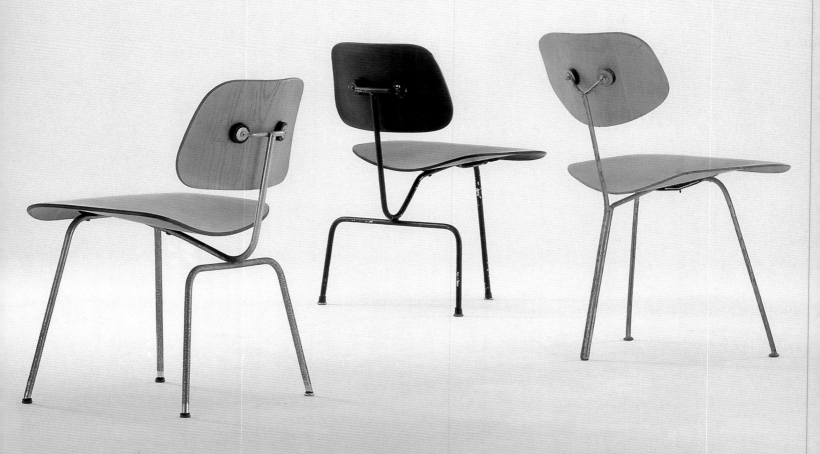

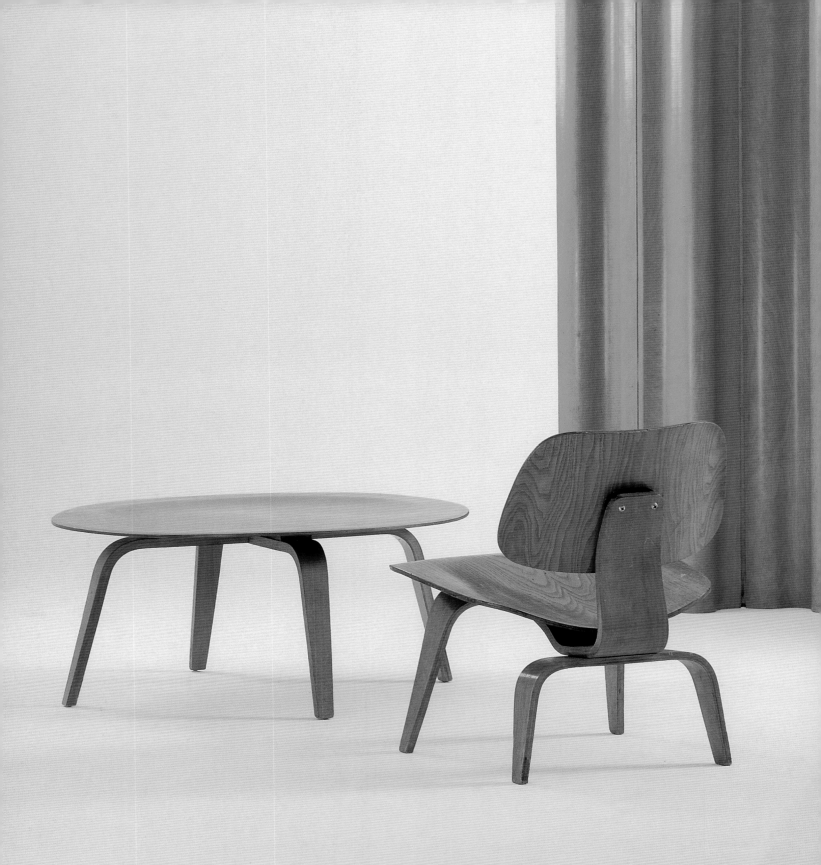

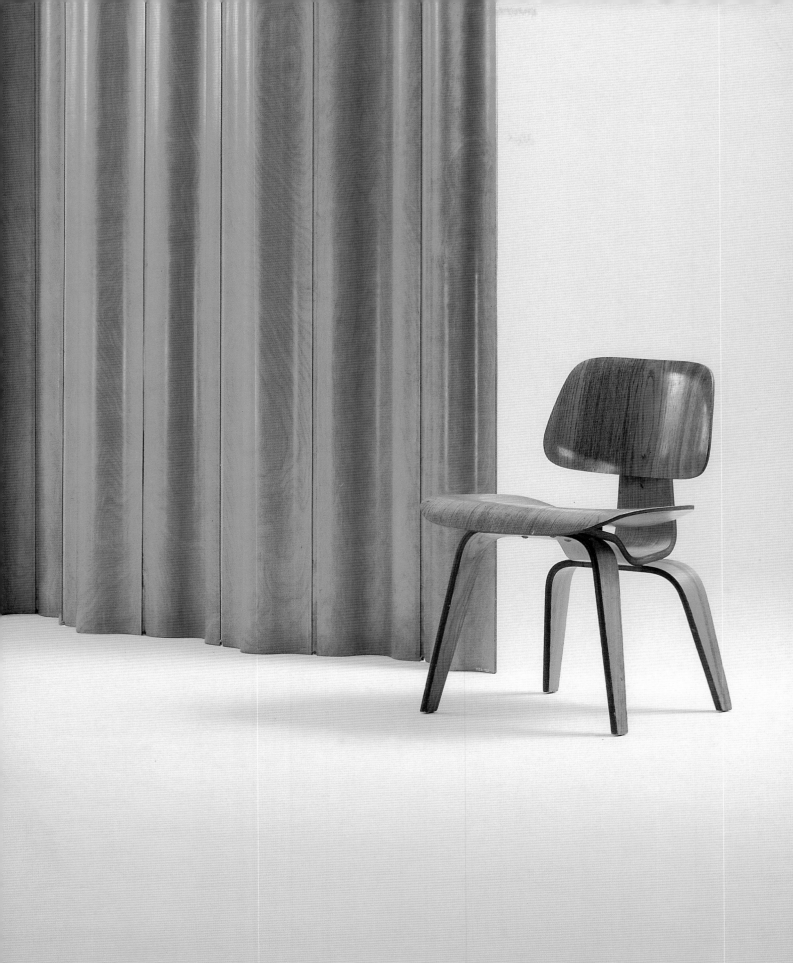

Suite of molded-plywood furniture. Left to right:
Coffee table with wood legs (CTW), 1945; prototype of
lounge chair with wood legs (LCW), 1945; folding wall
screen (FSW), 1946; dining chair with wood legs
(DCW), 1945

Lounge chair and precedents

In the Eameses' continuous quest for new furniture concepts, seemingly dead-end experiments could resurface with surprising results. In 1945 and 1946, for example, the office developed ideas for lounge chairs made with interlocking pieces of curving molded plywood. Lying dormant for nearly a decade, this concept reached fruition in the Eameses' 1956 leather and molded-wood lounge chair.

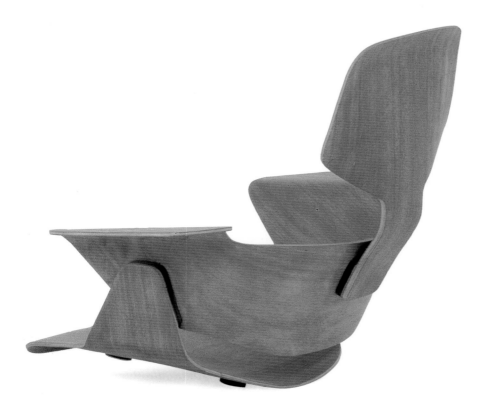

opposite: Experimental three-piece molded-plywood
lounge chair, 1946

below: Lounge chair and ottoman, 1956

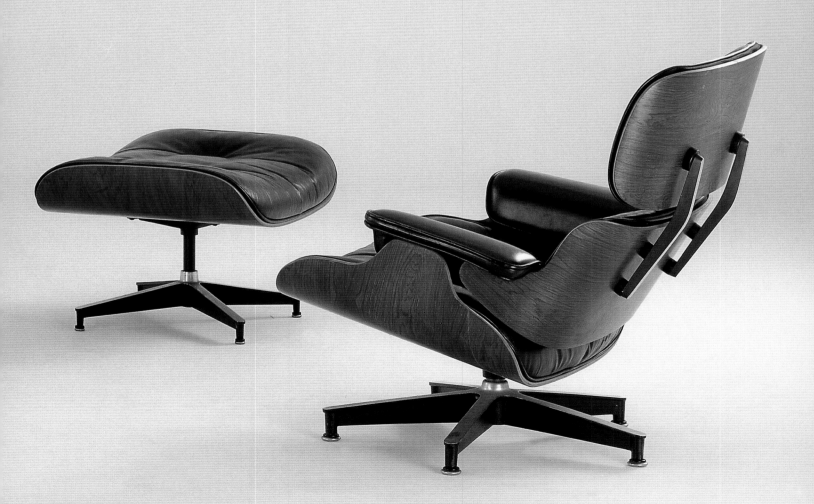

Fiberglass

The Eameses' fiberglass-reinforced plastic chair solved the problem of how to make a seat out of a single shell. In 1948 the office decided to collaborate with a research team of engineers from UCLA and enter The Museum of Modern Art's "International Competition for Low-Cost Furniture Design." Striving for a chair that was cheap, lightweight, versatile, and suitable for young families, the office produced a single-shell design to be stamped out of sheet metal, an industrial technique adapted from the automobile industry. Staff members developed special equipment to stamp and test the metal shells, specifically, a drop-hammer device using molds and weights. Metal stamping proved too expensive for low-cost production, and intrigued by fiberglass— a moldable material that had seen extensive wartime use—the office contacted Zenith Plastics of Gardena, California, which made fiberglass-reinforced plastic radar domes during the war. Working together, Zenith and the Eames Office reconceptualized the use of the material and developed one of the first one-piece plastic chairs whose surface was exposed rather than upholstered. Zenith began mass-producing armchair versions in 1950 for Herman Miller, which offered them for sale that year. The basic technology of these chairs involved forming liquefied plastic and fiberglass reinforcement with male-female molds using a hydraulic press. The chairs were initially available in only three colors; a broader palette was later offered, as were upholstered versions in fabric and vinyl. They have also been available with a wide variety of bases — rod legged, cast aluminum pedestal, swivel, wire strut, wood legged, and wood rocker on wire strut. Bases are attached to the shells with rubber shock mounts. The standard version of the chair has only recently gone out of production.

Stack of fiberglass-reinforced plastic chairs, 1954; dining armchair, produced 1950–89

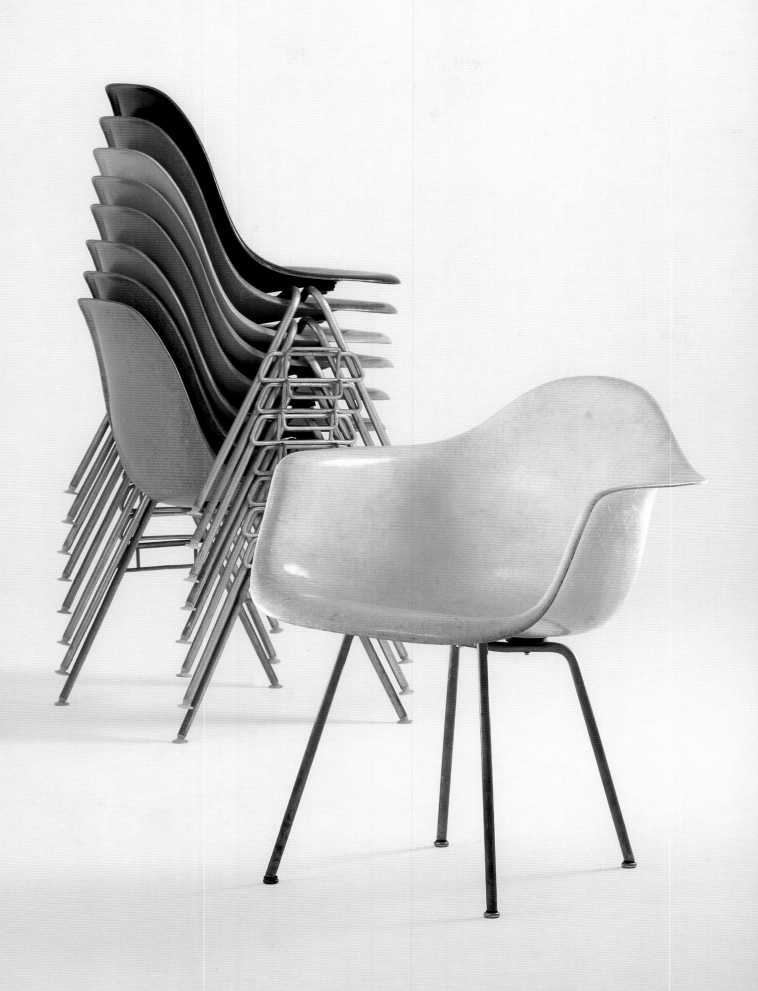

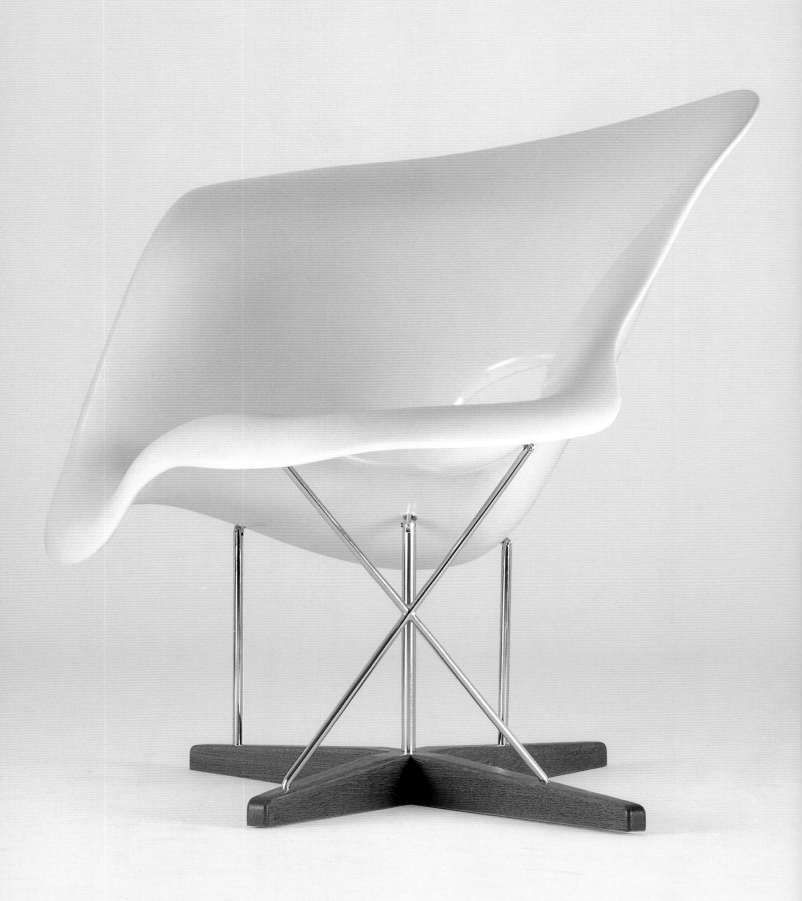

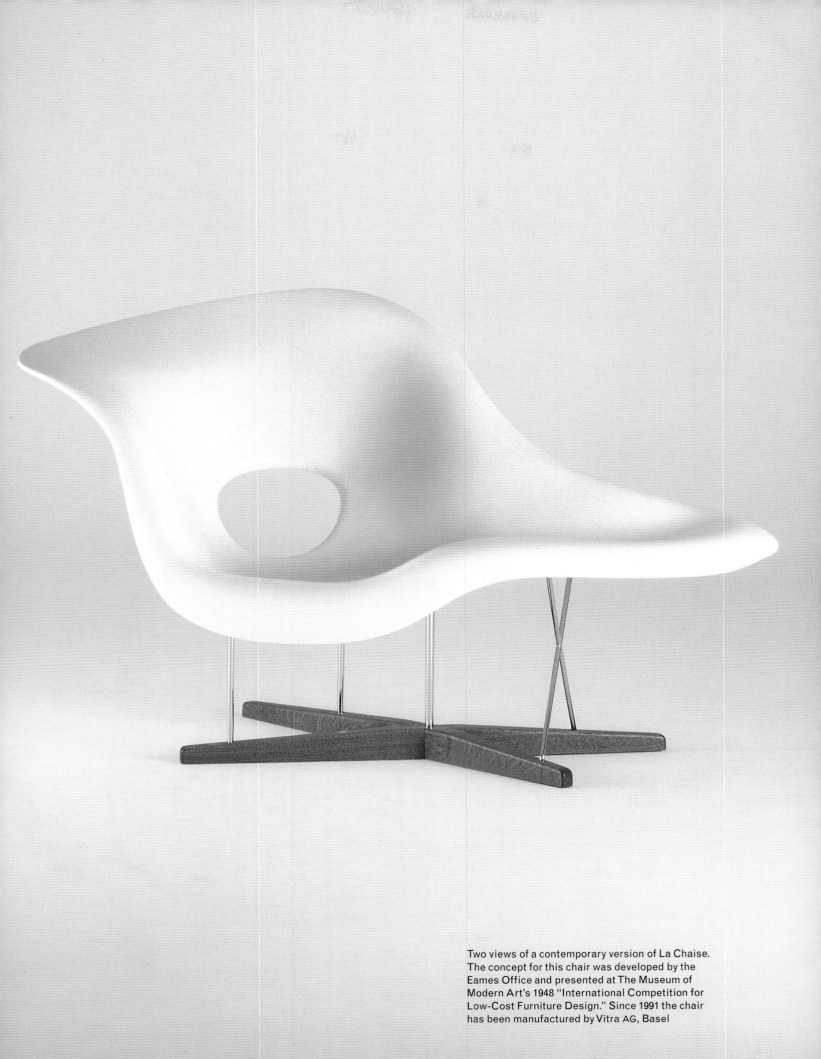

Two views of a contemporary version of La Chaise.
The concept for this chair was developed by the
Eames Office and presented at The Museum of
Modern Art's 1948 "International Competition for
Low-Cost Furniture Design." Since 1991 the chair
has been manufactured by Vitra AG, Basel

Wire

The Eames Office also investigated bent and welded wire as the basis for furniture designs. Inspired by trays, dress forms, baskets, and animal traps, the office developed experimental pieces as well as chairs and bases that were mass-produced. Like the molded-fiberglass chair, the wire-mesh chair is a uni-shell design. (Harry Bertoia, who worked with the Eameses in the mid-1940s, designed equally beautiful wire-mesh chairs for Knoll Associates in 1952–53.) The Eameses' chairs were marketed by Herman Miller from 1951 to 1957 and are today made by Vitra AG. The shell can be adapted to various base configurations and upholstery types. Ingenious techniques were developed for mass-producing this thin upholstery, and special molds were developed as a form over which to weld the wire shells. The office adapted a resistance-welding technique used for making drawers, developing an innovative method for reinforcing the shell's rim with a double band of wire.

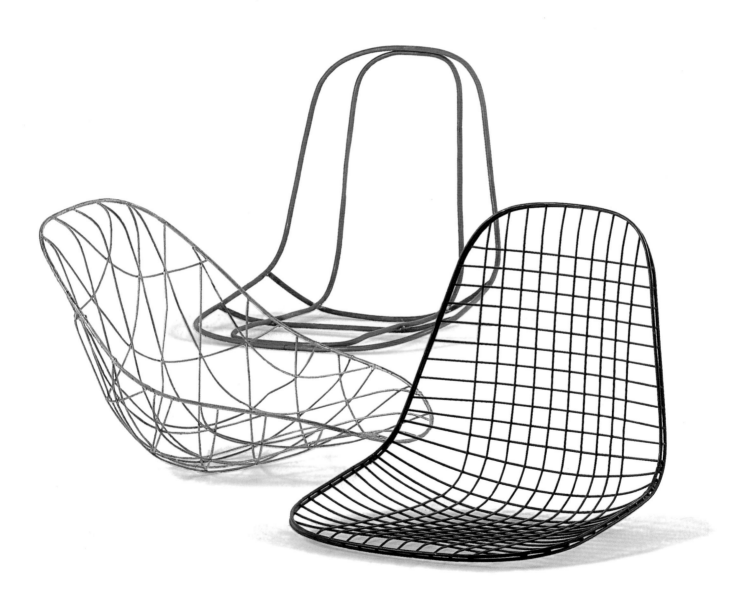

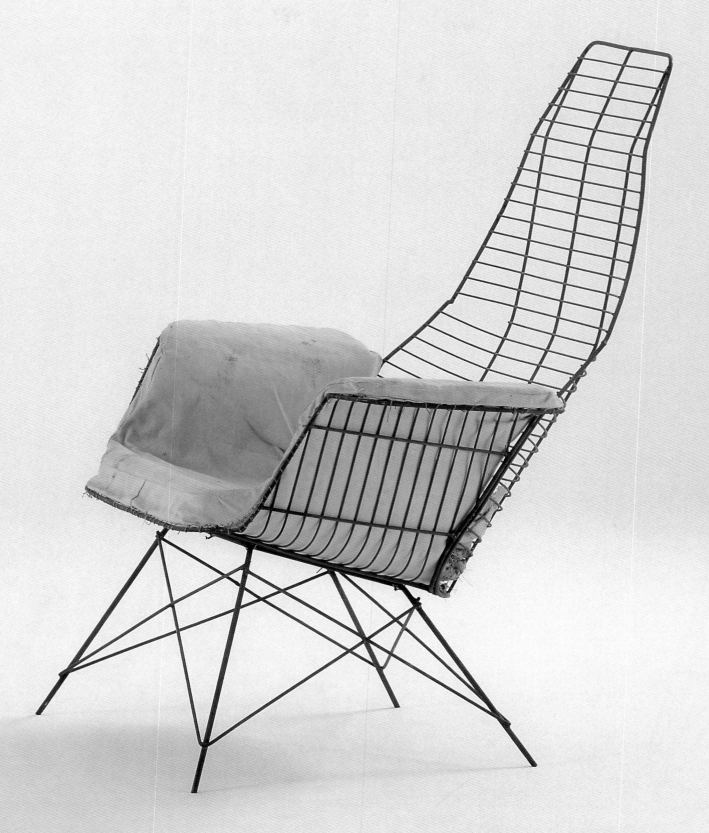

opposite left and right: Experimental bent and welded
wire chair shells, 1951

opposite center: Experimental metal rod chair shell, 1951

above: Experimental wire armchair, 1951

As was true of the design process for the plywood and fiberglass furnishings, the Eameses' mass-produced wire chairs and tables were created after considerable experimentation at the outer limits of the fabrication technique. Designs for a high-backed wire armchair and a folding, demountable sofa proved too complex to be manufactured economically. The latter's collapsibility and do-it-yourself assembly returned in the simpler Eames Sofa Compact, which Herman Miller introduced in 1954.

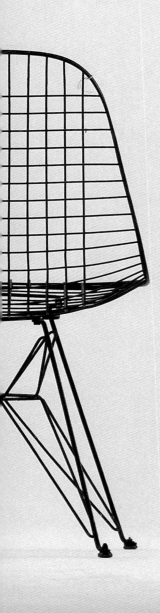
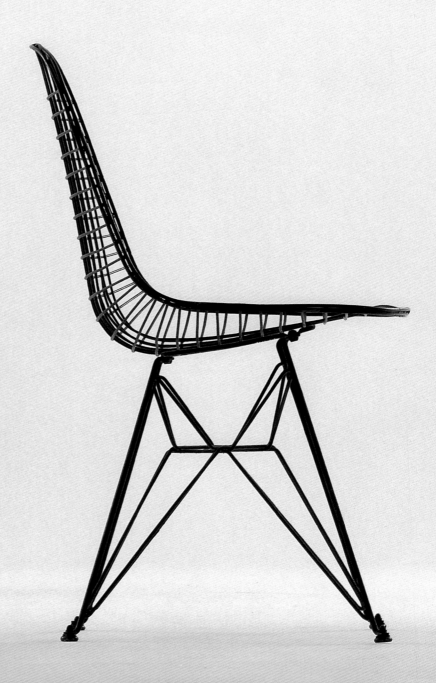

opposite: Bent and welded wire side chairs with "Eiffel Tower" bases, 1951

below: Frame of experimental folding wire sofa, 1951. Collection Lucia Eames, on loan to the Vitra Design Museum

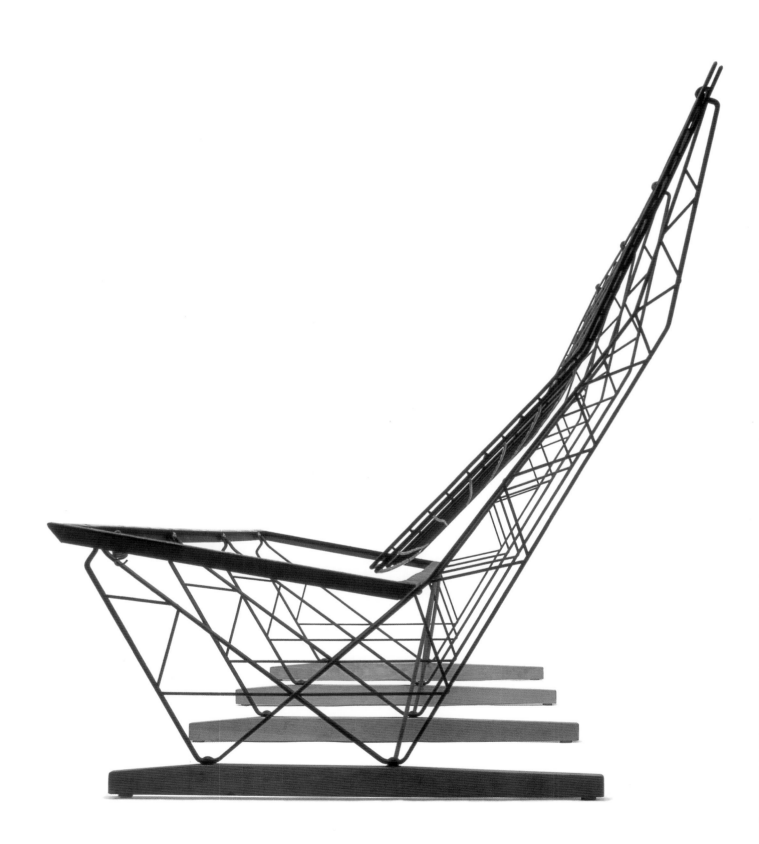

Aluminum

The aluminum chairs of 1958 were intended to be usable both indoors and out. The Eames Office created full-scale mock-ups in wood and metal over a three-year period in order to make a chair of minimal material and mass. The chair featured elegant, sculptural one-piece cast aluminum side frames between which upholstery was slung. Held within grooves in these side frames, the upholstery was reinforced in three places with stiff material hidden in folds to create a kind of flexible textile "sandwich"— another variation on the Eameses' body-fitting chair concept. To solve the problem of sagging, the fabric was rolled tightly at the top and bottom of the chair's frames. The aluminum chair's concept formed the basis of the office's 1962 Eames Tandem Sling Seating, an institutional multiple-seating system first installed in Chicago's O'Hare and Washington's Dulles airports.

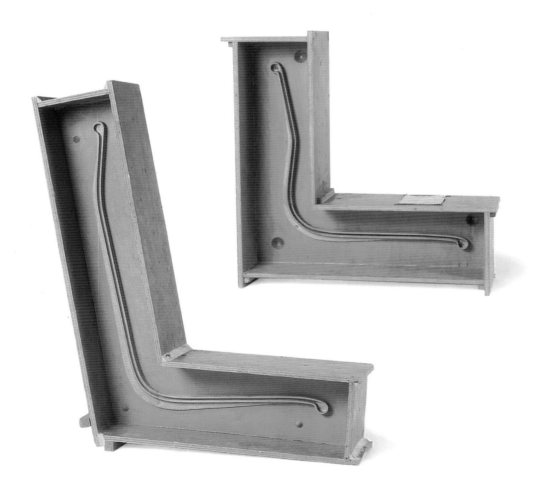

above: Wood casting patterns for aluminum chairs, 1958

opposite: Aluminum dining chair, 1959

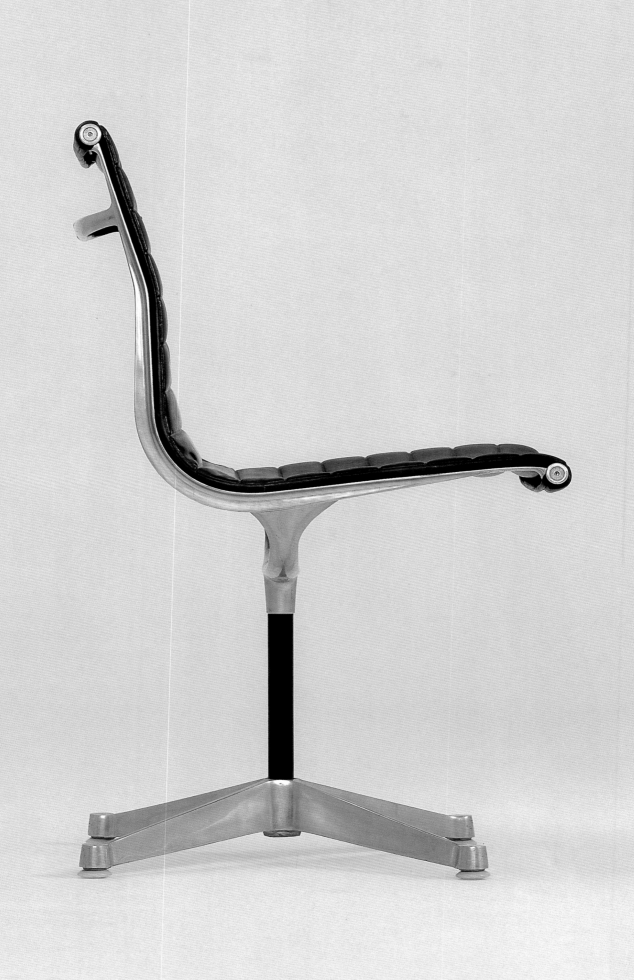

Aluminum dining chair, 1959, details

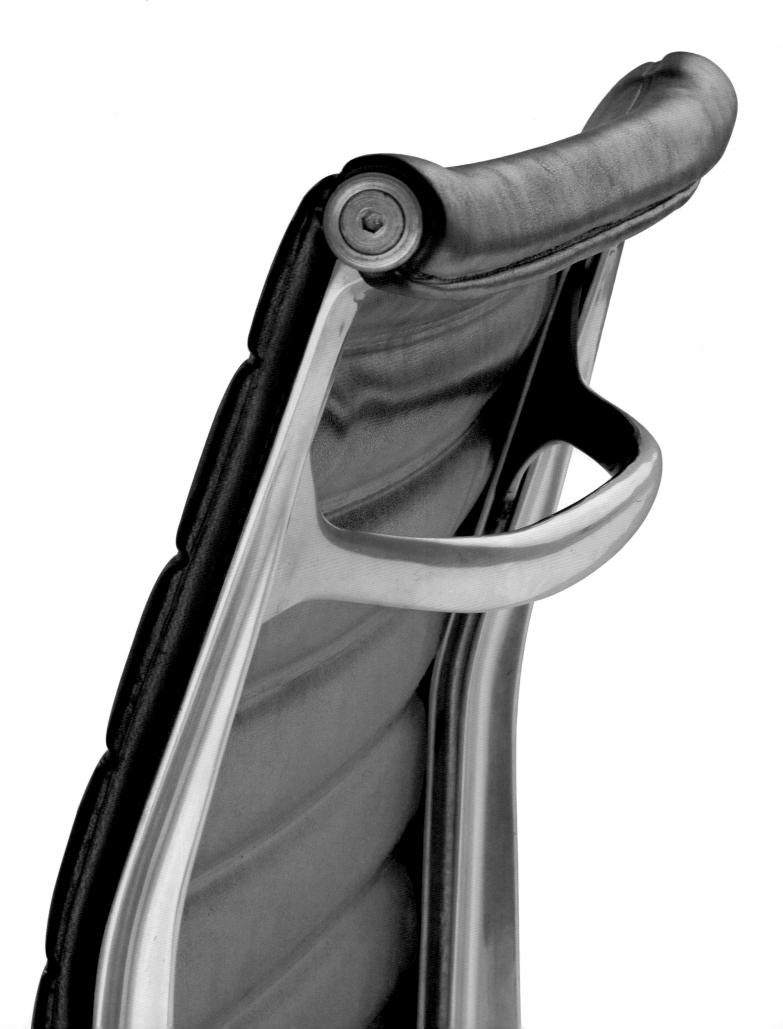

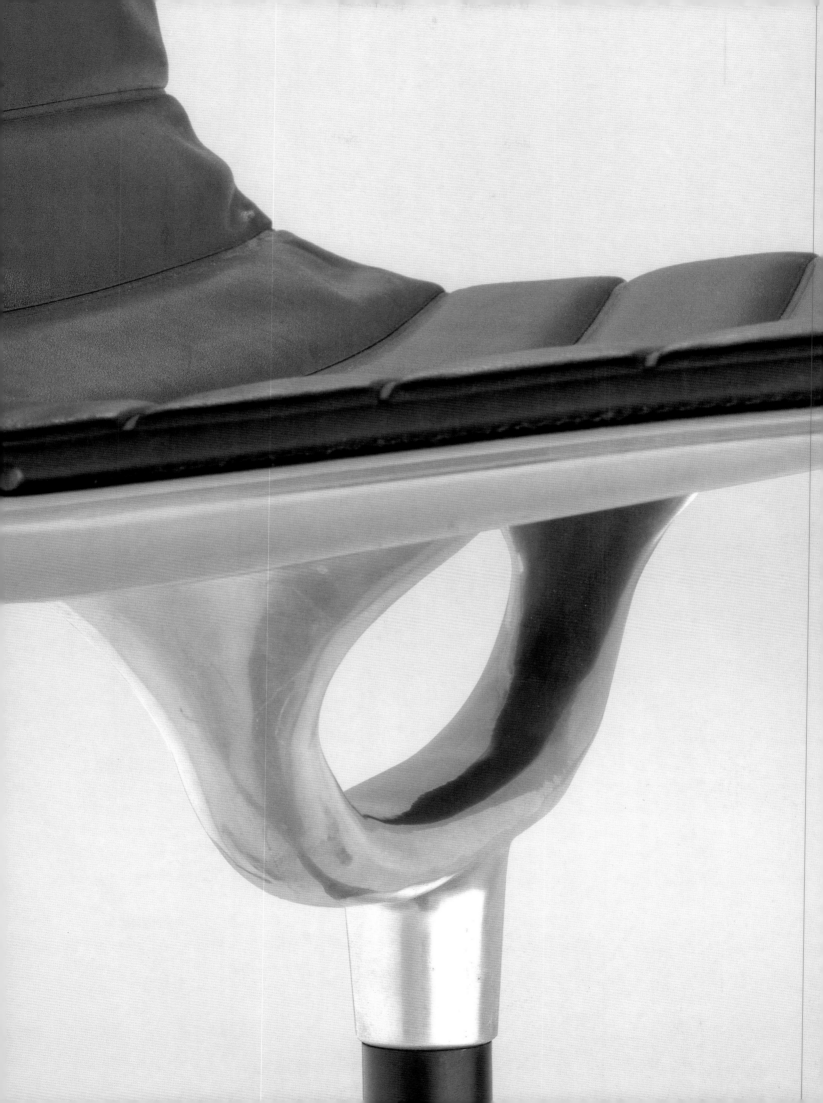

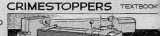

DICK TRACY

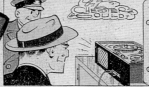

CRIMESTOPPERS TEXTBOOK

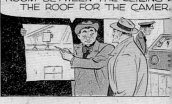

GETAWAY CAR, WHICH STOOD IN ONE SPOT F
SEVERAL MINUTES, HAD A LEAKY RADIATOR
DEPOSITED A BROWN RESIDUE. SAMPLE RES
FROM SUSPECT'S CAR, WHEN COMPARED BY
SPECTROSCOPE, PROVE TO BE THE SAME

Panel 1: YES, NEWSUIT NAN ADMITTED BUYING THE RIFLE — GOT IT AS A GIFT FOR A FRIEND OF HERS, WHOSE NAME, NATURALLY, SHE HAD "FORGOTTEN."

OH, SURE.

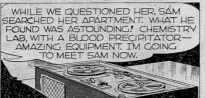

Panel 2: WHILE WE QUESTIONED HER, SAM SEARCHED HER APARTMENT. WHAT HE FOUND WAS ASTOUNDING! CHEMISTRY LAB, WITH A BLOOD PRECIPITATOR — AMAZING EQUIPMENT. I'M GOING TO MEET SAM NOW.

SNAP

Panel 3: MEANWHILE —

YES, THE TELEGUARD TV CAMERA IS ALL SET. EVERYTHING'S READY, SAM.

Panel 4: LATER IN A BASEMENT ROOM

HER APARTMENT IS ON THE TOP FLOOR AND HAS FLUSH CEILING LIGHTS. THERE WAS PLENTY O ROOM BETWEEN THE CEILING A THE ROOF FOR THE CAMER.

Panel 5: HEY! SOMEBODY'S COMING INTO HER PLACE NOW.

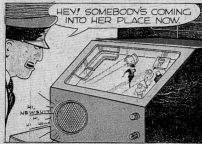

HI, NEWSUIT
HI, HEL

Panel 6: BE SEATED, GENTLEMEN.

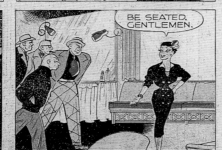

Panel 7: THAT HOSPITAL TYPE CENTRIFUGE OF HERS CONTAINED FOUR TUBES FILLED WITH COLORED WATER, A GREEN, YELLOW, RED AND BLUE.

WHAT IN THE WORLD WOULD SHE DO WITH THAT?

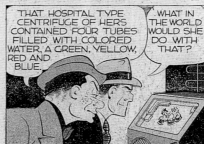

Panel 8: I TAKE YELLOW. GREEN RED

BLUE

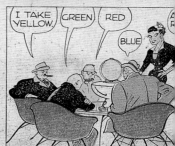

Panel 9: THE CENTRIFUGE IS SNAPPED ON AND **OFF!** THE TUBES WHIRL —

BEE

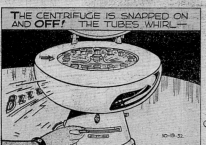

10-19-52

Panel 10: THEN, AS THEY LOSE THEIR SPEED, EACH MAN WATCHES HIS COLOR INTENTLY.

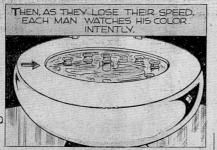

Panel 11: YELLOW! THAT'S ME.

YEAH, YOU'RE THE CHOSEN ONE, HANK.

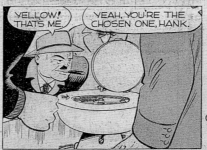

Panel 12: IT'S GOT TO BE A CLEAN JOB. A COUPLE OF WELL-PLACED SLUGS OUGHT TO DO IT.

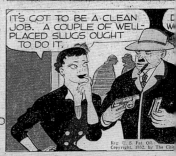

The Eamesian Aesthetic in Popular Culture

A TIMELINE OF CHAIRS

Charles and Ray made, and the world received. These advertisements, magazines, comics, and other ephemera trace a unique visual history of the Eameses' chairs as they echoed through the media of popular culture. Created by contemporary illustrators and art directors from the mid-1940s to the 1980s, the images demonstrate the assimilation of the Eameses' aesthetic into the realms of art, commerce, industry, and fashion. They have been selected primarily from the Eames Office's vast publicity files, which are now housed at the Library of Congress. *D.A.*

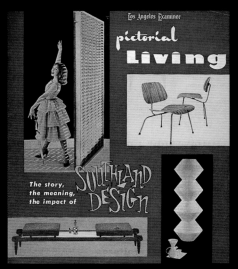

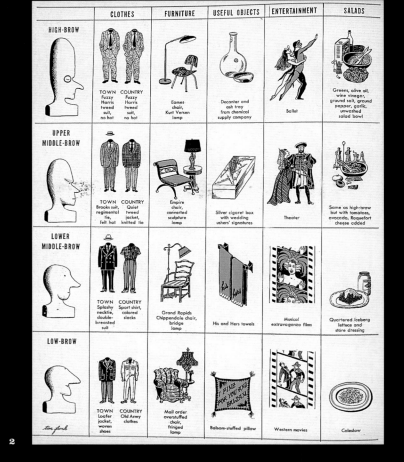

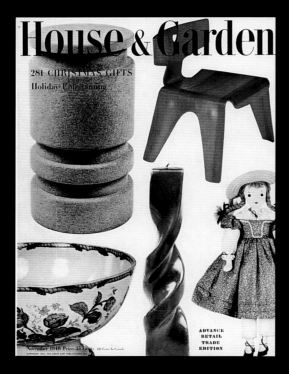

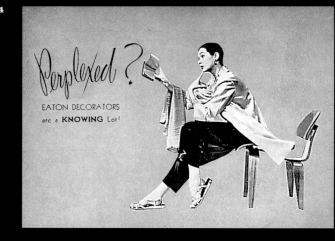

1 Plywood chair in "Pictorial Living" section,
   Los Angeles Examiner, January 24, 1960

2 Plywood chair representing "highbrow" taste
   in Russell Lynes's 1949 book *The Tastemakers:
   The Shaping of American Popular Taste*. The
   illustration later appeared in the April 1949
   issue of *Life*, a detail of which is shown here

3 Child's plywood chair, *House & Garden*,
   November 1946

4 Plywood chair in Eaton's advertisement,
   Perspective, 1955

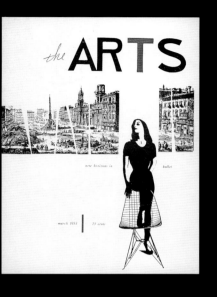

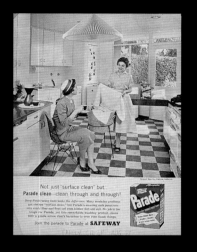

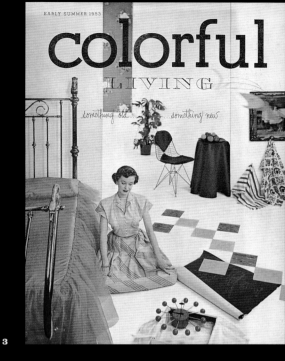

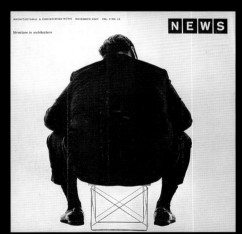

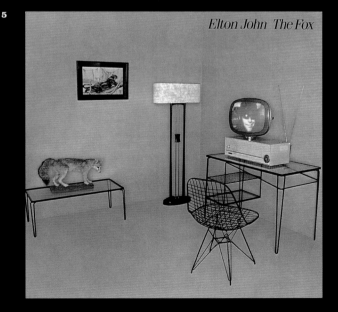

1   Wire chair in *The Arts*, March 1953

2   Wire chair in Parade detergent advertisement,
      Family Circle, August 1955

3   Wire chair in *Colorful Living*, Early Summer 1953

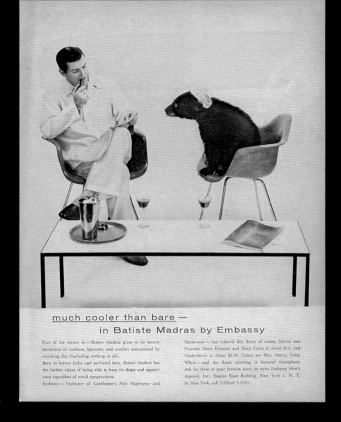

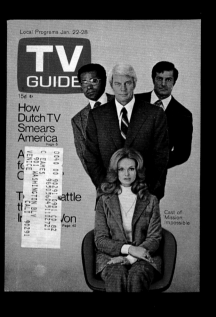

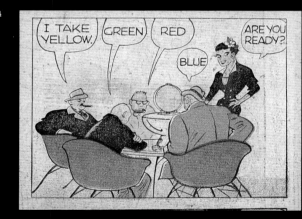

1 La Fonda chair and cast of "Mission Impossible," *TV Guide*, January 22–28, 1965

2 Fiberglass chair in Embassy menswear advertisement, *The New Yorker*, May 2, 1954

3 Fiberglass chair in *Business Week*, October 30, 1954

4 Fiberglass chair in "Dick Tracy" cartoon, detail, by Chester Gould

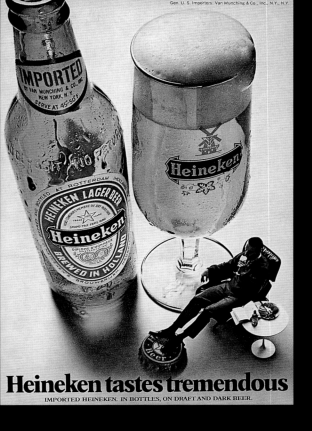

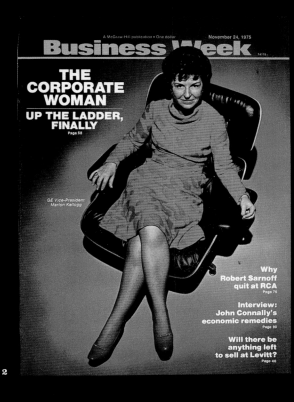

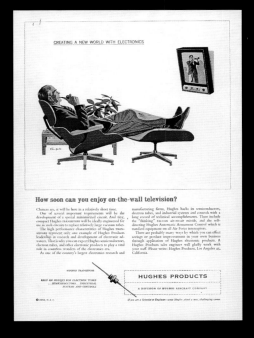

1   Lounge chair in Heineken beer advertisement,
Esquire, November 1971

2   Lounge chair in *Business Week*,
November 24, 1975

3   Lounge chair and ottoman in Lebow men's
suits advertisement, *Vogue*, May 15, 1956

4   Lounge chair and ottoman in Hughes products
advertisement, *U.S. News & World Report*,
August 10, 1956

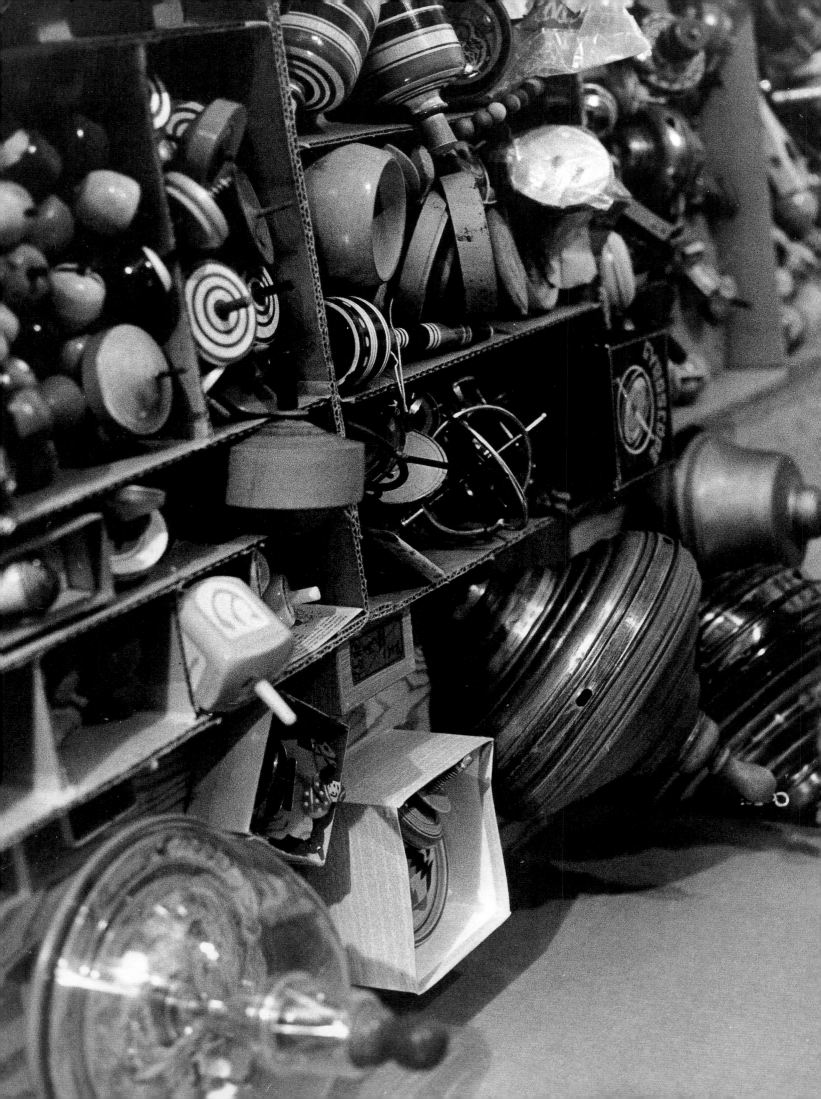

A Happy Octopus

CHARLES AND RAY LEARN SCIENCE AND TEACH IT WITH IMAGES

Philip and Phylis Morrison

Tops at the Eames Office, 1966

To the Screening Room

The ocean was out of sight behind low dunes paved over long ago, but on occasion its tumult could still be heard. The train tracks at the next corner that mark Electric Avenue were by those years deserted, an old change strongly underlined by the sight of two gas stations. The visitor rang at the office door to alert the lively receptionists, walked in past the *faux* palace background from a Bombay photographer's studio, down the long corridor, across the space of the big exhibit models and their busy modelers, on to the screening room, stopping just before reaching the active shop where the furniture prototypes found their form.

The small screening room was windowless, with a welcoming, comfortable, and diverse choice of the office's own chairs. In that room the entire optical path, projector lamp to screen, was just as flawless as the sound reproduction, both given devoted attention by one or another of the local experts at hand, prepared to make up at any moment for the deficiencies of work in progress. This was not Hollywood, pomp and pretense were absent, but that room was plainly the domain of technical mastery over a powerful technology. Only the results appeared effortless. Lights out, the films would begin. Usually an old one or two were offered as openers upon eager request, and then the current work was shown at whatever level of completion it had reached.

This essay—no substitute at all for the silvery screen—will outline some of the films (there are nearly one hundred of them) in which we see the secure basis for the admiring claim we make in the subtitle of our essay. Because the films are so widely accessible, the most enduring gift of this celebrated workshop is the two dozen of their films that move toward enhancing the public understanding of science. That need is greater today than ever. In later pages we shall give some account of the exhibitions and other Eames creations that address the same need.

Pure Cinema

The Eameses' film *Tops* (1969) is a rare specimen of pure cinema, only seven and a half minutes long. It has an apt and original musical score that partners the intricate dance of images. (The talented composer for this and most of the films was Elmer Bernstein, an old friend and understanding collaborator.) But the film speaks out not at all, not even one murmuring word, nor does it show any text (other than the title and credits) or diagram (a few printed words can be made out among the familiar markings of toys). Without symbols it transmits a depth of instruction in real science that is hard to match, a charming view of one striking portion of physical reality, transmitted with unspoken but gripping internal drama made plain by the sharp and steady view. Most shots are tight close-ups, their field of view desktop size or smaller. The pageant of these diverse toys seen in action becomes a riveting display of the unexpected, everywhere in engaging ceaseless flow.

Plenty of tops! A top or two is made of transparent plastic, a cavity filled with colorful liquids that separate like cream from milk in the little spinning centrifuge. Tiny bells made by the hand of some dexterous Indian silversmith spring stiffly out from the whirling carrier, to make even more tangible the very same forces. An elegant little ballerina of metal pirouettes past; does she come from some Danish ballet? A plump and self-satisfied top of sheet metal, in gold, red, and blue and a foot high, grand enough for any Victorian drawing room, hums loudly. A toy gyroscope is wound for spin with loving care, a common thumbtack magnified on the screen stands steadfast on its sharp point, set artfully spinning as if a draftsman had paused to launch it across his own tidy

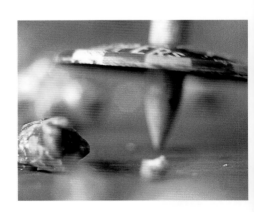

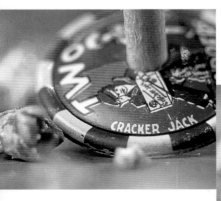

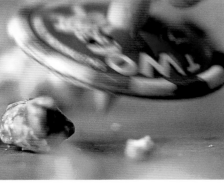

lettering. A trickier top inverts itself before our eyes, and a matched squad of conical tops weaves its way toward us. Half a dozen of the people from the Eames studio, ready for any playful task, had rehearsed their cooperative skills until they were able to set the tops spinning all at once. Cameraman and editor completed the wonderful shot with no sign on camera of human presence, though deft hands were only inches away.

The visual narrative of this wordless little epic is strong. Tops are born in spin, then they enjoy their life in motion, until the spin begins to fail. They gyrate aimlessly for a while as the once-decisive whirl dwindles to its wobbling, rolling end. A few human beings, youthful masters of the top, initially share the screen, launching and steering tops they know well. One is a charmer too young for school; others, more adept still, surprise us with their smooth skills. The actors remind us by dress and appearance that the tops come from far-flung cultures; some may be as old-fashioned as a few disks of low-fired clay, some are novel industrial products of our own times. Altogether several dozen tops perform before us, with the most disparate of origins, materials, designs, and scale.

The human ingenuity and variety of tastes displayed throughout this lighthearted processional is complemented by the sure unity of top behavior. That unity is inbuilt; it owes much less to the choices of the designer-craftsman than it does to the universal laws of gravity and motion. The close views are compelling. Side events abound, from musical sounds and centrifugal action to the psychological phenomenon of persistence of vision seen both in form and in color mixing. These trials are not austere lab experiments with a single end; rather, they open a rich and enjoyable world, long singled out by the playful. Innocents can hardly miss the wonder of tops even when they do not yet perceive the ordering principles. The more experienced will find cause and meaning sharply revealed amid larger implications.

The film is always well received by physicists and astronomers, who find in it examples of the same spin that is everywhere, in sea and air, in planets, comets, stars, galaxies—in every proton. In 1995 we showed *Tops* to a number of school audiences in South Africa. After one showing a boy asked why we felt the film was part of science. We began an awkward reply by saying that, after all, doesn't the earth spin? "Oh," he broke in, "I see: the planets are tops, too."

Frames from the film *Tops* (1969)

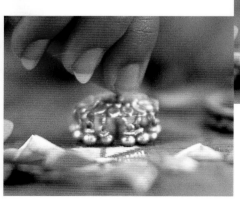
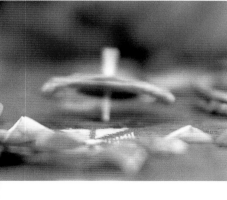
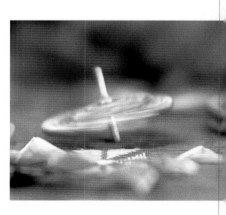

Powers of Ten: A Journey Across the Modern Cosmos

The 1977 film *Powers of Ten*, almost the last one the office produced, has become their most widely viewed production. It is much used in high schools and colleges, and travelers often report that they hear it playing all day long—automatically repeated—on little screens in the corners of science museums from Sydney to the Washington Mall. Since nearly all of it is carefully made animation, it is among the most ambitious, labor-intensive, and costly of all the films the Eameses made. It deserves its global acceptance as a miniature masterpiece, its screening time nearly nine minutes.

As with *Tops*, we will describe *Powers* to offer some sense of what is in it. We worked hard on the script and the narration. It engrossed Charles and Ray, who devoted a great deal of thought to this work. (Alex Funke, assisted by Michael Wiener, did the shooting, frame-by-frame, over the course of a year on a forty-foot-long animation stand. The two recorded their heroic efforts in an exposure log with nearly fourteen thousand frames.)

Powers is a superb science-teaching film. The intellectual and temporal structures are remarkably tightly disciplined. All is animation, except half a minute of live cinema that shows the two picnickers who are implicitly at the center of every screen. Most of the images on the screen are color photographs of artwork. In this way the entire film is indirect, reflexive: photos of photos, photos of composites, or photos of original paintings based on scientific photos. The final artwork—about forty meticulously prepared images, repeatedly photographed in precise register to produce the unbroken animated motion we follow—embodies the cosmic synthesis by Ray and Charles that comprises the final film. The artists used many scientific images and drew on the technical judgment of a number of advisors, all working scientists from a variety of disciplines.

The film is rigidly designed, almost sculptured. Clock tick by clock tick we share a metronomic journey moving along one straight line in space, out from the hand of one of the picnickers to the far galaxies, then back to tiny quarks deep within an atom of that same hand. Each step either expands or contracts the previous field of view by a factor of ten. Discipline is unbroken, not only in the meaning and position of what we see, but also in the time allowed to view it. Only the picnic is shot from life; the rest is all art.

Tops is a quite different enterprise. Every shot in *Tops* records a real physical scene of real motion, though sometimes filmed at a magnified scale not available even to eyewitnesses. Without words or text, diagrams or exposition, by the powerful processes of cutting and ordering alone, *Tops* was given a subtly structured narrative. No symbolic basis is present. The revealed unity is implicit. Both great unifying topics, the physics of rotation and the worldwide ethnography of top-making, go unmentioned.

Powers, less poetic, throws us into a realistic yet imaginary journey that can be taken only thanks to images created with the help of expert handwork informed by mapping, calculation, and photography. It would be too strong to say that the two films are polar opposites in terms of pedagogy, but they do lie rather far apart. One reports an open-eyed view of a very limited world as seen through the camera, with scale and time comparable from one scene to the next. The other uses the motion picture

   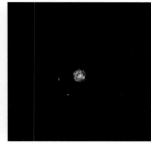

10^{+25} meters
~1 billion light years   **10^{+24} meters**
~100 million light years   **10^{+23} meters**
~10 million light years   **10^{+22} meters**
~1 million light years

Frames from the film Powers of Ten:
A Film Dealing with the Relative Size
of Things in the Universe and the
Effect of Adding Another Zero (1977)

camera to induce the illusion of smooth motion among a large number of contrived, still scenes based on well-founded inference. We see so much: a picnic, a city, streets of clouds that are the "day's weather in the Middle West," the blue sea of earth, the planets in their orbits, the stars of our galaxy, and whole clusters of galaxies far beyond. We see the intimate world within, from the red and white cells of the blood to the cell nucleus and the tangled helix of DNA. Then we are carried into the abstract particle clouds of the atom, down to the end of our present understanding, among the quarks. What will we see some day at still more distant scales?

Scenes made through an electron microscope often simulate the visible even when they differ very much from the human scale, for they resemble a direct view of forms and boundary surfaces, albeit strange ones. But in *Powers of Ten* the final seven main images, each one approached steadily over a ten-second viewing time, present what can never be seen by human eyes. Mostly they cannot even be given a uniquely compelling diagrammatic image. We see what is beyond color, forms without defined boundaries, structures constantly in swift random motion. We are thus given to "see" electrons in the atom, the nucleons in a nucleus, finally even some representation of transient quarks within a nucleon. All of these views use visual conventions to describe the remarkably unfamiliar quantum properties. Those conventions are more or less evident, and they have wide appeal, but they do reflect deliberate choices of the filmmakers. The filmmaker's conventions turn out to be plausible ones for the scientist-viewer as well. Only instruments and not the human senses enable us to grasp every step of that long journey out and back again. It is the unbroken coherence of the entire context that carries us credibly into the invisible. That idea of a cosmic journey, made quantitative in an astonishing and widely acceptable way over the magnitudes of all the cosmos, we—the Eameses included—owe to the Dutch educator Kees Boeke. He and his middle-school students first worked out such a journey of tenfold steps not on film but in drawings, during the first years after World War II. The final credit of the Eames film is a tribute to Boeke.

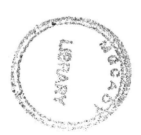

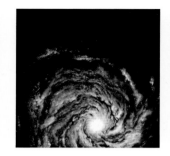

10⁺²¹ meters
~100,000 light years

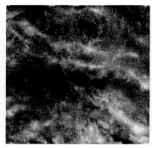

10⁺²⁰ meters
~10,000 light years

10⁺¹⁹ meters
~1,000 light years

10⁺¹⁸ meters
~100 light years

10⁺¹⁷ meters
~10 light years

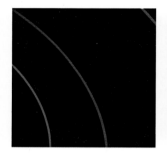

10⁺¹¹ meters
100 million kilometers

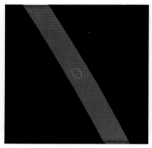

10⁺¹⁰ meters
10 million kilometers

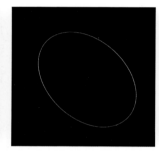

10⁺⁹ meters
1 million kilometers

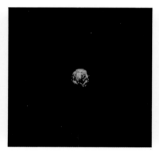

10⁺⁸ meters
100,000 kilometers

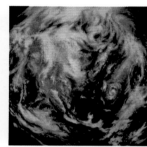

10⁺⁷ meters
10,000 kilometers

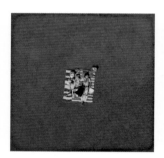

10⁺¹ meters
10 meters

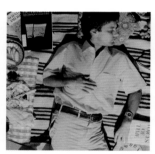

10⁰ meters
1 meter

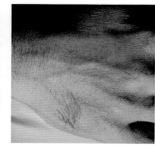

10^{−1} meters
10 centimeters

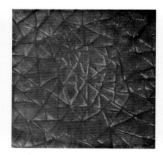

10^{−2} meters
1 centimeter

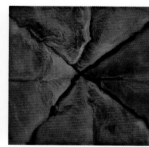

10^{−3} meters
1 millimeter

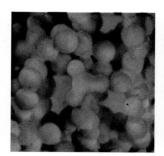

10^{−9} meters
10 angstroms
(1 nanometer)

10^{−10} meters
1 angstrom
(100 picometers)

10^{−11} meters
10 picometers

10^{−12} meters
1 picometer

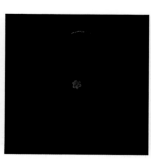

10^{−13} meters
100 fermis

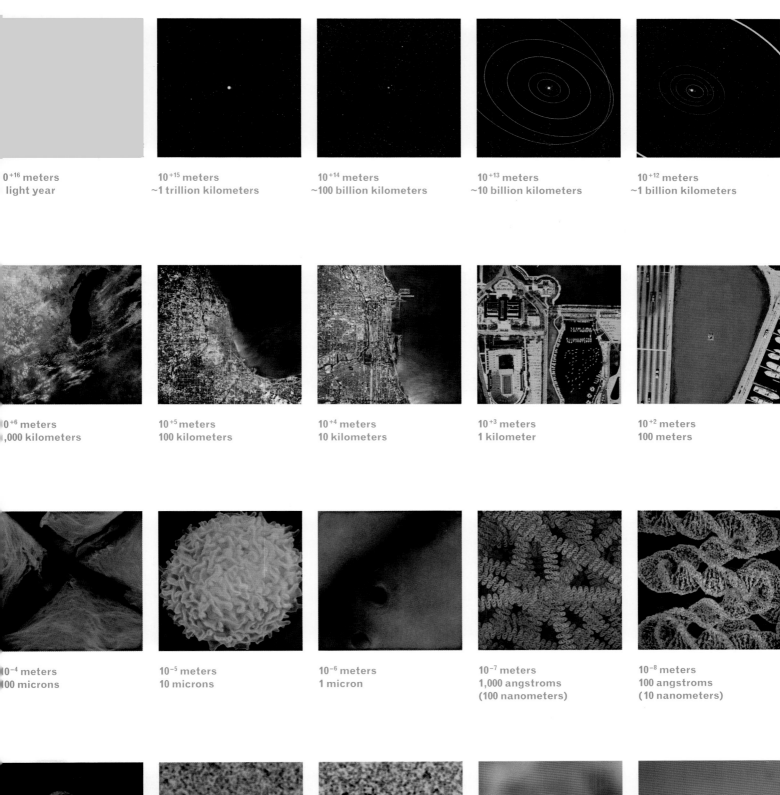

10⁰⁺¹⁶ meters
light year

10⁺¹⁵ meters
~1 trillion kilometers

10⁺¹⁴ meters
~100 billion kilometers

10⁺¹³ meters
~10 billion kilometers

10⁺¹² meters
~1 billion kilometers

10⁰⁺⁶ meters
1,000 kilometers

10⁺⁵ meters
100 kilometers

10⁺⁴ meters
10 kilometers

10⁺³ meters
1 kilometer

10⁺² meters
100 meters

10⁻⁴ meters
100 microns

10⁻⁵ meters
10 microns

10⁻⁶ meters
1 micron

10⁻⁷ meters
1,000 angstroms
(100 nanometers)

10⁻⁸ meters
100 angstroms
(10 nanometers)

10⁻¹⁴ meters
10 fermis

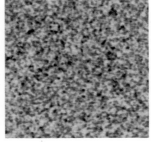

10⁻¹⁵ meters
1 fermi

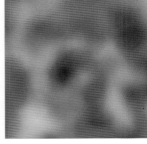

10⁻¹⁶ meters
0.1 fermis

10⁻¹⁷ meters
0.01 fermis

10⁻¹⁸ meters
0.001 fermis

A Communications Primer

The third film we examine is *A Communications Primer* (1953). It is an early film for the Eameses, the fifth of all the films they would make. It is striking that this clear and cogent account of the brand-new theory of information came out four years after Claude Shannon's defining book, *The Mathematical Theory of Communication*. While the ideas were still new even to the scientists, this film explained and illustrated such notions as signal, channel, noise, code, redundancy, even the bit. (The byte was not yet current.) It thanks as sources, among others, the pioneers of these concepts, mathematicians Shannon, Norbert Wiener, and John von Neumann.

Seriousness of purpose does not make this film sober. It is full of simpler images and symbols. The Eameses' icons, the heart and the rose, are here already well used. Noise is extended into a general concept from merely an auditory one. We see the carbon copies of a single typed text, a first carbon, a second...until the sixth becomes quite illegible from the distortions by the padded pages above it. Redundancy is made lucid by a brief text on the screen, modified step-by-step by omission, but retains meaning. As worth watching more than four decades later as it ever was, the work illumines today's world, where its terms have become common parlance.

While they worked they learned. Perhaps that was their surest genius; they grasped this science faster than almost any outsider to the profession. This early film records the strength with which they entered purposeful teaching of current science. It is more theoretical and didactic, and draws on less experiential evidence than most of their films. The topic, applied mathematics, was then a source of new conceptual order of great importance. *Primer* does not lack for winning and imaginative examples, and the power and generality of the ideas are made quite real. It is a foreshadowing of the *Mathematica* exhibitions, but centered on novel mathematics.

Primer set the office on a new path. Certainly, the Eameses, who had met at Cranbrook, had long felt the attraction of teaching and had tried their hand at it. They knew that this film was a pioneering piece of exposition, and Charles published a letter in an architectural journal to point out how relevant the new mathematical discipline was for students of design and architecture. The film was widely shown, and it reinforced the value of Eames films in the professions' schools. The Eames name carried most easily to that sort of classroom, and it is in the design community that their teaching films are still best known.

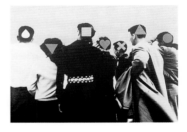

Frame from the film *A Communications Primer* (1953)

IBM at once found in *A Communications Primer* a way to introduce its employees to the new ideas in the field. The film's quality seems to have been responsible for beginning the Eameses' long relationship with the most generous and influential of their clients. For a long time IBM was the loaning source of Eames films for public use in the schools. Most of the films the office made were closely related to various proposals, projects, or exhibitions in the United States and overseas, and some were not even released for outside use. Fewer—but some of the best known—like the second version of *Powers*, were financed by IBM or another wealthy corporation and were intended from the start for wide educational use in classroom, museum, even theater. Television was never a major exhibitor of their swift, thoughtful style. Even today the science films are not all easy to obtain, though the most successful have become ubiquitous.

The Dual Goals of Science

How can we purport to put forward such distinct styles of presentation as admirable models for the visual teaching of science? Our reason is clear, but perhaps not as familiar as it should be. It is that the Eameses' styles are artfully suited to the aims of science as a whole, for those aims are not single but dual. The opening sentence of a reflective essay by the celebrated Danish physicist Niels Bohr is a statement of what science in fact attempts. In 1929 this leader of the quantum interpretation of the microworld wrote, "The task of science is both to extend the range of our experience and to reduce it to order." Both—not one task, but two.

The task usually assigned to science is the ordering one. That is what the philosophers say. Of course, that is exactly their own task in the world of the mind. But what beginners in particular must have—and this is truly central to the understanding of science as part of human activity—is not mainly an ordering of what they know about the world. What they thrive on is the new experiences science brings, those that pass beyond the scope of the everyday. For example, if we regard only the face of the TV screen and its content, and give no thought whatever to what lies behind it, both physical and purposeful, we will never know much about television or the world in which it has such appeal. The schoolbooks and the examinations are complacent in their emphasis on a single goal of order. Order is compact, ready to be well expressed in words or other symbols. It stands still for examination. But new experience is the reverse. It changes, enters anew through every perceptual channel, and demands more clearheaded reasoning, which in the end must include each novelty, minor or major, as part of a widened order. Most of what science orders was once unknown and was newly grasped while it remained in a more or less extended period of doubt and uncertainty.

Consider a few of the discoveries and concepts of science. Take the once controversial moons of Jupiter. Now we list new ones, probe them one by one, and admire a few erupting volcanoes on little Io. Take the idea of energy. Kids who have learned the narrow definition in the texts— "Energy is the capacity for doing work"—know little indeed until they have expanded the idea by experience, used the power of the constancy of energy throughout all its transformations, and recounted the experience in a variety of contexts.

As painter and architect Ray and Charles Eames were devoted builders of the new. As filmmakers they worked from the beginning not with words and icons only but with the world's image in detail. The three films we have discussed are examples of high achievements in meeting the dual goals of science, of course to differing degrees. It was the Eameses' own understanding and their joy in it that led them to present anew the evidence they had grasped, and to share their sense of wonder, which they never ignored.

The Design Setting

The kind of understanding of science that the Eameses shared was not professional; they were not scientists, though they knew and enjoyed the company of many. Indeed, the same is true of their relationship with specialists of many kinds, from opticians to bakers, tailors, artists, historians, film producers, and authors. What seems to have been theirs is the belief that knowing what we have learned is not the most useful test of learning. Rather, our new knowledge should be productive, that is, it should allow us to make something new, if only small, with what we learn.

The Eameses' gift of design implies that style of learning. The setting of any design, its wide context, lies around and underneath it; successful designers must know more than the work shows. The Achilles' heel of many an effort at popular science instruction is that the producer's understanding does not go far beyond the exposition itself; the consequences, the origins, the preconditions, even the limitations, all escape us. A narrow display is all we get; it is usually topical, timely, perhaps memorable, but it fails the stringent test of long-run utility, just what good education should provide.

As designers the Eameses always recognized the need for real depth, even unseen depths. When they prepared their proposal for a National Fisheries Center and Aquarium near the Mall—an ambitious project that was never realized—they began to try out the husbandry of sea creatures for themselves. A fine little film soon came of it, a nearly three-minute close-up of the dance of a fingernail-sized marine creature, titled *A Small Hydromedusan: Polyorchis Haplus*. The joy of direct experience is here given its power by loving and beautiful visual details: the camera magnifies the crinkling of the double membrane that surrounds the little tentacled medusan swimmer, and sets out the relationship of this animated life to its symmetries of form. Only one of myriad examples in the sea, *Polyorchis* opens up for the viewer the teeming diversity of plankton life.

There was more. A living half-pint octopus became a hero of the office, famous for being the longest-lived member of its species in tank captivity. They wanted it, too, to thrive in the office over time—no easy task! Sam Passalacqua, one of the office's graphic artists, became the caretaker who managed a dozen or more residential glass tanks of cool, airy, uncontaminated seawater. In one, there grew thumb-sized hermit crabs, who moved reclusively within their houses of shell. They became dinner for the octopus who dwelt grandly alone and declined to dine on anything less tasty than live crabs. The crabs fattened on algae in their tank, and the intelligent, fastidious little octopus enjoyed stalking and eating them, one after another.

What a drama! We were soon persuaded by what we saw never again to eat octopus. The little creature in its tank would usually change color when anyone entered the room. (Phylis recalls that it turned pink whenever she came by.) When Sam entered the door of the room, the animal would first dance on curly tentacle tip along the tank bottom. As Sam came nearer, the octopus would adorn itself with a kind of peacock-eye pattern, a colorful work of invertebrate art to welcome the hand that fed him. Such was the intense engagement of the Eames Office in a project that never came to be, and such was their habit of design in depth. What an exhibit the octopus and its food chain would have made! It was from that sort of productive understanding that their best films emerged.

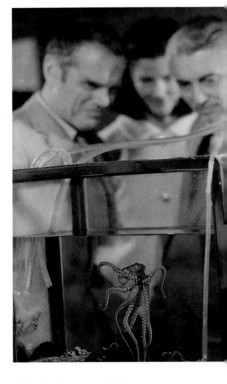

Charles Eames and visitors observing an octopus in the Eames Office, 1968

The Aesthetics of Finish

One authentic trait of the Eameses' work was what we may call the aesthetics of finish. This is quite apart from their strong attachment to meaning, or their admirable unwillingness to use filler, those empty images and soothing half-blank backgrounds. Instead, they packed their story lines with a richness of accessory information that amounts to deliberate overload, in particular from the viewpoint of those who seek a compact and easily learned formulation, even for complex ideas. The Eameses knew that richness is part of the universality of science to be encountered along every trail. But their concern for and their unfailing provision of high polish in every design is not part of the consistent regard for meaning. It is something they themselves brought to their expositions, part of what we can call taste. No picture lacked its frame, no edge was ignored, no visual implication was left unstated.

An example helps us see the nature of this commitment. For the IBM Corporate Exhibit Center in midtown Manhattan, the Eameses designed exhibitions large and small on topics in the history of science. Part of their aim was to amass a full-fledged museum of the subject over the long run. One small show (made to travel) sampled the English Enlightenment and was a miniature beauty, with the perfect title *Philosophical Gardens.* It is an ideal specimen for our look at finish.

The display presented in a very small area the "vegetable staticks" of Stephen Hales. The seventeenth-century naturalist had examined the growth of plants with the overall quantitative approach of physicists, through number, weight, and measure. In the exhibition the Eameses

Illustration from *Vegetable Staticks*, Stephen Hales's 1727 treatise on plant physiology, included in the 1974 exhibition *Philosophical Gardens* included a wonderful photo of a big green leaf, marked with a grid of red spots. As the leaf had increased in size the spots had moved apart to reveal directly the pattern of growth. This was Hales's own investigation brought alive. Of course the display also included information on Hales's era.

But the office provided more. They framed the sharp leaf picture: the small exhibition was organized around an airy gazebo with latticework panels. Fresh green plants and potted spring flowers sat at the base of the panels. The ensemble of visual motifs evoked the period. The result was beautiful, and hard to forget. The charm and detail of the display impressed passersby and scientists alike. Without clashing, always related in some honest way to the main ends, the aptness and pleasure offered by the Eameses' presentations often stood a little upstage from more sober and difficult issues.

This engaging style suited many people, but it imposed a burden, both visual and economic, that not everyone could appreciate and profit by. A rival approach, much more casual, was used in the large hall of the Exploratorium, the museum of art, science, and perception in San Francisco that was founded by Frank Oppenheimer. There a dazzlingly varied set of unfinished and roughly framed demonstrations and activities set an opposite course. Again, many visitors were put off by this presentation, but many were won over by its evident economy, simplicity, and inviting air.

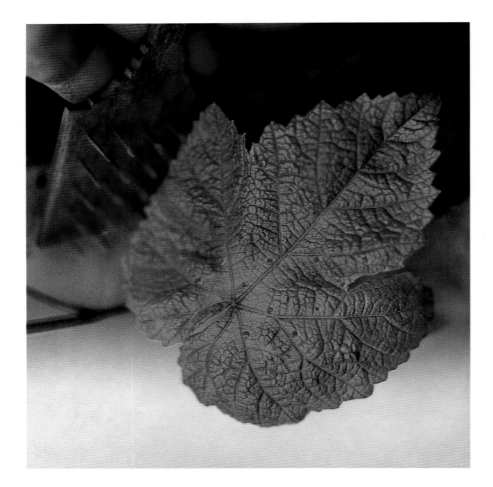

Photograph of leaf painted with grid of red dots, featured in *Philosophical Gardens*

There is room for both styles. A wider look adds new meaning to the contrast. One might say that the issue is how involved the fine arts and the refined crafts should be in functional displays of experience and order in science. History has given its answer; the early scientists—with noble patrons—always found rich finish, even ornament, proper for their instruments. More to the point, the Exploratorium, though itself the home of the "casual" style, has had a half-dozen resident artists at work throughout the years. Their finished works of art, as diverse as glowing plasma columns and whirling balls of fluid currents, are benchmarks of the beautiful among the museum's examples of studied simplicity.

How hard Ray worked to achieve that fitting quality of finish—never slighted, never showy, always important! The Eameses carried on a lifelong campaign to bring scientists and specialists themselves directly into the design of expositions of their work. The best examples from the Eames Office are several brief and unusual films made by UCLA mathematician Raymond Redheffer, such as *Exponents* and *Alpha*.

"Q. To whom does design address itself...? A. To the need."
Such was Charles's response to a question posed to him in a laconic half-debate, half-interview that formed the basis of the 1972 film *Design Q & A*. In that spirit the office produced about twenty-five films out of their total of some one hundred that we judge as useful contributions to education in science and technology. Our sorting is a strict one: we excluded a handful of films that support specific architectural proposals, a number of slide shows, and a few films made outside the office for Hollywood or television. We omitted films like *Clown Face* and *Bread* because they seem to be part of an ethnography of our place and time, and not centered either on the natural sciences or on the technologies that derive from modern science. There are more than a dozen relevant exhibitions as well, recorded mainly in still photographs and drawings.

We see the corpus of the works of Ray and Charles and their large, shifting team as a loving gift to genuine education in science and technology. Plainly, the future holds a cornucopia of new media. Digital modularity is soon to unite all sensory channels. Interactivity is by now a major element of this new world (itself anticipated by the office in the 1960s). What we can hope for is the rise of designers in the Eames tradition: working out of understanding and not only out of technique, able to unite text and vision, art and science with attention "to the need."

General references:

Niels Bohr, *Atomic Theory and the Description of Nature* (Cambridge, England: Cambridge University Press, 1934).

John Neuhart, Marilyn Neuhart, and Ray Eames, *Eames Design: The Work of the Office of Charles and Ray Eames* (New York: Abrams, 1989).

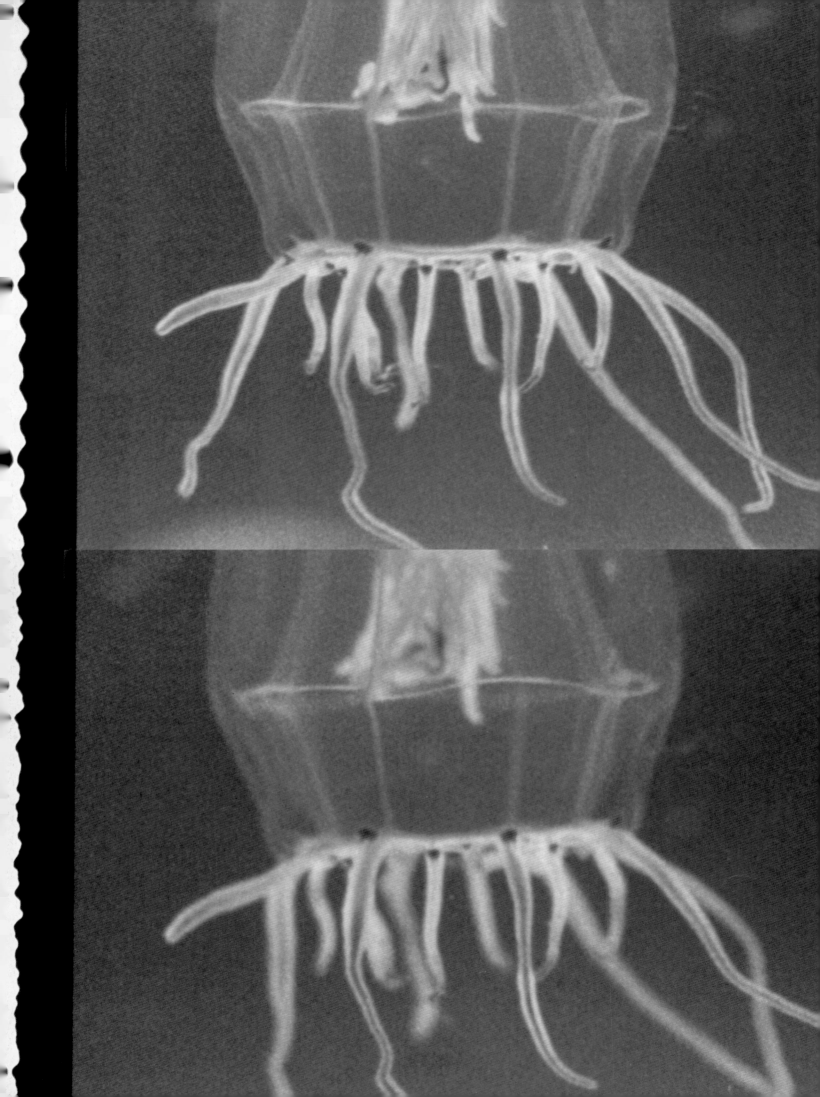

A Sense of the Mysterious

Alan Lightman

Frames from the film
*A Small Hydromedusan:
Polyorchis Haplus* (1970)

First Encounters

Ray and Charles Eames's first film, *Traveling Boy* (1950), was conceived about the same year I was. Thus, very indirectly, I like to consider myself one of their spiritual offspring, the next generation, an inheritor of some small part of their vision of art mixed with science. Yes, but let me start over, with less pretension. *Traveling Boy* has nothing to do with science. I have never met the Eameses. I have never visited the Eames Office in California. A few years ago I did receive an unexpected telephone call from their grandson Eames Demetrios, arriving like a private message from outer space, but that was my only contact with the great designers themselves.

I was just becoming interested in science education, in the late 1970s, when I encountered my first Eames creation, the magnificent film *Powers of Ten* (1977). It is a mark of Ray and Charles's famous good taste that they enlisted Phylis and Philip Morrison to help produce this short film. I will not say much about *Powers*, as it is discussed well and at some length in the Morrisons' essay in this volume. However, I do want to note that this one film probably accounts for the Eameses' greatest impact on science education. Without equations and even without words, *Powers* shows how a profound idea of science can be conveyed visually and emotionally while preserving the utmost accuracy and precision. The particular idea here is the vast range of sizes in nature, from quarks to clusters of galaxies, all miraculously conceived by the human mind. To portray the idea for the nonscientist it is not necessary to dilute, to simplify, or to disguise in uncertain metaphors. What it takes is an artistic vision. I am certain that *Powers* has not only brought pleasure and understanding to the countless students who have seen it but also served as a model to science educators all over the world.

Hydromedusan

Another of my favorite Eames science films is the two-and-a-half-minute *A Small Hydromedusan: Polyorchis Haplus* (1970). As the Morrisons say of *Tops* (1969), *Hydromedusan* is almost pure cinema. There are no words, no script. However, there is sound. As *Polyorchis*, a tiny and translucent jellyfish-type creature, leaps buoyantly like a ballerina performing sautes in slow motion, we hear the languid strains of a Chopin étude in the background. Sounds and images mesh exactly. Indeed, most of the film consists of these graceful aquatic jumps and then the slow descent of the creature back to the ocean floor of small pebbles and debris. We are now accustomed to seeing great underwater photography on HBO and the Nature Channel, but this brief film was made over twenty-five years ago, and it still surprises. The ocean water is so transparent, and the magnifying camera lens so precise, that the little creature appears to be dancing right in our living room.

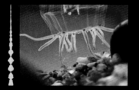

Here is natural science of the most beautiful kind. What a strange and delightful creature is our minute *Polyorchis*. Most of its body is an aqueous and nearly transparent membrane, shaped like a bell or a round tent. Inside the bell hangs a diaphanous material, highly articulated, some kind of digestive system. Floating down from the bottom of the bell are a dozen tentacles or "legs," each capped with an artist's splash of red color. No doubt, these last features account for the Latin name *Polyorchis*. The creature ambles slowly along the ocean floor, walking on its legs, then pushes up into liquid space with those same legs. Once above the ocean floor, *Polyorchis* transports itself from one place to another by contracting and expanding its bell, as if its entire body were a single translucent muscle. The camera work and cropping are done so that the delicate creature fills up half of the viewing screen, walking and dancing and occasionally trembling in some invisible ocean current. Occasionally, we see a bit of debris in the water beside *Polyorchis* and are reminded that the animal is floating in a liquid, not hovering weightless in empty space. Above all is a certain leisurely and intimate mood, as if we have caught the ballerina practicing after hours in the dim theater and are welcome to watch as long as we are respectful and discreet.

While *Polyorchis* dances, several areas of science are quietly in view. There is biology, of course. Can we see how the creature eats and processes its food? How does *Polyorchis* differ from a polyp, which also has tentacles but remains anchored in one place? Why does it need its watery environment? What might be the purpose of color in its body? There is physics. How do the contractions of the bell propel the animal through the ocean? How does the buoyancy of the water reduce the effective gravity, allowing the creature to descend gently from its leaps like an astronaut on the moon?

Part of the beauty of the film is that none of these questions is explicitly asked. We are not hit over the head by a scowling schoolteacher, who then expects us to bolt upright with the answers. We are not given explanations. Instead, we are invited to enjoy a visual spectacle, a ballet of the natural world. We are reminded that much of science is careful observation and appreciation, not number crunching. In his excellent little book *The Character of Physical Law*, physicist Richard Feynman suggests that the language of nature is mathematics and that one must be adept at mathematics to understand nature's laws. However, we know that the young Feynman made trips to the American Museum of Natural History to look at dinosaur bones, took his younger sister to a golf course one night to gaze up at the wine-green streaks of the aurora borealis, studied the whirling motions of lawn sprinklers. It is this tactile and immediate experience with science, absolutely essential in the maturation of every scientist I have known, that is conveyed in *Hydromedusan* and in many of the other Eames films on science. Their science films do visually what good laboratory experiments do. We see the pendulum swinging back and forth, we see the weight oscillating on the spring, we see the insides of the frog.

The Mysterious in Science and Art

The Morrisons, in their essay on the preceding pages, quote the great atomic physicist Niels Bohr as saying that the goals of science are to order the world and to extend the range of our experience. At the time of his comment, in the late 1920s, Bohr was himself embarked on a theory of the atom called quantum mechanics. Quantum mechanics was not only probing nature on a scale unimaginably smaller than anything in human experience, but it was also producing a new understanding of the behavior of matter at odds with millennia of recorded thought. (For example, an electron can be at two different places at the same time.) Thus, we can understand what was on the Danish physicist's mind when he referred to "extend[ing] the range of our experience." Extrapolating on Bohr's comment, the Morrisons go on to say that students of science must have a wide range of new experiences with the world, passing beyond the scope of the everyday. Such novelty and surprise are necessary for success in science education. To these novel experiences, I would add a sense of the mysterious.

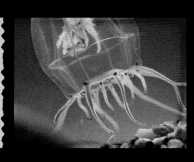

In an article published in 1931, Albert Einstein wrote, "The most beautiful experience we can have is the mysterious. It is the fundamental emotion which stands at the cradle of true art and true science."[1] Interesting that Einstein should link art and science in this way, so appropriate to the work of the Eameses, and I will return to the point. But first, what did Einstein mean by "the mysterious"? I do not think he meant that science is full of unpredictable or supernatural forces. I do not think he meant teleological or even unknowable. I believe he meant a sense of awe, a sense that we do not have all the answers at this very moment, a sense that we can stand right at the edge of what is known and unknown and gaze into that vast cavern and be exhilarated rather than frightened. And when we do stand right at the edge, we might "learn to love the questions themselves," as the poet Rilke said, "like locked rooms and like books that are written in a foreign tongue."[2] Of course, we are determined to find the keys to those rooms, we are determined to find the Rosetta stone that allows us to translate the language, and that determination is what eventually produces the new law of physics or the new painting. But, for the moment, we tingle with our glimpse of the unknown, with the potentiality, and we rejoice in that tingling. That, to me, is Einstein's mysterious. He refers to it as an emotion, and indeed it is. He refers to it as a germinal force, and it is, as every scientist or artist knows.

The Eameses understood the mysterious. They did make some cut-and-dried (but elegant) pedagogical films for the *Mathematica* exhibition (called "peep shows") in 1961, with everything neatly buttoned up, but many of their science films, like *Powers of Ten*, *Tops*, and *Hydromedusan*, have an open-ended, searching, haunting quality to them. In *Hydromedusan*, as I have said, a great many interesting questions and phenomena are suggested but not discussed. Instead, we are presented with a striking visual spectacle, we are invited to sit back and simply enjoy the strangeness before us. I say strangeness because very few of us have seen an aquatic creature such as *Polyorchis*, much less at close range and while the animal is doing its liquid jumps undisturbed. At the same time, we are aware that the spectacle is not fundamentally derived from unusual camera angles or cartoon animation; *Polyorchis* is an actual organism of nature, swimming in the same ocean that we swim in, part of the same great evolutionary chain of life as Homo sapiens. In this way strangeness connects to us, goes deep and demands our attention, captures our imagination. Finally, there is the ocean world itself, below the dry world that we know well. The ocean seems to have an unlimited power to haunt with its mysteries and to spur exploration ("Having nothing particular to interest me on shore, I thought I would sail about a little and see the watery part of the world,"[3] says Ishmael at the beginning of *Moby Dick*). The ocean is the home of *Polyorchis*, and the camera never once leaves that home. We are awed and delighted that we live on the same planet as this strange little creature, and we want to know more. For me, a film of something more common, such as a cat jumping in slow motion, would not evoke nearly the same sense of the mysterious.

If I may break my promise and say more about *Powers of Ten*: here the unknown shouts at us from all sides. At the opening of the film, the camera finds us sitting comfortably in the middle of the known, on a blanket in a park. It is a warm day, we are happy to have escaped the city for a few hours. We have our familiar comforts around us, perhaps a few magazines, a book, a picnic lunch. We are in control of our world. Then the camera goes to a tenfold larger scale, and we are smaller, then tenfold larger again, and the entire park shrinks to the size it once was. Still, the view is not too surprising, we have seen it from low-flying airplanes. Another few powers of ten larger, however, and we are looking at the earth from the view of an orbiting satellite, another few powers after that and we see the earth from the distance of the moon. Now it happens that, in the age of space exploration, we have seen pictures of the earth from the moon before, so we may hold back on our enthusiasm, but grudgingly admit that things are beginning to look strange and not all that familiar. A few more powers of ten and we are looking from the distance of the sun, a view we have definitely never seen, and we begin to get a feeling of the vastness of our solar system, our planet a tiny speck in space. As we continue going up in powers of ten, we see things on the scale of our Milky Way, then galaxies of a hundred billion stars that are mere islands in space, then great clusters of galaxies orbiting each other. We feel dizzy and overwhelmed. Suddenly, the camera begins compressing, shrinking in powers of ten: we fly through galaxies, solar systems, planets, are back in our park, back to the familiar and the

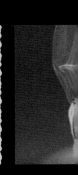

comfortable. We want to stop here and recuperate in the warm sun, but the camera won't let us, it keeps galloping to smaller and smaller scales: to microscopic tissues, molecules, atoms, the interior of atoms, and we see the unknown grinning at us from this side as well. The unknown has surrounded us. The world of the everyday seems now like an illusion.

Designers First

If you look up the entry on Charles Eames in the *Encyclopedia Britannica*, there is a mention of his contributions to the International Business Machines exhibition at the New York World's Fair in 1964, but you will find no other reference to science or science education. It is not even clear that Ray and Charles Eames considered themselves science teachers. Of their stunning traveling exhibition *Mathematica*, which presented a history of mathematics, Charles commented, "I don't believe 'Mathematica' should be looked on as a teaching device—it was never intended to be. We have perhaps thought of it more as a door opening situation where each visitor can find something that hopefully he will pursue later."[4] Charles and Ray Eames were first and foremost designers. They began all their projects, including their films on science, with attention to the need, as Charles would say, and an eye for the visual design. The visual image was central.

Consider, for example, one of the *Mathematica* peep shows, the short film 2^n (1961), which demonstrates the nature of exponentiation and how quickly numbers increase when raised to successive powers. (In some ways, 2^n is a forerunner of *Powers of Ten*.) The film begins with a story. King Sharam of India is given a gift of a beautiful chess set by his "grand bazair." To thank the grand bazair, the king promises to give him one grain of wheat for the first square on the board, two grains of wheat for the second, four grains for the third, and so on, doubling the number of grains for each successive square until all sixty-four squares have been accounted for. Seems like a modest return gift, does it not? While a sitar is played in the background, we see the requisite number of grains being placed on each square. By the time we reach the seventeenth square, the 2^{16} grains of wheat for that square have completely buried the chess board. By the forty-second square, we see wheat pouring out of every window and opening of the palace. At this point, the king becomes anxious and consults the court mathematician, who calculates that 2^{64} grains of wheat, approximately the total from all sixty-four squares, would cover the whole of India to a depth of fifty feet. Next we see another stunning display. The narrator asks what would happen if all these wheat grains were arranged end-to-end in a straight line. We see the line of wheat grains forming, extending past the moon, past the sun, and out to the star Alpha Centauri. But this is not all! The astronomical chain of 2^{64} grains of wheat loops around Alpha Centauri, returns to earth, goes back out, and makes four round trips. A description in words hardly does justice to this impressive visual spectacle.

Patterns in Creativity

There is some evidence that Ray and Charles Eames thought of the scientific enterprise, and all human endeavors, as originating with an artistic vision. This belief is stated explicitly in their film *The Information Machine* (1957), produced for IBM. It presents a history of human achievement, ending with the need for immense computational ability and the resulting development of the computer. In the beginning of the animated film, we see humans at the complete mercy of their world. They cut down trees but cannot predict where they will fall. When given three wishes by a generous genie, the first puny human's wish is never wise, and the second overcompensates for the first error. If he is lucky, his last wish will leave him no worse off than when he began. Eventually, according to the narrative, humans mature into "artists," whose wishes are "prudent and have the habit of coming true." Artists are never bored, and they are constantly building up a store of information. Artists can speculate and predict and produce; they can relate different factors; they work in architecture, mechanics, science, medicine, and politics.

For the Eameses, the artist was the playful creator, the conceiver, the designer, the visionary. Art, in this sense, comes before everything else and lies at the center of every noble human achievement. It is well known that many of the great scientists have been guided by aesthetic criteria and vision. The great physicist Paul Dirac, who developed the first successful theory combining relativity and quantum mechanics, was propelled by his belief in mathematical beauty. A favorite saying of Dirac's was, "Find the mathematics first, the physics will come later." The development of the successful "electroweak theory" in the 1960s, unifying the electromagnetic and weak nuclear forces, was guided by a belief that the separate forces of nature should be unified in a single force. What could be more artistically unifying, or visionary, than Charles Darwin's principle of natural selection, at once explaining countless variations and adaptations among species?

The artistic vision is a powerful force in science education as well as in scientific research. One of my favorite science writers was the philosopher and secretary of the French Academy of Sciences, Bernard le Bovier de Fontenelle. In his masterwork, *Conversations on the Plurality of Worlds* (1686), Fontenelle sets himself the daunting task of conveying to the general educated public the new astronomical ideas of Nicolaus Copernicus and René Descartes. Rather than make this some dry treatise, Fontenelle conceives an artistic and literary approach. He creates a fictitious cultured lady, whom he meets on several evenings in a public park. As they stroll through the gardens, he unfolds before her the new universe in witty and poetic language. Another favorite practitioner of the imaginative approach to science education was the physicist George Gamow. In his two Mr. Tompkins books, published in the early 1940s, Gamow conveys the effects of relativity and quantum mechanics by imagining first a world in which the speed of light is very much smaller than it really is, and then a world in which Max Planck's quantum constant is very much larger. The result of this literary device is that relativistic and quantum phenomena become apparent in everyday life. Bicyclists become visibly shortened and squashed in the direction of their motion. Moving billiard balls spread out into waves.

Returning finally to Einstein's comment linking art and science through the experience of the mysterious, the creative force embraced by the Eameses must surely be part of that link. The best scientists have been enormously creative. So, too, the best science educators. Toward the end of *The Information Machine*, the Eameses make it clear that the computer is only a tool. And with any tool, says the narrator, the concept and

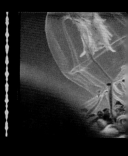

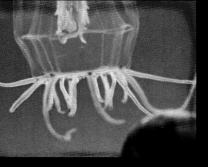

directions must come from humankind. We see, finally, dozens of images of men and women in factories running machines, at drawing boards, in laboratories, at crafts tables, artists and scientists, and in every frame there is a small sign saying "Think." For the ultimate computer is our own mind. Out of our minds we create, we imagine, we see. We experience the known and the unknown.

Science Education Today

I want to end with a few brief remarks about new directions in science education today, some of which can be seen as a legacy of Ray and Charles Eames. Ever since the congressional report "A Nation at Risk" was published some fifteen years ago, there has been a national awareness that our science education needs great improvement at all levels. In the last ten years, the American Association for the Advancement of Science, the National Research Council, and the National Science Foundation, among other institutions, have begun developing new national science curricula and standards for science education. Project 2061 of the AAAS is one example. These new curricula are guided by the belief that science education should include many more "hands-on" experiences, that a thorough understanding of a few basic principles is far more valuable than a large collection of facts, that science and technology should be understood in a human context. In addition to such developments within the formal educational experience, there has been an explosion of popular books on science, written by scientists as well as nonscientists. To name just a few of my most imaginative favorites: Jearl Walker's *Flying Circus of Physics with Answers* provides hundreds of intriguing questions (and brief answers) from the world of experience, such as why chalk squeaks, why you sometimes see spots before your eyes, what causes volcanic lightning. Douglas Hofstadter's *Gödel, Escher, Bach* uses stories, music, and the playful human imagination to discuss profound ideas in science and mathematics. Primo Levi's *Periodic Table* tells a number of human stories, each triggered in the literary imagination by one of the chemical elements.

Fresh ideas in science education have permeated other media as well. Dozens of science museums across the country now employ the "hands-on" type of exhibits pioneered by the Exploratorium in San Francisco. Imaginative series of programs on science, such as Carl Sagan's "Cosmos" and Phil Morrison's "The Ring of Truth," have come to public television. Huge kinetic sculptures, with moving gears and steel balls traveling the gauntlet, sit in the lobbies of airports.

If one could somehow distill into a single word the legacy of Charles and Ray Eames for science education, and perhaps for all of their endeavors, it might be imagination. Seeing with the mind. In the human imagination, our art and our science come together.

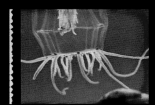

1. Albert Einstein, *Ideas and Opinions* (New York: The Modern Library, 1994), 11.
2. Rainer Maria Rilke, *Letters to a Young Poet* (New York: Norton, 1954), 35.
3. Herman Melville, *Moby Dick or the Whale* (New York: Random House, 1950), 1.
4. Charles Eames's narration, May 30, 1971, for a slide show produced by Tom Woodward for the California Museum of Science and Technology in Los Angeles, presented at the opening of the Los Angeles Convention Center in July 1971. Box 159, The Work of Charles and Ray Eames, Manuscript Division, Library of Congress.

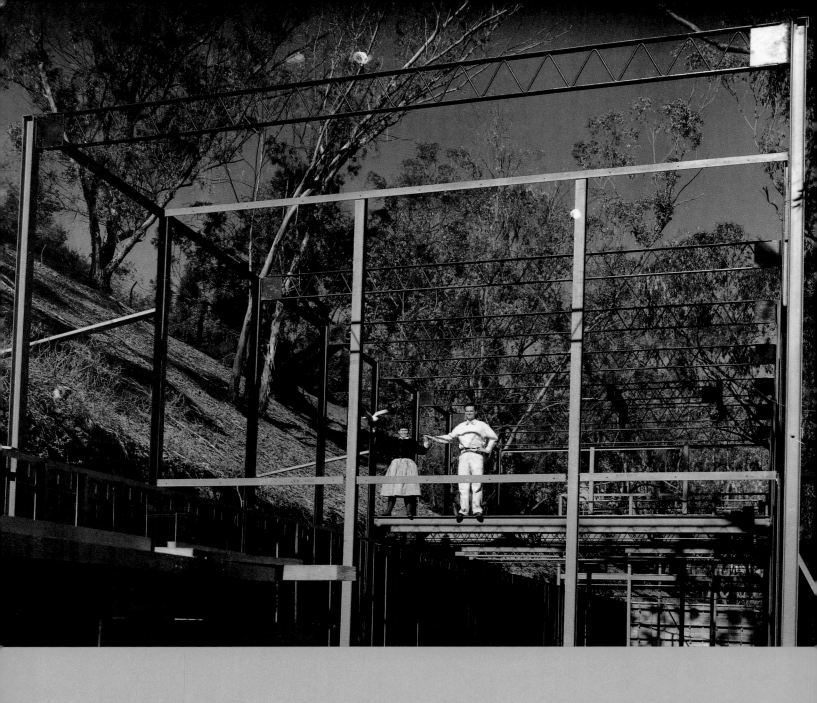

Reflections on the Eames House

Beatriz Colomina

Ray and Charles on the newly
constructed steel frame of
their house in Pacific Palisades,
California, 1949

The Eames House under
construction, 1949

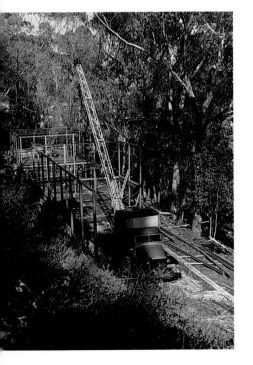

"So, somehow through Mies, through a rejection of much of Mies,
but still through Mies, or so it seems to me, we get the 1949 house—
something wholly original, wholly American."
Peter Smithson[1]

The oldest published photograph of the house shows a truck on the site,
occupying the place of the house, taking its place, anticipating it.
The windshield happens to lie exactly where a glass facade will terminate
the building. The steel frame of the house is being assembled from a
crane on the back of the truck as it steadily moves down the narrow site
carved out between a steep hillside and a row of eucalyptus trees. It is
said that this process took only a day and a half.[2]

The Eameses immediately celebrated. A sequence of photographs
shows the ecstatic couple holding hands under the frame, then stepping
off the retaining wall onto a thin beam suspended like a tightrope across
the space, and finally posing in the middle of the beam, still holding
hands. Ray has a white bird in her raised hand.[3]

The Eameses liked to celebrate things. Anything. Everything. This was
not just whimsy, a distraction from work. It was part of work itself. Walking
along the beam of the house under construction was the beginning of the
occupation of the house. They were literally moving in, even if the crafting
of the basic fabric of the building would take almost a year. The house
became an endless process of celebration over the course of their lives.
When they walked across the steel tightrope before the tent had even

been pulled up over the frame, they were launching an intense program of construction through festive play. Every stage of the play was recorded, photographed, and disseminated to an international audience.

Circus, it turns out, was one of their fascinations. In 1970 Charles was made Charles Eliot Norton Professor of Poetry at Harvard University. As part of this appointment he gave a series of six lectures, and he concluded the first of them by presenting a three-screen slide show of circus photographs he had been shooting since the 1940s. The 180 images were accompanied by a sound track featuring music and other sounds recorded at the circus. The theme of the lectures was that "the rewarding experiences and aesthetic pleasures of our lives should not be dependent solely upon the classic fine arts, but should be, rather, a natural product of the business of life itself."[4] Eames turned to the circus because what "seems to be a freewheeling exchange in self-expression, is instead a tightly knit and masterfully disciplined organic accumulation of people, energies and details."[5] In a talk given before the American Academy of Arts and Sciences in 1974, he elaborated on the point:

> The circus is a nomadic society which is very rich and colorful but which shows apparent license on the surface....Everything in the circus is pushing the possible beyond the limit....Yet, within this apparent freewheeling license, we find a discipline which is almost unbelievable. There is a strict hierarchy of events and an elimination of choice under stress, so that one event can automatically follow another. The layout of the circus under canvas is more like the plan of the Acropolis than anything else.[6]

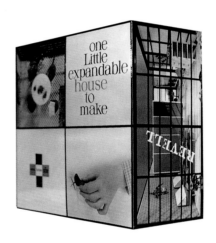

In many ways, this is what Eames thought architecture was—the ongoing theatrical spectacle of everyday life, understood as an exercise in restrictions rather than self-expression. The endless photographs of the ridiculously happy Eameses displaying their latest inventions were part of an extraordinarily precise and professional design practice. We see them on top of the frame of their house, "pinned" by metal chair frames, holding Christmas decorations, waving to us from inside a Christmas ball, wearing Easter hats or masks, photographing their own reflections in the house, and so on. In almost all of the early photographs they wear matching outfits as if to emphasize the performative aspect of their work. The Eameses were very precise about their clothes, commissioning them from Dorothy Jeakins, the Oscar-winning designer who did the costumes for many films, including *South Pacific, The Ten Commandments, Night of the Iguana,* and *The Sound of Music* (Ray Eames's distinctive pinafore dresses are even reminiscent of Julie Andrews's dresses in that film). The effect of the Eameses' costume was the professional couple as a matching set, carefully positioned like any other object in the layout. The uniform clothes transformed the couple into a designer object that could be moved around the frame or from picture to picture. It was always the layout that was the statement, not the objects. And the layout was constantly reworked, rearranged.

If design was not the self-expression of the designer, it was the occupant's daily life that would leave its mark on the house. Eames houses used "industrial technology to provide...an 'unselfconscious' enclosure that would satisfy the essentials for comfortable living. Such a

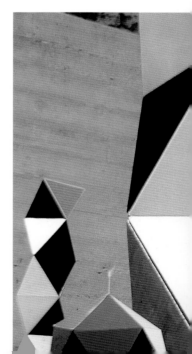

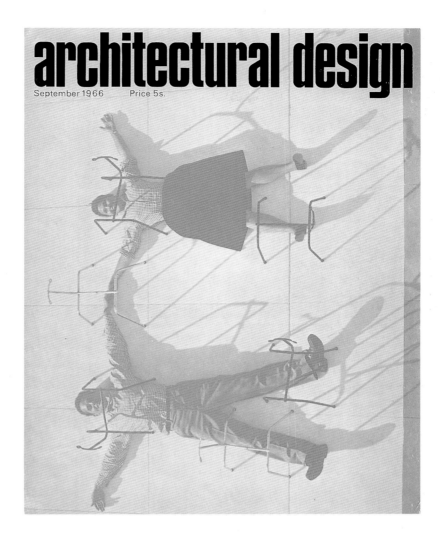

architectural design

September 1966   Price 5s.

Charles and Ray, pinned by chair leg bases to a sidewalk, photographed from the roof of the Eames Office

The Little Expandable House, prototype version designed for the Revell Company in 1959

Ray at home with an early prototype of The Toy, a kit of geometric panels for creating three-dimensional structures, 1951

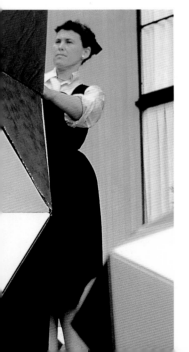

structure could then be made into a personal statement by the occupant, who could fill it with the accessories of his or her own life."[7] All the ephemera of daily living would take over and define the space.

For Eames, everything was architecture, from the setting of a table for breakfast to a circus performance. Everybody was a designer. He trusted, sometimes to later disappointment, the choices craftsmen would make.[8] If they knew their trade, he believed, they would know what a good solution was. Even without experience, the individual's capacity to choose well was respected: "I don't believe in this 'gifted few' concept, just in people doing things they are really interested in doing. They have a way of getting good at whatever it is."[9] Employees arriving at the Eames Office were routinely assigned tasks for which they had no previous experience.[10] It was thought that anybody who applied his or her attention totally, obsessively, to a problem would come up with a good solution, especially if there were many restrictions, such as limited time, materials, or money. Eames spoke nostalgically of his days at the MGM studios, where he often had only one night to make a whole new set out of a limited range of props.

This idea of design as the rearrangement of a limited kit of parts was constant in their work. Everything they produced could be rearranged; no layout was ever fixed. Even the formal lectures were sometimes rearranged in midstream. Kits of parts, movable partitions, The Toy, the plywood cabinets, the House of Cards, the Revell Toy House, the Kwikset House were all infinitely rearrangeable.

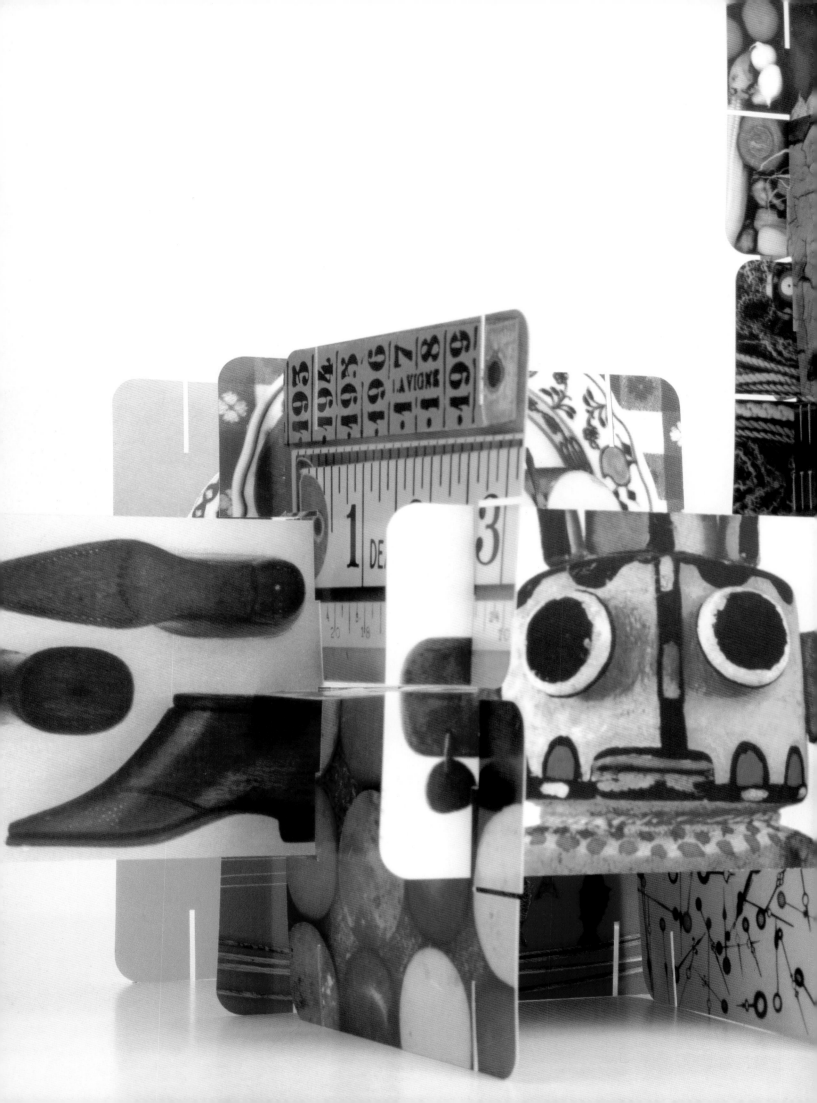

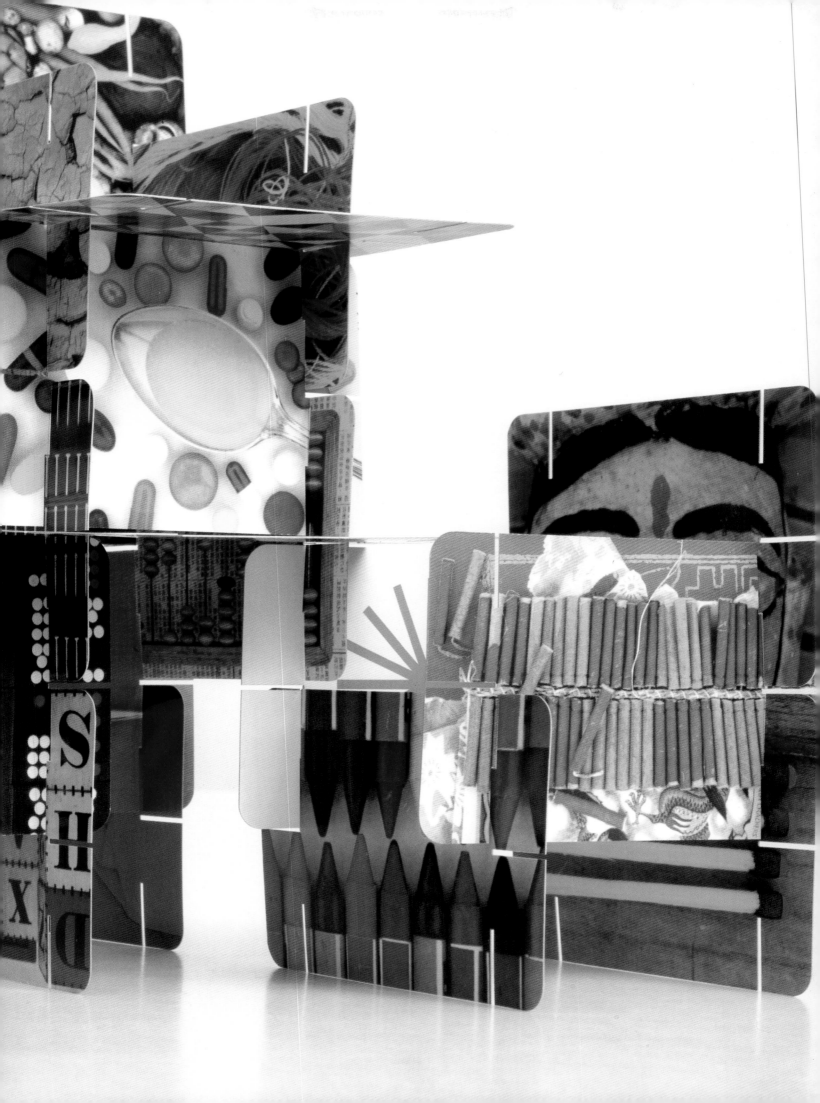

The Eames House is a good example. Not only was it produced out of the same structural components as the utterly different Entenza House (designed by Charles Eames with Eero Saarinen), but the Eames House was itself a rearrangement of an earlier version. After the steel had already been delivered to the site, Eames decided to redesign the house. He put the same set of steel parts together in a completely new way.[11]

The structure exhibits the same logic of rearrangement that would soon dominate its interior. The Eames House blurs the distinction between designer and occupant, accommodating structure and mobile accessories. Where does the work of the designer end and that of the occupant begin in this house? Are the famous colored panels on the facade ephemera (picked up from the history of modern art like the pieces of driftwood the Eameses were always gathering and rearranging) or "unselfconscious" structure? In fact, the colors of the panels were meant to change. Ray said that they chose the cheapest kind of paint from Sears, Roebuck so that they could experiment, but the original colors remain.[12] Eventually the panels became fixed in the mind of the architectural community and taken to be the architecture. But for the Eameses the real architecture of the house was to be found in their endless rearrangement of collectibles within it. The real space was to be found in the details of their daily life.

Charles constantly reflected on what "quality" makes a good architect. In an interview with Digby Diehl, Eames recalled a conversation he had with Saarinen on the subject: "One of the things we hit upon was the quality of a host. That is, the role of the architect, or the designer, is that of a very good, thoughtful host, all of whose energy goes into trying to anticipate the needs of his guests — those who enter the building and use the objects in it. We decided that this was an essential ingredient in the design of a building or a useful object."[13] The house had to efface itself in favor of the creative choices made by its occupants. Its only role was that of the "shock absorber" that protects a unique and ever-changing lifestyle: "The house must make no insistent demands for itself, but rather aid as background for life in work. This house… acts as re-orientator and 'shock absorber.'"[14]

It is difficult not to think of the war. Domestic life could no longer be taken for granted. It became an artform carefully constructed and marketed by a whole new industry. A form of art therapy for a traumatized nation, a reassuring image of the "good life" to be bought like any other product. Rather than offer a complete environment to the postwar consumer, the Eameses presented a variety of components that individuals could construct and rearrange themselves. The Eameses insisted that life was making choices. They left most of them to the occupants, rejecting the role of the artist in favor of that of the industrial designer and catalogue distributor.

The idea of the house as shock absorber was also literal. The Eameses devoted a lot of research to perfecting the rubber shock absorbers in their furniture. In the 1946 exhibition of their plywood furniture at The Museum of Modern Art, New York, a rotary device was used to show the strength and flexibility of the rubber shock mount, and a tumbling drum containing the plywood "Eames chair" demonstrated its durability. A house is likewise meant to absorb the eccentric movements of everyday life. In the Eames House, panels shifted, furniture moved in and out. It became a kind

on the preceding pages:
The House of Cards,
designed in 1952

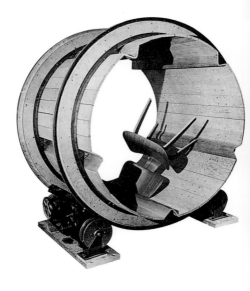

Rotating drum made by the Eames Office to demonstrate the durability of their molded-plywood chairs; displayed in the exhibition *New Furniture Designed by Charles Eames* held in 1946 at The Museum of Modern Art, New York

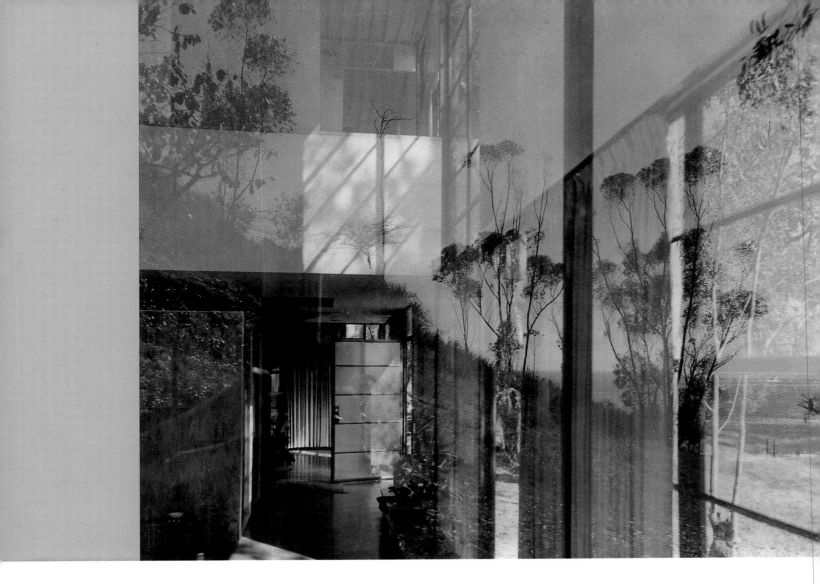

Reflections of trees on the glass
facade of the Eames House,
photographed by Charles

of testing ground for all the work of the office. Everything moved in the
end. Only the basic frame stayed still and this frame was meant to be
almost invisible. A necessary prop—no more than that. As Esther McCoy
wrote, as a caption for an image of trees reflected on the glass walls
of the Eames House, "After thirteen years of living in a house with
exposed steel frame, Ray Eames said, 'The structure long ago ceased
to exist. I am not aware of it.' They lived in nature and its reflections—
and reflections of reflections."[15]

The house dissolved itself in a play of reflections, restless images that
immediately caught the eye of the world. The Eames House was published
everywhere, exposed, scrutinized.[16] The images multiplied and became
the objects of reflection. Their appeal was part of the general fascination
with postwar America that extended from pop-up toasters to buildings.

It was beautiful while it lasted. For a brief period, the span of about five
years following the end of the war, America seemed to embrace modern
architecture. It wasn't, as with MoMA's so-called International Style
exhibition of 1932, the importation of some European ideas repackaged as
a style. It was the development of a whole new mode of operation, one
that fascinated Europe in the same way that European models had once
fascinated the U.S.A. And it was not just Europe. The war seemed to have
opened the frontiers, particularly to the Pacific. The Eames House held a
special place in this new geography. Reyner Banham wrote:

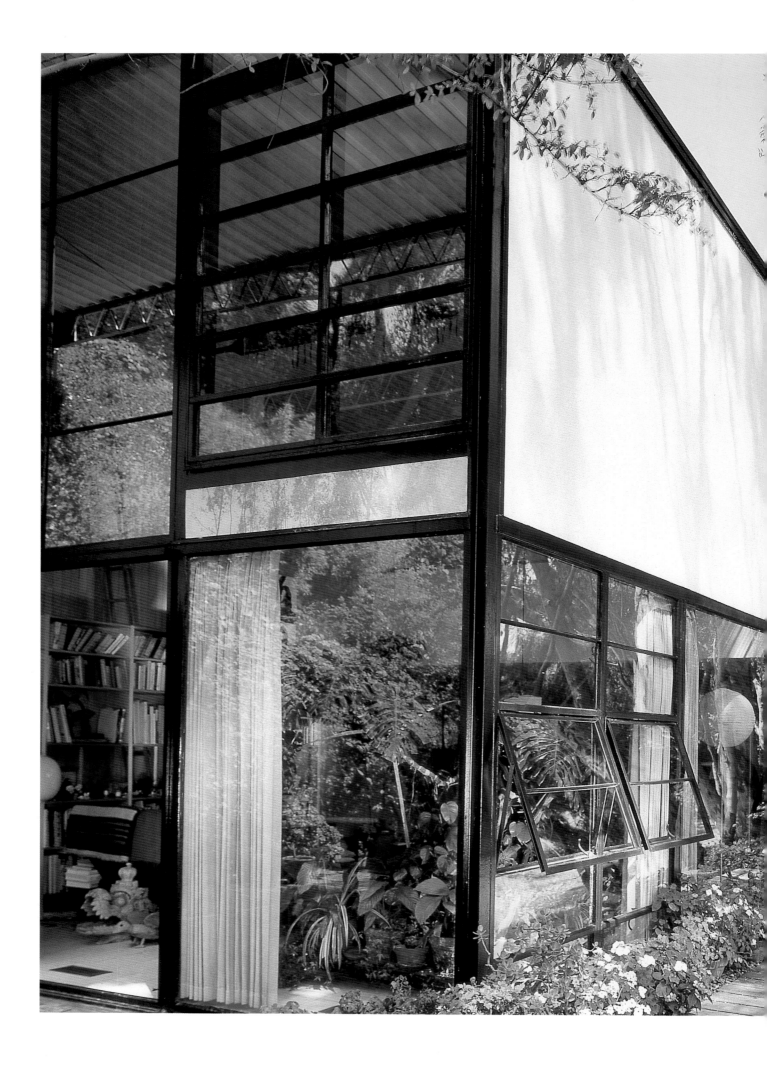

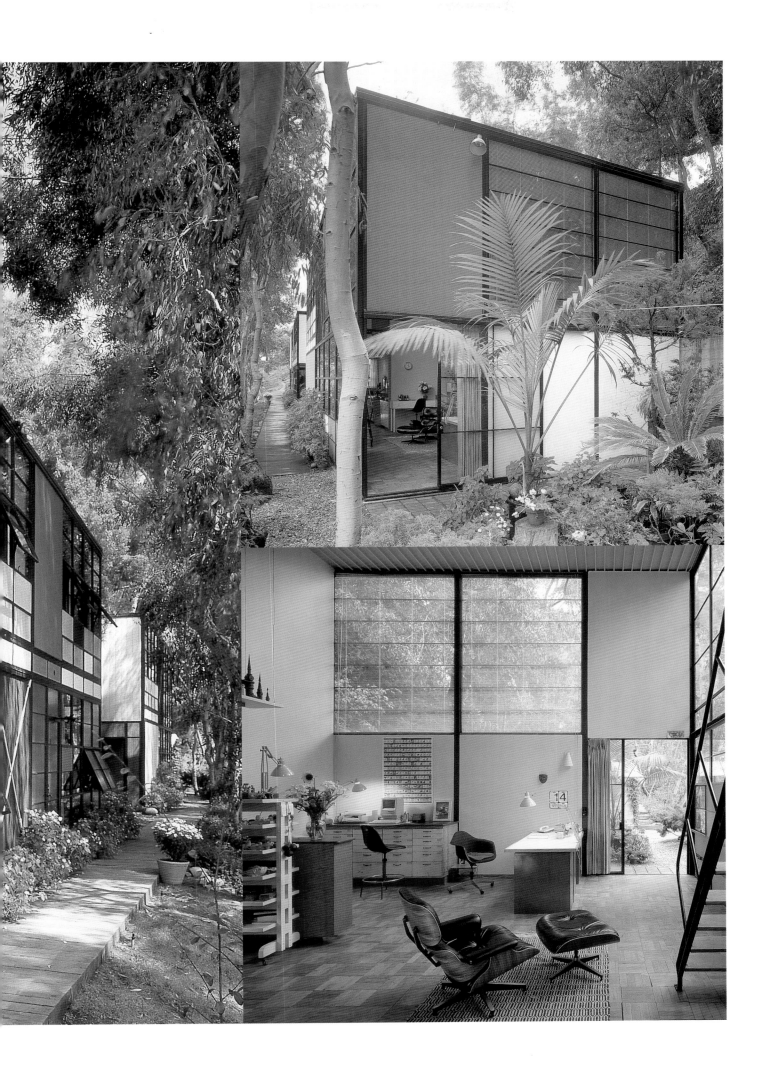

For most Europeans—and some Africans, Australians, and Japanese to whom I have spoken—the Case Study era began around Christmas 1949. By that time the magazine *Arts & Architecture* had achieved a sufficient degree of penetration into specialized bookstores and architectural libraries for the impact of the first of the steel-frame Case Study houses to trigger—as British architect Peter Smithson said—"a wholly different kind of conversation."[17]

The first steel house that Banham referred to was the Eames House, #8 of the Case Study House Program, into which the Eameses moved precisely on Christmas Eve, 1949. The Case Study House Program was, as Banham noted, "overwhelmingly Charles and Ray Eames in foreign perception."[18] That explains that foreigners thought of it as 1949, even if the program had started in January 1945, a few months before the end of the war.

The Case Study House Program was sponsored by the magazine *Arts & Architecture* under John Entenza.[19] The journal commissioned a number of architects to each design a house as a prototype for a new way of living—the postwar way of living. The assumption was that the soldier returning from war had become a "modern man," a figure who would prefer to live in a modern environment utilizing the most advanced technology rather than return to live in "old fashioned houses with enclosed rooms." The twenty-six houses resulting from this program were not only published in *Arts & Architecture* but were, for the most part, built. They were open to the public for six to eight weeks before their occupation. Each was to be completely furnished under an arrangement with the manufacturers. Like so many of the houses of the modern movement in Europe, the Case Study houses were exhibition houses. The program was enormously successful both professionally and among the wider public. The first six houses to be opened received almost four hundred thousand visitors.

The program was preceded by two competitions organized by *Arts & Architecture*: the 1943 "Designs for Postwar Living," and a second such competition in 1944, sponsored by the U.S. Plywood Association. These competitions encouraged participants to arrive at a "pattern of living for the American worker" and his family. The "worker," they said in their call for entries, "conditioned by the war-time years and including the members of the armed forces who will become a part of the working population...is likely to have an enormous respect for the machine both as creator and as a weapon of destruction...and it is very likely that he will not only accept but demand simple, direct, and honest efficiency in the material aspects of the means by which he lives."[20] The Second World War, *Arts & Architecture* implied, provided the context for the acceptance of modern architecture. It was as if the war had educated the taste, the aesthetic sensibility, of the public.

A historical reference for the Case Study houses can be found in Le Corbusier's fascination with the technologies developed during World War I and his dream of an architecture that would "recycle" these materials and techniques into the mass production of houses. This was most obvious in his relationship with Gabriel Voisin, who after the war was looking to transform his war aircraft factories by breaking into the building industry.[21] The Case Study program likewise exemplifies the impact of the war on both architectural discourse and the specific techniques and materials employed in the production of housing. On the one hand, the industry was recycling the products and techniques that it had developed and tested at war. On the other hand, and this is what is new, the architects themselves, unlike their European counterparts, had been involved in the development of these military products.

During the war Charles and Ray Eames had formed a company with John Entenza to mass-produce plywood war products. In 1941–42 they developed a molded-plywood splint for the United States Navy to replace a metal leg splint used in the field that did not sufficiently secure the leg and led to gangrene. The navy accepted the Eames prototype and they, with the financial support of Entenza and the help of other architects such as Gregory Ain (who later became involved in the Case Study program), designed the equipment needed for mass production, and eventually put 150,000 units into service. In addition the company designed and developed a body litter, an arm splint, aircraft parts, and other products, all in molded plywood. By 1946 the Eameses were producing lightweight plywood cabinets and molded-plywood chairs and tables with the technology they had developed for the military. A photograph of the plywood lounge chair of 1946 shows Charles reclining in it, the position of his leg indicating that he has not forgotten where it comes from. The Eameses also produced molded-plywood children's furniture, molded-

Eames House, ca. 1952

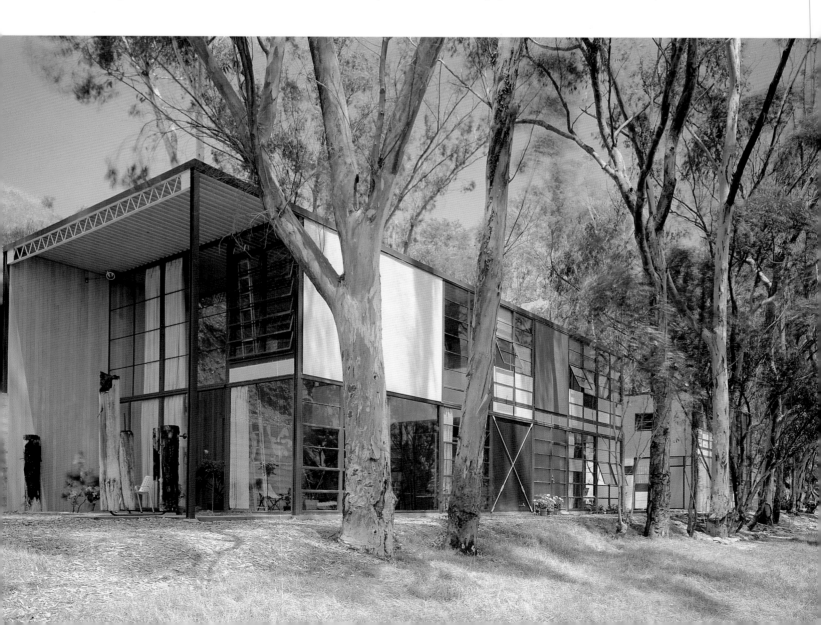

plywood animals, and even plywood Christmas decorations cut out of leftover splints. Military and medical equipment had become the basis of domestic equipment.

This obvious displacement from war to architecture can be found throughout the Case Study House Program in more subtle forms. The very idea of standardization, which had been perfected by the military, was very much part of the program's agenda. Every component of the Eames House was selected from a steel manufacturer's catalogue and bolted together like a Meccano set.

One is reminded again of Le Corbusier, who in relation to his potential collaboration with Voisin had written (with Amédée Ozenfant) in *L'Esprit nouveau*, "Houses must go up all of a piece, made by machine tools in a factory....It is in aircraft factories that the *soldier-architects* have decided to build their houses; they decided to build this house like an aircraft, with the same structural methods, lightweight framing, metal braces, tubular supports."[22] From that point of view, the Eames House represents the realization of Le Corbusier's dreams. While Le Corbusier theorized the factory-made house, or at least new materials and building techniques, the houses he managed to build in the meantime used the most conventional techniques. Like Le Corbusier, Charles Eames was an avid reader of catalogues on marine and aviation equipment. He later said about the house that he regretted having "stuck so close to the building industry," neglecting several offers from outside quarters, and that if he were to do it all over again, "he might treat this house more as a job of 'product design,' less architecture in the traditional sense."[23]

But how could the house be less architecture in the traditional sense? It seems to be one of their plywood cabinets blown up in scale. It is built out of off-the-shelf components, assembled off the back of a truck, in just over one day. It is hard to imagine a more radical gesture. It was precisely its radicality that attracted worldwide attention.

Perhaps nobody was so captivated by the Eameses, and more lucid about their work, than their buddies the British architects Alison and Peter Smithson. In a 1966 *Architectural Design* issue devoted exclusively to the Eameses and prepared by the Smithsons, they wrote: "There has been much reflection in England on the Eames House. For the Eames House was a cultural gift parcel received here at a particularly useful time. The bright wrapper has made most people—especially Americans—throw the content away as not sustaining. But we have been brooding on it—working on it—feeding from it."[24] The house as an object, a gift all wrapped up in colored paper. This comment reflects so much of the Smithsons' obsessions, so much of what they saw as new in the Eameses: the attention to seemingly marginal objects (which the Smithsons perceptively understood as "remnants of identity"), the love of ephemera, of colored wrapping paper, and the like.

For the Eameses, gifts were all important. They maintained that the reason they began to design and make toys (the House of Cards, The Toy, the masks) was to give them to their grandchildren and the children of staff members and friends. But the concept of gift extended far beyond the toys. Not only were the Eameses extremely generous with their friends (they once paid for airline tickets so the Smithsons could visit them in California), but they understood all their work as a gift. In an interview Charles said: "The motivation behind most of the things we've

"Life in a Chinese Kite," published in *Architectural Forum*, September 1950

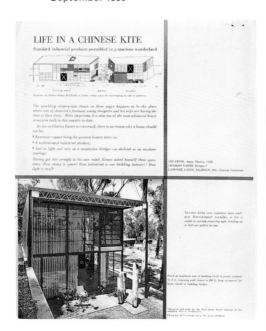

done was either that we wanted them ourselves, or we wanted to give them to someone else. And the way to make that practical is to have the gifts manufactured....The lounge chair, for example, was really done as a present to a friend, Billy Wilder, and has since been reproduced." Wilder wanted "something he could take a nap on in his office, but that wouldn't be mistaken for a casting couch."[25] In addition to the "nap" chaise, the Eameses designed a "TV chair" for Wilder. An article in a 1950 issue of *Life* magazine shows a multiple-exposure photograph of Billy Wilder moving back and forth on the plywood lounge chair of 1946, claiming that it was designed so that the "restless Wilder can easily jump around while watching television."[26]

From the toys, to the furniture, to the houses (which were either designed for their closest friends, John Entenza and Billy Wilder, or as toys, like the Revell House and the Birthday House designed for Hallmark Cards in 1959), to the major productions (such as the film *Glimpses of the U.S.A.*, which was understood as a token of friendship to the Russians), to their most complex exhibitions, the Eameses always concentrated on what they were giving and how it should be presented. Everything was thought of as a gift. Design was gift giving.

No one has understood the Eameses better than the Smithsons. They took it all personally, seeing the Eames House as a gift wrapped in colored paper, the Eames chair as "a message of hope from another planet,"[27] and the Eames cards as giving them "the courage to collect whatever pleases us."[28] These gifts transformed their own practice:

> The prettiness of our lives now I attribute to Ray even more than Charles; we would not be buying flower-patterned ties but for the Eames card game....I like to think it is to Ray and Charles Eames we owe the debt of the extravagance of the new purchase. The penny whistle, the Woolworth's plastic Christmas decoration and toy, on to the German pressed metal toy and the walking robots: fresh, pretty, colorful ephemera.[29]

The Smithsons were eager to return the favor. "Eames Celebration," the special issue of *Architectural Design* prepared by the Smithsons, was a gift given in return for so many others. They wrote: "The essays on the work of Charles and Ray Eames which make up this issue are very personal, and the impulse behind them was to repay the debt the authors felt they owed to the Eames in a way that would be both pleasurable and useful to the Eames themselves."[30]

The sense of the Eames House as a gift also points to the constant shift in scale in their work: from house, to cabinets, to children's furniture, to toys, to miniatures. Even the architectural models were treated like toys, played with by excited architects and clients acting like curious children. Eames once said that in the "world of toys he saw an ideal attitude for approaching the problems of design, because the world of the child lacks self-consciousness and embarrassment."[31] In Eames architecture everything is a toy, everybody is a child. Perhaps this explains the constant presence of children in the photographs of their work. Since when have we seen so many children in architecture?

Charles and Ray saw everything through the camera. This accounts for the astonishing continuity between work in so many different scales. If

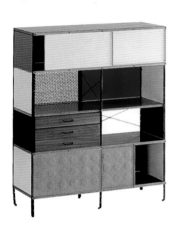

An early version of the Eames Storage Unit, produced by Herman Miller, 1950–52

on the following pages:
The Eames House living room with tatami mats, 1951

Ray and Charles in their living room, 1958

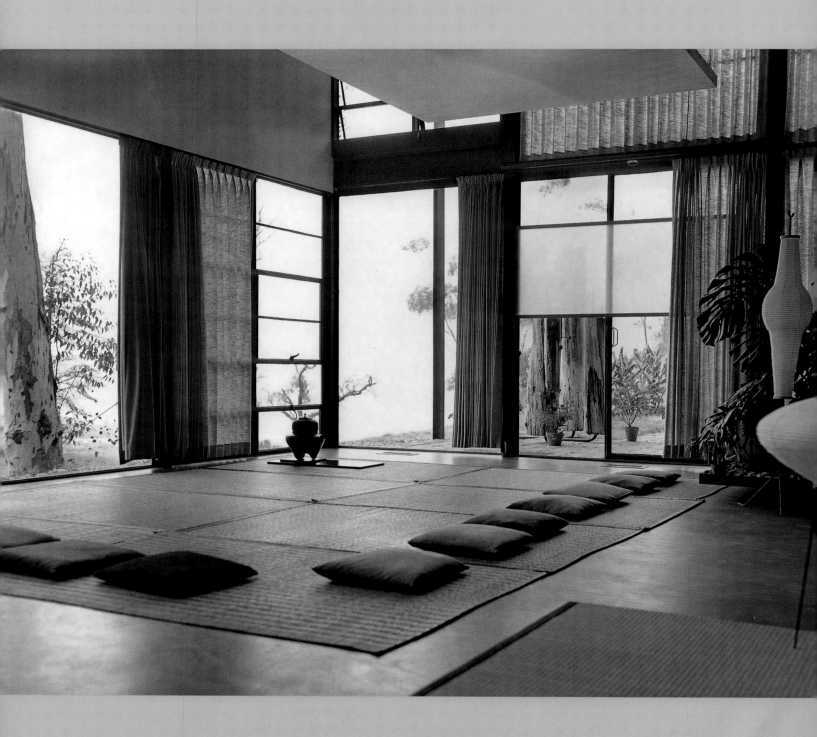

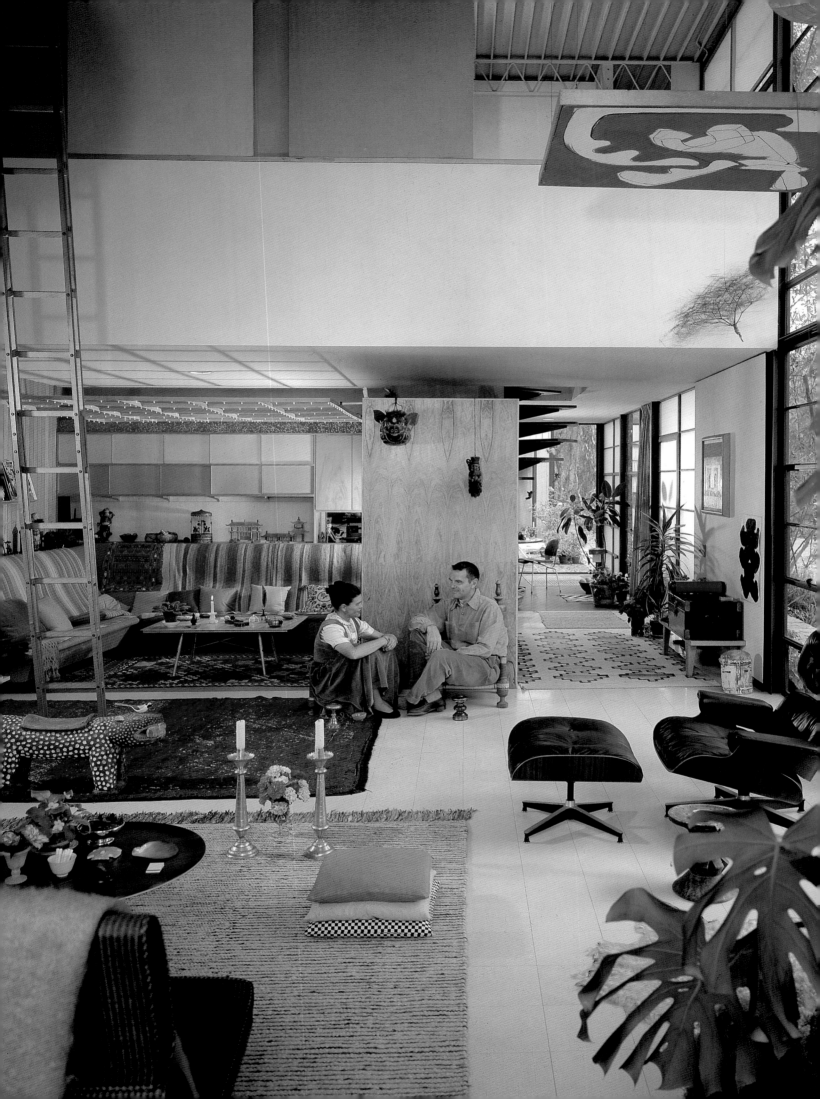

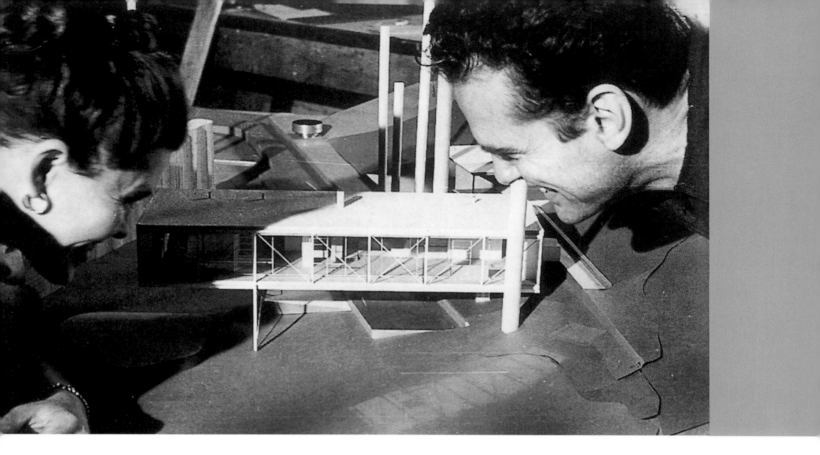

the eye is the eye of a camera, size is not fixed but continuously shifting.
They used to shoot everything. This was surely not just an obsession with
recording. There is that, no doubt, but they also made decisions on the
basis of what they saw through the lens, as is evident in Ray's description
of the process of decision making in the Eames House:

> We used to use photographs. We would cut out pieces from
> photographs and put them onto a photograph of the house to see
> how different things would look. For instance—there was a space
> in the studio we wanted filled. It was between the depth of the
> floor where it opens for the stairs (this is not so in the house,
> where there is a balcony rail). We wondered what to do. We had
> some pier pylons from Venice pier (we had wanted to keep
> something of it to remember it by). Well, we had pictures of it,
> glued it onto a photo and decided it worked so we went ahead
> and did it.[32]

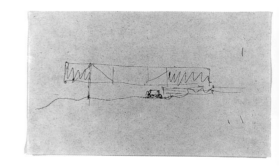

Ink sketch of a glass house on a
hillside, by Ludwig Mies van der
Rohe, 1934

To remember the Venice pier they took a piece of it with them. This is
characteristic of the Eameses, who over the years accumulated an
astonishing quantity of objects. The pylons can be seen standing outside
the house. But to see if they could keep a memory of the object inside
the house they used photographs and collage. Indeed, a photograph of
the Venice pier ended up filling the space in the house they had tested
using collage.

The photocollage method had already been important to architects
from the early European avant-garde. Ludwig Mies van der Rohe
photocollaged a drawing of his office building of 1919 onto a photograph
of the Friedrichstrasse; glued photographs of landscape, materials, and

Klee's painting *Bunte Mahlzeit* to the Resor House drawings, 1938; and glued together pictures of water, trees, sculptures, and Picasso's mural *Guernica* in the collage of the Museum for a Small City of 1942. The structure of the building gives way to a juxtaposition of photographic images. But it would be important to understand in what sense the Eameses transformed the strategies of the avant-garde. How was the Eames House able to "trigger," in Peter Smithson's words, "a wholly different kind of conversation"? As Smithson wrote:

> In the 1950s the Eames moved design away from the machine aesthetic and bicycle technology, on which it had lived since the 1920s, into the world of the cinema-eye and the technology of the production aircraft; from the world of the painters into the world of the lay-out men.... The Eames-aesthetic, made definitive in the House at Santa Monica Canyon, California, 1949 (as the machine-aesthetic was given canonical form in the "dwelling unit" in the Esprit Nouveau Pavilion, Decorative Arts Exhibition, in Paris, 1925), is based on an equally careful selection, but with extra-cultural surprise, rather than harmony of profile, as its criteria. A kind of wide-eyed wonder of seeing the culturally disparate together and so happy with each other. This sounds like whimsy, but the basic vehicle—the steel lattice frame and in the case of the house, the colour film and colour processing in the graphics work, the pressing and mouldings in the case of the furniture— are ordinary to the culture....Charles Eames is a natural Californian Man, using his native resources and know-how— of the film-making, the aircraft and the advertising industries— as others drink water; that is almost without thinking.[33]

This shift from the machine aesthetic to color film, from the world of painting to that of the layout men, from Europe to California, can be traced in the shift between the first and second versions of the Eames House. The first version, the so-called Bridge House, published in *Arts & Architecture* in 1945, seems to be based on Mies's 1934 sketch of a glass house on a hillside. The scheme was rejected in 1947, after Charles went to MoMA to photograph the Mies exhibition, in which the sketch was first made public. Charles must have known it before 1947. In fact, he said that he didn't see anything new in the projects that were exhibited, but he was impressed by Mies's design of the exhibition itself. Shortly after his visit to the show, the Eameses came up with a new scheme for their house.

The first version, which Charles designed with Saarinen, faithfully follows the Miesian paradigm in every detail. The house is elevated off the ground as a kind of viewing platform. The sheer glass walls are aimed at the landscape, lined up with the horizon. In the original drawings, published in *Arts & Architecture* in December 1945, we see the occupant of the house standing behind the glass, an isolated figure looking out at the world that is now framed by the horizontal structure. The interior is almost empty. In the model of the house published in March 1948, the only thing occupying the house is the reflections of the surrounding trees, which the Eameses went to considerable trouble to photograph by placing the model on the actual site and carefully superimposing an image of the trees in the foreground. The effect is classic Mies. As in the Farnsworth

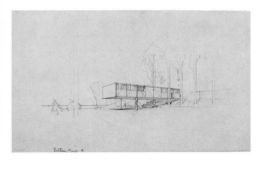

Pencil drawing of the Bridge version of the Eames House

House, there is a stark elevated interior with at most a few isolated pieces of furniture floating near the glass in a fixed pattern prescribed by the architect.

In the second version the house is dropped to the ground and swung around to hug the hillside. It no longer faces the ocean. The view is now oblique and filtered by the row of eucalyptus trees in front of the long east face. A low wall is wrapped around the patio on the south facade, partially blocking the ocean from the view of someone sitting in the space and focusing attention on the patio as an extension of the house, as an interior. The dominant focus is now in rather than out. The house abandons the Miesian sandwich, where floating slabs of floor and ceiling define a strictly horizontal view. The floor is treated like a wall with a series of frames defined by rugs, tiles, trays, and low tables on which objects are carefully arranged. In fact, floor, wall, and ceiling are treated in a similar way. Not only are they now given the same dimension (the sandwich being replaced by a box) but they start to share roles. Hans Hofmann paintings used to hang horizontally from the ceiling. Ray said that it was necessary to protect them from the strong light, and that they "would be able to see them well from that position."[34] Many photographs of the house were taken from a very low angle, and we often see the Eameses sitting on the floor surrounded by their objects. The west wall is clothed in birch because they needed something they could hang objects on. On the east wall much of the glass has become translucent or is wired ("to make people realize it is there"[35]) or replaced with opaque colored panels. The sheer surface is broken up with louvers. The occupants can only see fragments of the outside, fragments that have the same status as the objects that now take over the interior. The view is there but restricted to a few of the many frames. Everything overlaps, moves, and changes. The singular unmediated view is replaced by a kaleidoscopic excess of objects.

The eye that organized the architecture of the historical avant-garde has been displaced by a multiplicity of zooming eyes. Not by chance the Eameses' 1955 film *House: After Five Years of Living* is made up entirely of thousands of slides. Every aspect of the house is scrutinized by these all-too-intimate eyes. The camera moves up close to every surface, every detail. But these are not the details of the building as such, they are the details of the everyday life that the building makes possible.

Le Corbusier also considered film the best medium to represent his architecture. In his 1931 movie *L'Architecture d'aujourd'hui,* directed by Pierre Chénal, he moved through the space of his houses (Villa Savoye, Garches, Villa d'Avray) without taking his jacket off. In *House: After Five Years of Living* the Eameses took the opposite approach. Everything, as the title indicates, is about living in the house. The focus is extremely close: flowers, bugs, eggs, pots and pans, crockery…While Le Corbusier had included figures to provide the scale, and perhaps to insist that he was just visiting, in the Eames film there are no figures, only traces of ongoing life.

Le Corbusier's film is all horizontal panning—like the modern house, which frames a horizontal view. The Eames film is just a collection of slides. This is consistent with the house itself. It is impossible to focus in the Eames House in the same way that we do in a house of the twenties. Here the eye is that of a TV-watcher. Not the fifties TV-watcher but closer

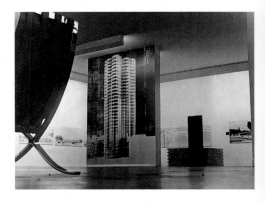

Installation photograph by Charles Eames of the exhibition *Mies van der Rohe*, held in 1947 at The Museum of Modern Art, New York

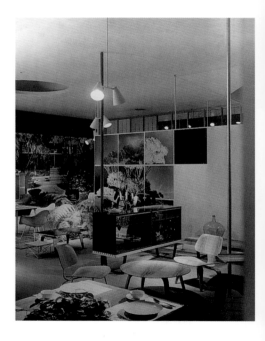

Herman Miller furniture showroom, Los Angeles, 1949

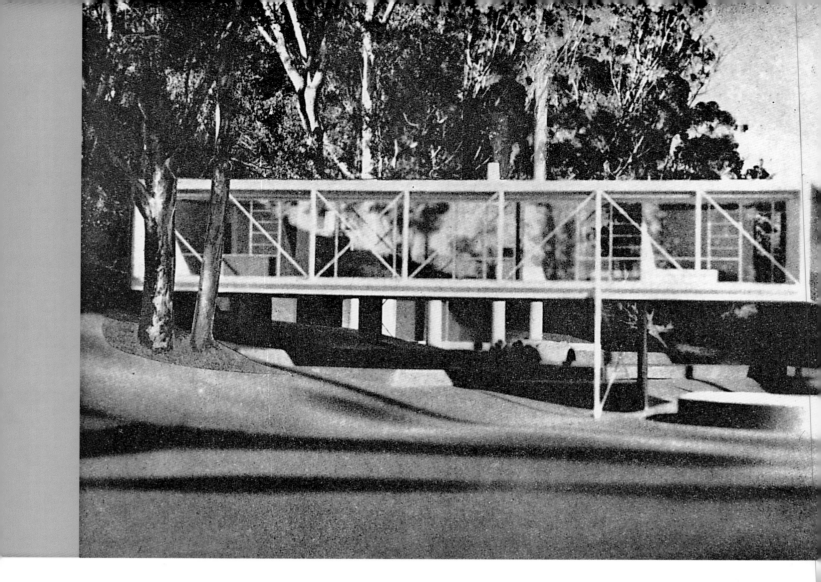

Model of Case Study House #8,
published in *Arts & Architecture*,
March 1948

CASE STUDY HOUSES
8 AND 9
BY CHARLES EAMES AND EERO SAARINEN, ARCHITECTS

Case Study Houses #8 and #9,
published in *Arts & Architecture*,
December 1945

to that of today—multiple screens, some with captions, all viewed simultaneously. It helps to follow more than one story at once.

To some extent the Eameses pioneered this mode of viewing. They were experts in communication. In 1959 they brought *Glimpses of the U.S.A.* to Moscow, projecting it on the seven screens suspended within R. Buckminster Fuller's geodesic dome. Twenty-two hundred still and moving images presented the theme of A Day in the Life of the United States. Fuller said that nobody had done it before and advertisers and filmmakers would soon follow.[36] The Eameses used the technique repeatedly:

> Having come upon the use of multiple images, we exhibited a tendency to find new uses for it. If you give a young boy a hammer, he'll find that everything he encounters needs hammering. We found that everything we encountered needed the multiple-image technique....I used the process with triple slides in the Norton lectures at Harvard, in order to give a depth of view. In each lecture I would talk for five minutes and then show three minutes of imagery, and then talk seven minutes more.[37]

The Eames House is also a multiscreen performance. But Mies is not simply abandoned. Indeed, the house takes an aspect of Mies's work to its extreme. When Eames gave up on the first scheme after seeing the

Mies exhibition at MoMA, he did so because he saw something else there. In fact, it was the exhibition technique that inspired him. When he published his photographs of the exhibition in *Arts & Architecture* he wrote: "The significant thing seems to be the way in which he has taken documents of his architecture and furniture and used them as elements in creating a space that says, 'this is what it is all about.'"[38]

Eames was very impressed by the zooming and overlapping of scales: a huge photomural of a small pencil sketch alongside a chair towering over a model next to a twice-life-size photograph, and so on. He also noted the interaction between the perspective of the room and that of the life-size photographs. The visitor experienced Mies's architecture, rather than a representation of it, by walking through the display and watching others move. It was a sensual encounter: "The exhibition itself provides the smell and feel of what makes it, and Mies van der Rohe, great."[39] What Eames learned from Mies, then, was less about buildings, more about arrangement of objects in space. Exhibition design, layout, and architecture are indistinguishable, as Mies had demonstrated in his layout for the magazine *G*, his numerous exhibitions with Lilly Reich, the Silk Café, the Barcelona Pavilion, and so on. Eames picked up on the idea that architecture is exhibition and developed it.

Once again, the Eames House takes something from history and transforms it. The house is an exhibition, a showroom, but it is a different kind of showroom from those of the modern movement. The multiple eye belongs to a completely different kind of consumer. It is the eye of the postwar acquisitive society. While Mies is famous for his comment "Less is more," the Eameses said that their "objective is the simple thing of getting the most of the best to the greatest number of people for the least."[40] The glass box gives way to such a density of objects that even the limits of the box are blurred. The role of the glass changes. With Mies, reflections consolidate the plane of the wall. The complex lines of trees become like the veins in marble. With the Eames House, the plane is broken. The reflections of the eucalyptus trees are endlessly multiplied and relocated. Eames even replaced a panel on the south facade with a photograph of a reflection of the trees, confirming that every panel is understood as a photographic frame. Furthermore, he and Ray took photographs of the reflections on the exterior glass, switched some from positive to negative, and reassembled them into a panel. Apparently intended for the house, the panel ended up in the Los Angeles Herman Miller showroom.

Just as the house was a showroom, the showroom was a house. The Eames House and the showroom for Herman Miller, built at the same time, were in fact the same project. They used the same principles. A light unselfconscious enclosure, a minimum of architecture, provided a flexible frame for multiple interior arrangements. A wall-size photomural was used to construct the sense of an exterior, complete with patio, garden, trees, outdoor furniture, and a neighboring house. A complete lifestyle was laid out down to the smallest detail of cutlery and table settings. The space was even filled with personal objects: an African leopard and an early American weathervane loaned by Billy Wilder, a Herbert Matter photograph and a Hofmann painting loaned by John Entenza, and so on.[41] Gifts from friends.

The showroom quality of the Eames House is exemplified by its repeated use as the site of fashion photographs. Magazines such as *Life*

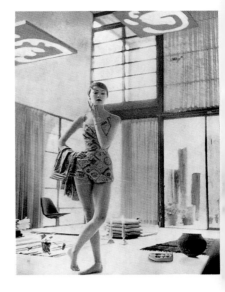

Ludwig Mies van der Rohe at the Farnsworth House construction site, Plano, Illinois, ca. 1951

Fashion photograph taken in the living room of the Eames House, published in *Vogue*, April 15, 1954

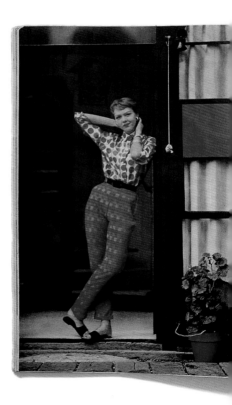

Fashion photograph taken in front of the Eames House, published in *Life*, June 15, 1954

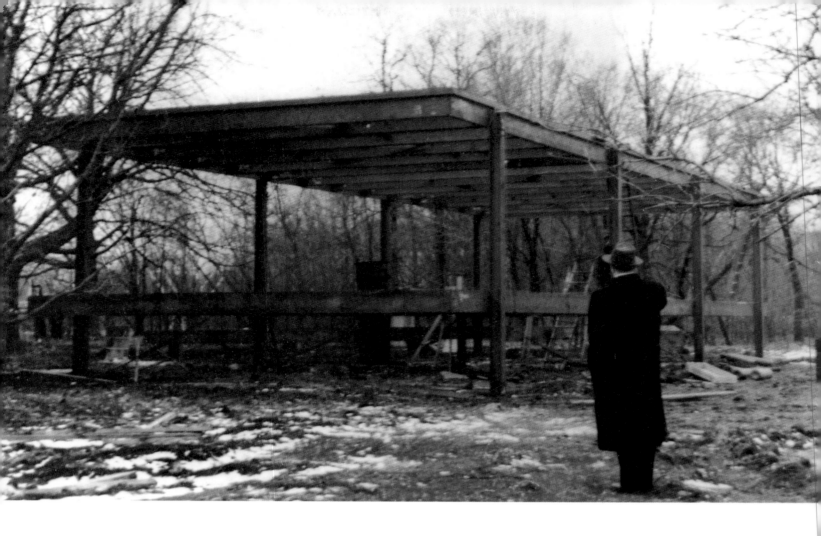

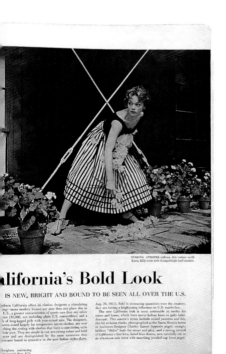

lifornia's Bold Look

IS NEW, BRIGHT AND BOUND TO BE SEEN ALL OVER THE U.S.

and *Vogue* inserted their models into the building, lining them up with the architecture, even merging them into the interior elements.[42] In this, the house participates in another long tradition of the historical avant-garde. Ever since the turn of the century, modern architecture has been used as a setting for fashion publicity. In fact, the history of modern architecture is the history of the showroom, the history of a blending of architecture and exhibition. But the Eames House was no longer just a uniform backdrop for fashion designs as discrete innovations. The garments were blended into the fabric of the house, mingling with the objects. The accompanying text bounced backward and forward between the "California bold look" of the architecture and the fashion. What was on display in the showroom was the equal status of all kinds of objects. The announcement of Case Study Houses #8 and #9 in the December 1945 issue of *Arts & Architecture* shows the silhouettes of both the Eameses and Entenza surrounded by the galaxy of objects that define their respective lifestyles. The role of the architect was simply that of happily accommodating these objects.

A photograph of the Farnsworth House under construction shows the lonely figure of Mies with his back to the camera somberly appraising the empty frame. His enormous figure cuts a black silhouette into the frigid landscape. With his coat on, he stands like a Caspar David Friedrich figure confronting the sublime. At about the same time, but a world away, the Eameses put on their new outfits, climbed into their frame, and smiled at the camera.

1. Peter and Alison Smithson, "Phenomenon in Parallel: Eames House, *Patio and Pavilion*," *Places* 7 (Spring 1991), 20.
2. The Eameses said that the structural shell of the house was raised by five men in sixteen hours. "Life in a Chinese Kite: Standard Industrial Products Assembled in a Spacious Wonderland," *Architectural Forum* (Sept. 1950), 94.
3. The first photograph was published in Elizabeth A. T. Smith, ed., *Blueprints for Modern Living: History and Legacy of the Case Study Houses* (Cambridge, Mass.: The MIT Press, 1989), 182, and credited to the Eames Office. The second, in "Steel in the Meadow," *Interiors* (Nov. 1959), 109, is attributed to Jay Connor. The third, reproduced here, was printed in John Neuhart, Marilyn Neuhart, and Ray Eames, *Eames Design: The Work of the Office of Charles and Ray Eames* (New York: Abrams, 1989), 108; it is attributed to John Entenza.
4. Charles Eames, interview with Digby Diehl, "Charles Eames: Q & A," *Los Angeles Times WEST Magazine*, Oct. 8, 1972, 14. Reprinted in Digby Diehl, *Supertalk* (New York: Doubleday, 1974).
5. Neuhart, Neuhart, and Eames, 356.
6. Charles Eames, "Language of Vision: The Nuts and Bolts," *Bulletin of the American Academy of Arts and Sciences* (Oct. 1974), 13–25. Quoted in Neuhart, Neuhart, and Eames, 91.
7. Neuhart, Neuhart, and Eames, 137.
8. Charles decided to leave the design of a door handle and lock for the home in the hands of a locksmith, "who, he felt, would handle the problem with a degree of sensitivity born of his own training and craftsmanship. He was later horrified to find a large and clumsy fitting placed in an awkward position on the door." John Neuhart and Marilyn Neuhart, *Eames House* (Berlin and London: Ernst & Sohn and Academy Editions, 1994), 56.
9. Charles Eames quoted in Bill N. Lacy, "Warehouse Full of Ideas," *Horizon* (Sept. 1980), 27.
10. Pat Kirkham, *Charles and Ray Eames: Designers of the Twentieth Century* (Cambridge, Mass.: The MIT Press, 1995), 89.
11. While many sources insist, following the Eameses, that the new version used only those parts already delivered to the site, with the exception of one additional beam, Marilyn and John Neuhart question this: "A count of the seventeen-foot vertical girders needed for both house and studio yields a total of twenty-two for the first and sixteen for the latter, considerably more than would have been needed for the first version of each. In addition, there do not appear to have been any seventeen-foot girders in the original house. Additional trusses would also have been required to accommodate the reworked plan." Neuhart and Neuhart, 38.
12. Ray Eames, interview with Pat Kirkham, July 1983, Box 61, The Work of Charles and Ray Eames, Manuscript Division, Library of Congress, henceforth WCRE. See also Kirkham, 115–16.
13. Diehl, 16.
14. "Case Study Houses 8 and 9 by Charles Eames and Eero Saarinen, Architects," *Arts & Architecture* (Dec. 1945), 43. Also quoted in *Portfolio Magazine*, no. 2 (Summer 1950), unpag.
15. Esther McCoy, *Case Study Houses 1945–1962* (Los Angeles: Hennessey & Ingalls, 1977), 54; first published in 1962 as *Modern California Houses.*

16. In addition to *Arts & Architecture,* the Eames House was published in *Architectural Forum* (Sept. 1950), *Architectural Review* (Oct. 1951), *Arquitectura* (Mexico, June 1952), *L'Architecture d'aujourd'hui* (Dec. 1953), *Interiors* (Nov. 1959), *Domus* (May 1963), and *Architectural Design* (Sept. 1966).

17. Reyner Banham, "Klarheit, Ehrlichkeit, Einfachkeit...and Wit Too!: The Case Study Houses in the World's Eyes," in Smith, 183.

18. Ibid.

19. On the Case Study House Program, see McCoy and Smith.

20. John Entenza, "Competition: Designs for Postwar Living," *California Arts & Architecture* (Apr. 1943).

21. See Beatriz Colomina, *Privacy and Publicity: Modern Architecture as Mass Media* (Cambridge, Mass.: The MIT Press, 1994), 159.

22. Le Corbusier–Saugnier, "Les Maisons 'Voisin,'" *L'Esprit nouveau* 2 (Nov. 1920), 214.

23. Charles Eames quoted in "Life in a Chinese Kite," 96.

24. Alison and Peter Smithson, untitled, in *Architectural Design*, special issue, "Eames Celebration" (Sept. 1966), 432.

25. Diehl, 17. The Wilder-inspired aluminum frame chaise was first manufactured by Herman Miller in 1968.

26. "A Designer's Home of His Own: Charles Eames Builds a House of Steel and Glass," *Life*, Sept. 11, 1950, 152.

27. Alison Smithson, "And Now Dhamas Are Dying Out in Japan," *Architectural Design*, speical issue, "Eames Celebration" (Sept. 1966), 448.

28. Alison Smithson, "Eames Dreams," paper delivered on the occasion of the opening of an Eames exhibition in Berlin, Sept. 1979. Published in Alison and Peter Smithson, *Changing the Art of Inhabitation* (London: Artemis, 1994), 84.

29. Alison Smithson, "And Now Dhamas Are Dying Out in Japan," 447.

30. Alison and Peter Smithson, untitled, 432.

31. Entry on Charles Eames in *Current Biography* (New York: Wilson, 1965), 142.

32. Ray Eames, interview with Kirkham.

33. Peter Smithson, "Just a Few Chairs and a House: An Essay on the Eames-Aesthetic," *Architectural Design*, special issue, "Eames Celebration" (Sept. 1966), 443.

34. "We hung them off the ceiling for two reasons—one was because they needed to be kept away from strong light and the second was because we thought we would be able to see them well from that position." Ray Eames, interview with Kirkham.

35. Charles Eames quoted in "Life in a Chinese Kite," 94.

36. R. Buckminster Fuller, letter to Ms. Camp, Nov. 7, 1973, Box 30, WCRE.

37. Charles Eames quoted in Diehl, 14.

38. Charles Eames, "Mies van der Rohe" (photographs by Charles Eames taken at the exhibition), *Arts & Architecture* (Dec. 1947), 27.

39. Ibid.

40. Charles Eames quoted in "A Designer's Home of His Own," *Life*, Sept. 11, 1950, 152.

41. "Furniture Show Room by Charles Eames," *Arts & Architecture* (Oct. 1949), 26–29.

42. "California's Bold Look," *Life* (June 1954), 90–97; "California Ideas: Spreading West to East," *Vogue*, Apr. 15, 1954, 60–87.

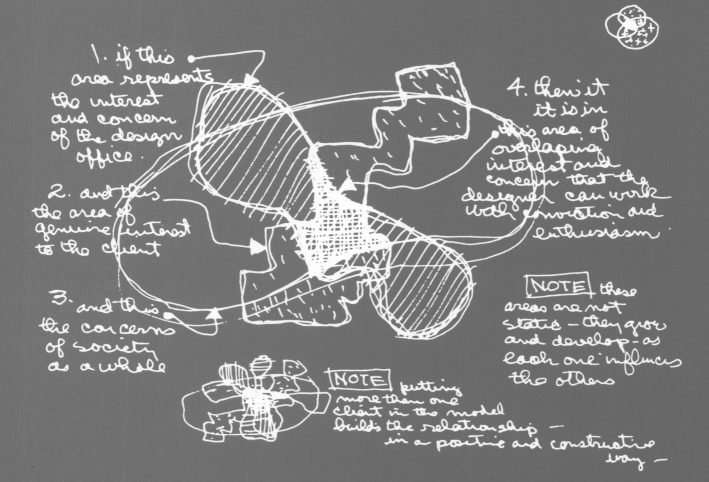

1. if this area represents the interest and concern of the design office.

2. and this the area of genuine interest to the client

3. and this the concerns of society as a whole

4. then it it is in this area of overlapping interest and concern that the designer can work with conviction and enthusiasm.

NOTE these areas are not static — they grow and develop — as each one influences the others

NOTE putting more than one client in the model builds the relationship — in a positive and constructive way —

"Natural Overlap"

CHARLES AND RAY EAMES
AND THE FEDERAL GOVERNMENT

Hélène Lipstadt

Conceptual diagram by Charles
Eames of the design process,
displayed in the 1969 exhibition
Qu'est-ce que le <design>?
(What Is Design?) at the Musée des
Arts Décoratifs, Paris

When asked "What is Design?" by the Musée des Arts Décoratifs, Paris,
in 1969, Charles and Ray Eames described their characteristically
inclusive approach: "Our interests have included many aspects of
communication—photography, exhibitions, writings, and motion pictures.
Our work in education has intensified this and has provided a natural
overlap to the interests of several government agencies."[1] The Eameses
described this "natural overlap" between their office and various
government agencies as mutual interests in the natural environment, the
objects of everyday life, and "conversations with other nations."[2] If the
first two natural overlaps fit with what we know of the Eameses, it is the
third claim that is especially intriguing, for it is a claim of another scale
and of much larger ambition. How did the Eameses come to be
responsible for conversations with nations on behalf of the government?
And why did they believe that the interests of the United States in this
domain naturally overlapped with their own?

Although their home and office were perched, culturally as well as
geographically, on the edge of the world, by the late 1950s the Eameses
were on familiar terms with its apparent center—scientists at American
universities, heads of American corporations, and directors of private
and public cultural institutions. While the benevolent patronage of the
Eameses by big business (most notably "Big Blue," or IBM), was typical of
a period in which large corporations embraced modern design, the
American government's sponsorship of these brilliant designers may
surprise us. Even their contemporaries, such as critic and editor Peter

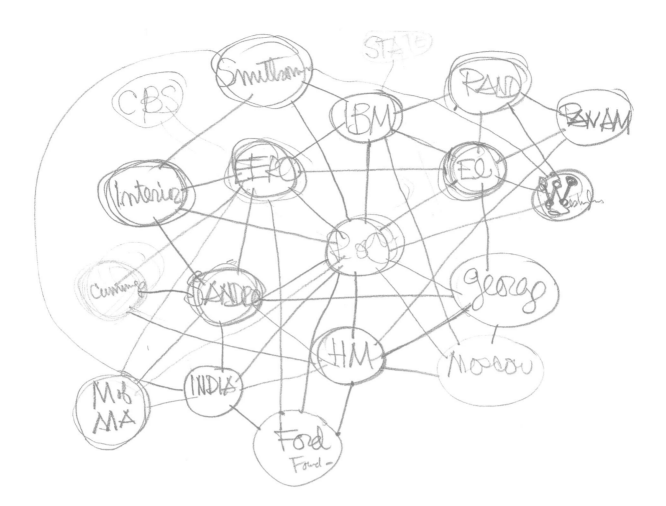

Blake, were astounded that "staid government agenc[ies]" patronized the Eameses, who were widely regarded as "cutting edge" and "hardly in the mainstream of American Culture."[3] Furthermore, while personally "very, very liberal," according to their friend the director Billy Wilder, they had carefully constructed a public persona that was apolitical and nonideological, one that suggested a "complete detachment from the outside world," as one observer noted, and a total disinterest in "aligning" themselves with political parties or causes.[4]

Two diagrams prepared by the Eames Office help us explore their work for the American government, an uncharted but important area of the Eameses' production. In a preparatory diagram for the 1969 exhibition *What Is Design?*, Charles and Ray appear as the nucleus of a system of interlinked friends and clients. Lines connect them to circles representing their government clients—the United States Information Agency (USIA), here called Moscow, the Department of State, the Smithsonian Institution, and the Department of the Interior; their corporate clients—IBM, Herman Miller, and Westinghouse; their designer colleagues and friends—Eero Saarinen, George Nelson, and Sandro (Alexander) Girard; and other powerful companies and institutions of postwar America—Pan American Airlines, the Ford Foundation, Columbia Broadcasting System, The Museum of Modern Art, the Rand Corporation, and Cummings Engines.

Another diagram prepared for *The World of Franklin and Jefferson*, a series of films and exhibitions created for the 1976 Bicentennial of

Diagram by Charles Eames showing the connection of the Eames Office to important clients, patrons, and colleagues

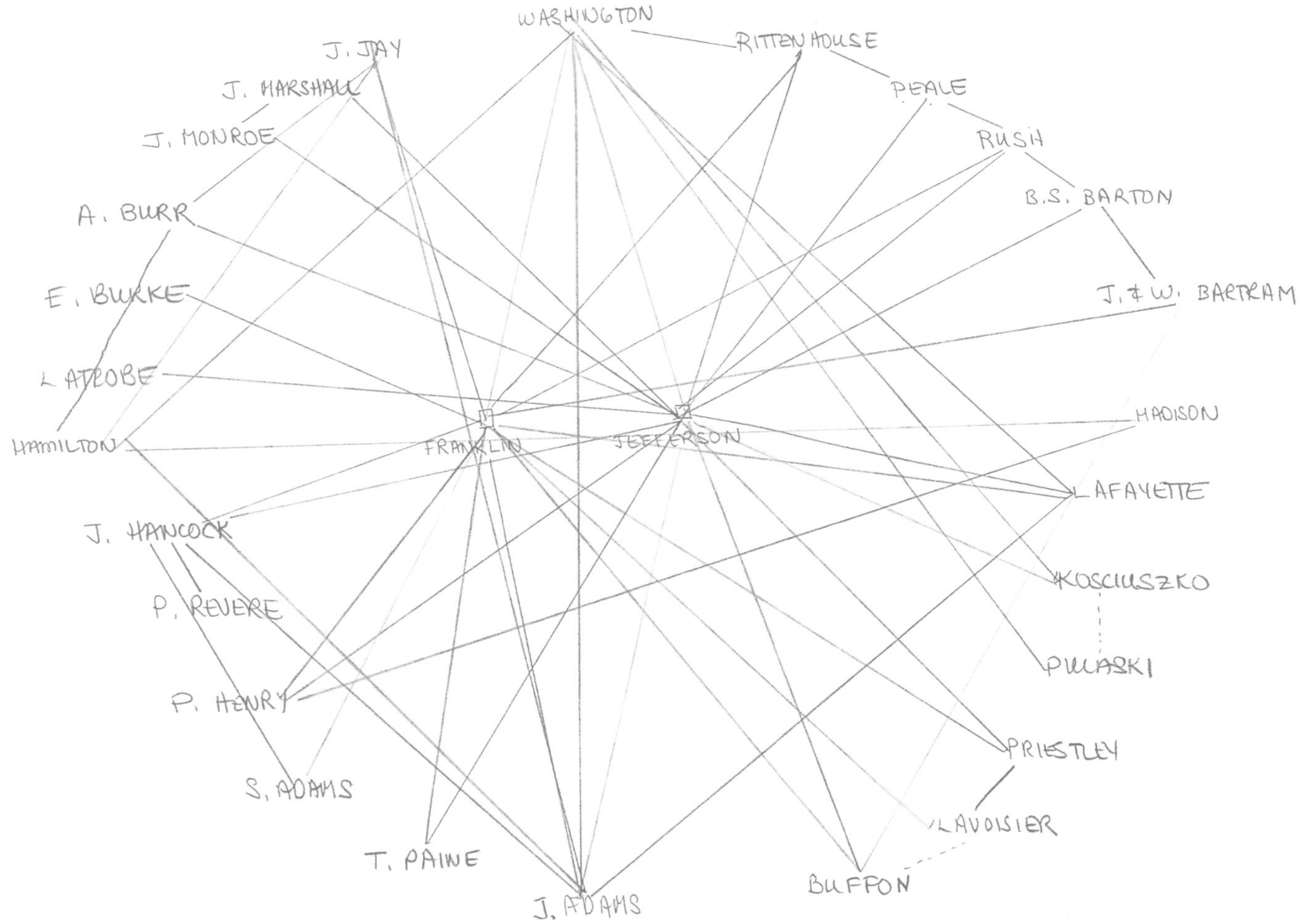
WASHINGTON
RITTENHOUSE
PEALE
RUSH
B.S. BARTON
J. & W. BARTRAM
MADISON
LAFAYETTE
KOSCIUSZKO
PULASKI
PRIESTLEY
LAVOISIER
BUFFON
J. ADAMS
T. PAINE
S. ADAMS
P. HENRY
P. REVERE
J. HANCOCK
HAMILTON
LATROBE
E. BURKE
A. BURR
J. MONROE
J. MARSHALL
J. JAY
FRANKLIN
JEFFERSON

Diagram by Charles Eames entitled "Friends and Acquaintances" for the Bicentennial exhibition *The World of Franklin and Jefferson*

the American Revolution, is remarkably like the earlier sketch. It depicts the American Revolution as a galaxy of American patriots, European and American scientists, and other cultural innovators who orbit around the twin suns of Benjamin Franklin and Thomas Jefferson. A cat's cradle of lines connects the galaxy's planets to each other and to the centers of the Enlightenment universe in America, represented by Franklin and Jefferson.[5]

The world of Franklin and Jefferson and the world of Charles and Ray Eames are similarly schematized. In each, the connectedness of individuals and the sharing of information represent and, at the same time, obscure complex relations of conflict and competition, of power, profit, and politics. In both, history is equated with biography, and the tangled skeins of the corporate world and of the Revolution are represented as open channels for clear communication and mutually beneficial exchange. In Charles and Ray Eames's rational world, communication always functioned in the same way. The two worlds could be depicted in the same fashion because they were similarly imagined. Designers more than historians, the Eameses viewed the past in a manner conditioned by their knowledge of the present. Their understanding of the origins of America and its government and of contemporary American society was predicated on their experience of that government and their place in that society. The second diagram is, like the first, about the Eameses' America, and government and politics were part of that America.

Contracts with the United States government bracketed the Eameses' career: their first paid assignment as designers—molded-plywood leg splints for the United States Navy in 1942—and what they considered their crowning achievement,[6] completed in 1977—*The World of Franklin and Jefferson*. However, the completed works directly commissioned by the federal government form only part of the relationship between the government and the Eames Office, which was far more extensive than the published record of the Eameses' federal projects suggests. Between 1959 and Charles's death in 1978, it is unlikely that the office ever went long without a direct or indirect commission from the government, or at least a request for advice or a proposal for a project that was never developed. Even before they made their first government-sponsored film, in 1959, Charles and Ray had received an award from the State Department for *The Information Machine*, their contribution to IBM's pavilion at the Brussels World's Fair.[7] Along with ongoing professional relationships with the USIA and the Smithsonian, Charles held appointments to the National Council on the Arts and a Library of Congress advisory committee.[8] His advice was prized abroad and at home by career diplomats and ambassadors appointed by both parties and by some of the government's cultural spokesmen.[9] Thanks to the USIA, libraries around the world were furnished with Eames films; photographs of their works were widely distributed; and traveling exhibitions, lectures, and cultural trips were sponsored regularly.[10] The Eameses were treated as representatives of American culture by the federal government, which acted sometimes as an agent and almost always as a fan.[11]

This essay charts the "natural overlap" between the Eameses and the American government by analyzing two ideal projects for imaginary government clients and two realized projects commissioned by federal agencies. The Eameses' political beliefs can be deciphered in these ideal and real projects. The imaginary projects—a city hall designed for *Architectural Forum* magazine and a competition entry for a memorial to Thomas Jefferson—suggest the Eameses' theories about the nature of government-citizen relations and the role of design in enforcing those relations. The real projects—a seven-screen film for the 1959 American National Exhibition in Moscow (later called *Glimpses of the U.S.A.*) and *The World of Franklin and Jefferson*—provide insight into how these "cutting edge" designers actually worked with a government agency (the USIA in both cases) to develop cultural products that represented American innovation at home and abroad.

Charles and Ray's USIA projects also offer a detailed look at works created for the government by leading modernists, undertakings that are often dubbed ideological without addressing their designers' political beliefs. The Eameses made a rule of collaborating only with clients whose objectives they shared. The notion of natural overlap suggests that the government's purpose and theirs were compatible: both wanted to enter into conversations with other countries. Since the American government entered these conversations for political reasons, it follows that the Eameses did so as well. Thus, in the USIA projects we find their work at its most explicitly political. This does not mean their beliefs were identical to those of the federal government, only that the Eameses did not shrink from using the USIA commissions as an opportunity for conveying political ideas, just as the USIA did not shrink from employing the Eameses to convey its own ideas. Similarly, these works are no less

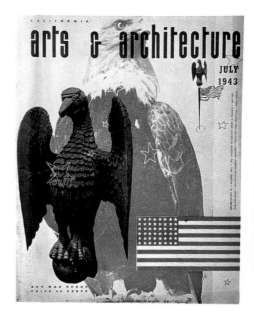

July 1943 *Arts & Architecture* cover designed by Ray Eames

interesting *as works*, no less quintessentially the Eameses' for having the federal government as sponsor. To the contrary, the Eameses' conversations with "other nations" proved, as the two diagrams suggest, to be with themselves and about themselves, to describe their place in the American nation and the place of their nation in the postwar and cold war eras. Thus, examination of the Eameses' government work in both its real and imagined dimensions illuminates motivating political beliefs obscured behind their carefully constructed apolitical public persona. Deconstruction of the natural overlap reveals the Eameses' unstated political vision for America of a participatory democracy based on direct communication between government and citizens in media provided by Charles and Ray Eames.

City Hall for 194X

In the middle of World War II, *Architectural Forum* invited Charles Eames and thirty-one other architects to imagine the "New Buildings for 194X" that a typical postwar community of seventy thousand inhabitants might need.[12] Eames's submission for an ideal City Hall, designed with John Entenza (editor of the vanguard California publication *Arts & Architecture*) provides a key to his views of the ideal government and its cultural role and of an ideal architecture and its political role.

According to the project text, "A city government should—must—be housed as the center of a mutually cooperative enterprise in which: "THE GOVERNMENT TALKS TO THE PEOPLE. AND THE PEOPLE TALK TO THE GOVERNMENT." In the town's "house of government," which Eames considered "the heart of the community," democratic government would be symbolized by a building that grouped together places of assembly for the city's representatives, offices for government services, and a community arts and media center. This City Hall expressed "the *idea* of government," which, "is never static and...can never be complete without the direct participation of the people who create it."[13] Conceived as a manifesto in the form of a prototypical building, this City Hall translated into built form Eames's ideals for government and its relationships with its citizens.

Illustration for City Hall for 194X project by John Entenza and Charles Eames, published in the May 1943 issue of *Architectural Forum*

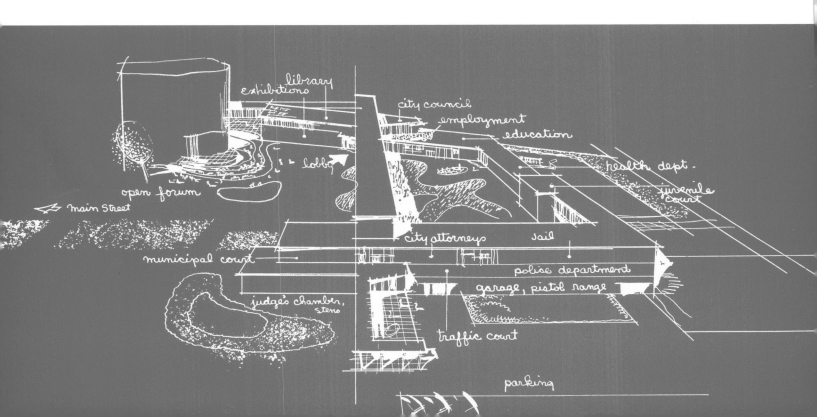

The hypothetical City Hall is arranged in one complete and two incomplete tetrahedrons, which, perhaps coincidentally, form an L and an A hinged together. (Its outdoor café and scrubby landscaping make this ideal town seem as if it could fit in a suburb of Los Angeles.) The A-shaped wing houses municipal services, and the L-shaped wing houses the activities of an unusual board of education. This board does not administer schools but provides the city with exhibitions, motion pictures, study and lecture groups, and open forums. Dominated by the towering stage house of the auditorium, the board of education's wing wraps around an open piazza, which spills out onto an outdoor meeting place called the "Open Forum." The forum, in turn, opens onto Main Street, a broad avenue with a grassy mall at its center, reminiscent of Washington, D.C. The municipal and juvenile court, the police department, health department and clinic, and the board of education's administrative offices are housed in the perimeter of the A-shaped wing. The wing's crossbar, raised on pilotis, is a bridge containing what Eames and Entenza called the "machinery of municipal planning and government": the law library and offices for the engineering, landscaping, and planning departments. At the intersection of the two wings is a belvedere that houses the see-and-be-seen council chamber for this dialogical government.

In their imaginary project, Eames and Entenza arranged what they considered the essential services of the government around the City Hall's main entry at the hinge of the L and A. In the heart of this "heart of the community" were the city's political power (the council chamber); its dispensers of information (the law library, the public library with a movie theater, the city clerk's offices, and, next to them, the offices of the board of education); its art life (the gallery); its facilities for the design and management of its infrastructure (the engineering and city planning offices); and its place for interactive public discussion of civic life (the piazza). In these interdependent indoor and outdoor spaces, government would become a "mutually cooperative enterprise," an Athenian democracy of participation. "WHEN THE GOVERNMENT TALKS TO THE PEOPLE AND THE PEOPLE TALK TO THE GOVERNMENT—IT IS ONE AND THE SAME VOICE." The "truly democratic type of government" was not only symbolized but also fostered by the architecture of the City Hall. Thus, in the Eames-Entenza formula for government, representative political government added to the science of urban and environmental planning and then multiplied by communication, arts, and media results in participatory and dialogical democracy.[14]

In plan the City Hall evokes the Dessau Bauhaus of 1925–26, designed by Adolf Meyer and Walter Gropius, which provided the basic concept of interlocking wings and bridge. In both designs the bridge provides a panoptic view of the entire institution and serves as headquarters for its intellectual leadership. Le Corbusier's project for an assembly hall for the League of Nations, 1927, probably inspired the wedge-shaped auditorium, while the oversized stage house and overall aesthetic resemble a low-cost version of the Saarinen, Saarinen, and Swanson design for the Smithsonian Gallery of Art of 1939, which Eames had worked on while at the Cranbrook Academy of Art.[15] Similarly, the partially enclosed quadrangle plan evokes parts of Eliel Saarinen's design for the Cranbrook schools, 1924–30, where Eames had been head of the academy's department of industrial design.[16]

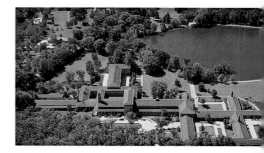

Kingswood School at Cranbrook Educational Community, designed by Eliel Saarinen, 1943

Thus Eames's City Hall joins the Bauhaus, the building considered the realization of modern architecture's aspiration to be both functional and abstract, with schemes by Le Corbusier and the Saarinens that heralded a new form of monumental modernism.[17] Together these models provided the formal vocabulary and means of expression and symbolism for Eames and Entenza's ideal City Hall. Eames's civic building was modeled on a museum and two art schools, underscoring his notion that creativity, achieved through education and popular media, was the key to ideal civic life.

Employing a strategy he applied to all his government projects, Eames "built" from his life experiences. The building's program and design not only incorporate Charles's ideology, but they also summarize his career up to then: his work for a Works Progress Administration (WPA) arts program measuring historic buildings, his teaching in Cranbrook's open-structured art school, and his participation in the design of a municipally sponsored artwork for the city of St. Louis (the Carl Milles fountain, *The Meeting of the Waters*)[18] and the Smithsonian's new Gallery of Art.

Eames and Entenza treated the imaginary City Hall for 194X as a demonstration project. While other architects in the 1940s were busy drawing word pictures of public spaces for public discourse, they designed one in which communication, information, planning, and media form the lynchpin of the "house of government." For Eames, the unity achieved by the war effort in 1940s America—the sense of participation, relative equality, and purpose created by fighting the "good war"—would be maintained by civic activities and buildings modeled on innovative art schools (Cranbrook and the Bauhaus) and a populist museum (the Smithsonian Gallery of Art). Democracy would thrive in a society where art and popular media become part of civic life. Here is the natural overlap of interests, writ small for the arts, and writ large for all society, with cultural programming as the vital link between them. The City Hall for 194X prefigured the cultural activities—the media, exhibitions, public presentations, and design of spaces for them—and the overarching philosophy of the Eameses' later work for the larger "house" of the federal government.

Entry No. 154, "Jefferson National Expansion Memorial" Competition

The architecture and arts programming of the City Hall for 194X made it the catalyst for a new kind of civic life and participatory democracy. Similarly, in 1947, in the Eameses' proposed "Jefferson National Expansion Memorial," competition entry number 154,[19] buildings designed for popular culture would sustain Jeffersonian participatory democracy and provide the education that Jefferson believed made individuals into citizens. The Jefferson National Expansion Memorial Association solicited designs for a national memorial dedicated both to the memory of Jefferson and to western exploration and settlement. Intended for an eighty-acre site in St. Louis, the program included a federally funded memorial representing the Louisiana Purchase and westward expansion and a hypothetical "Living Memorial," an institution that would provide social and cultural programs based on Jefferson's belief that men's knowledge of each other was "the instrument" with which to "improve the lot of men of all races and all creeds under Democracy."[20] How it would do so was left to the competition entrant.

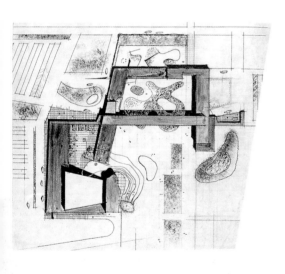

Illustration for City Hall for 194X project by John Entenza and Charles Eames, published in the May 1943 issue of *Architectural Forum*

Born and bred in St. Louis, Charles Eames was on home ground here in every way. He was familiar with the Mississippi River valley landscape, the cityscape of the nineteenth-century riverfront that had been razed to make way for the memorial, the local politics and civic activism that made it possible, and Missouri's image of itself as the "child of Jefferson" and its worship of the Louisiana Purchase as a second Declaration of Independence. Eames's Thomas Jefferson, whom he later described as a "kind of hero" for Ray and himself in the 1920s and 1930s, [21] was, however, closer to Franklin Delano Roosevelt's than Missouri's—a sponsor of big government projects like the WPA, which improved the lot of the "common man." The Eameses' Jefferson resembled the one whom many modernists believed was, in the words of a group of Columbia University School of Architecture faculty members, "not only a...liberal Democrat, but also... a progressive architect." [22]

While the Eameses' project (with a text by Entenza) scrupulously adhered to the program requirements, it played down the representation of westward expansion and Jefferson. Their design relegated it to a mural and a series of decidedly unmonumental works of sculpture that hovered between the vanguard and the whimsical, turning the figure of Jefferson into something that seems a cross between a Henry Moore sculpture and a leggy Betty Grable. Indeed, a "commemorative mound" was the only feature of their design that could be considered monumental, even as modernists understood the term: durable, sizable, expressive, and nonclassical. What the mound actually commemorated, however, is unclear. If it was truly inspired by the ancient Native American man-made land forms that had dominated the St. Louis landscape before urban development destroyed them, then the mound actually memorialized the losses incurred during westward expansion. The most monumental part of the project was what might be called an antimonument. In the Eameses' design, there was no central commemorative monument other than the Living Memorial, and no memorializing in the usual sense. This left the visitor free to have a "very personal experience" [23] of Jefferson's greatness, to build a mental and, especially, a political monument by participating in the activities of the Living Memorial.

Devoted to the production and dissemination of "information" (of unspecified content), the Eameses' Living Memorial used the arts and popular media to "express" Jefferson's "life and work of 'reason'... in terms of creative learning." Ideas would be drawn from an "immense reservoir" comprising the physical environment, the aesthetics of industry, planning, the nature of freedom, government, housing, propaganda, materials, and folkways. The institution was left without a subject or central theme, for this would be decided by "legitimate public concern," or public opinion. Its activities, however, were clearly established. Information would be presented through the media of popular culture—graphic art, motion pictures, radio and recordings, animated cartoons, music, dance, and exhibitions. A television and radio station would be included, but notably absent were the "high" arts of painting and sculpture or even studios for producing them.

The objective of this information center remained explicitly political and especially populist. As good modernists, the Eameses subordinated representation and regional identity to the greater good and more abstract goals of social improvement. As Depression-era populists and believers in the image of Jefferson forged by the New Deal, [24] they gave

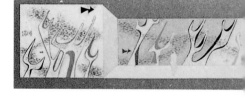

Detail of a presentation board submitted by Charles and Ray Eames to the 1947 "Jefferson National Expansion Memorial" competition, showing a mural symbolizing American westward expansion

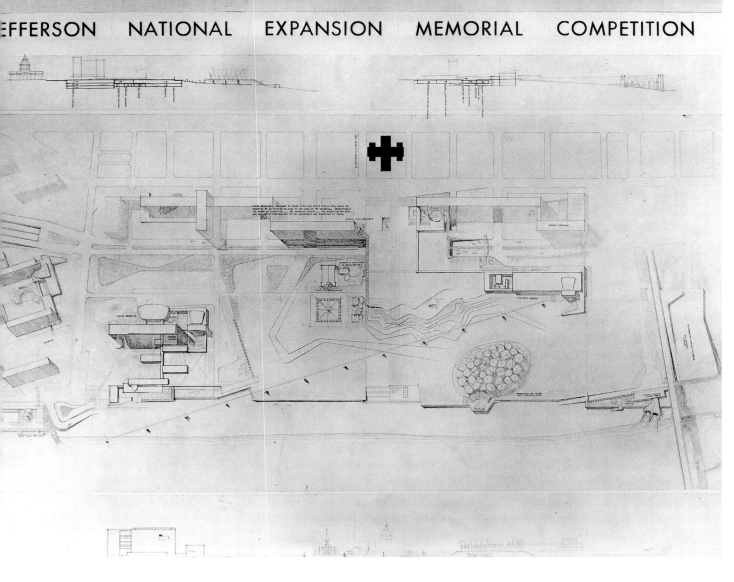

Presentation boards submitted by
Charles and Ray Eames to the
1947 "Jefferson National Expansion
Memorial" competition

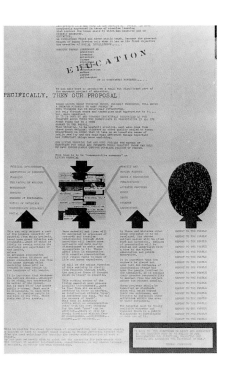

greater weight to the cultural Jefferson than to the political Jefferson, to the Great Commoner and democrat rather than the founder of the Democratic Party. Significantly, Jefferson is described in the Eameses' text as architect, inventor, scientist, farmer, statesman, mathematician, author, lawyer, and philosopher, in that order, and never as the author of the Louisiana Purchase treaty. By this omission, the Eameses inverted the competition program's priorities and sacrificed any advantage they might have gained from their intimate knowledge of St. Louis and familiarity with local politics.[25] They put their own personal ideology and idea of Jefferson first, emphasizing their modernist objectives for society (hinted at by words like "housing" and "nature of freedom") rather than the competition's goal of a monument to St. Louis's historic importance as Jefferson's child.

As Charles explained to George Howe, the professional adviser and author of the program, what he and Ray had "got down on paper was little to the richness we ourselves gained."[26] The competition entry can thus be read for what it tells us about their position on the much-debated architectural topic of monumentality.[27] This discussion was not about style, but about the nature of civic spaces and architecture's ability to represent government as participatory and democratic. What was wanted was a monumentality that could be modernist. What was feared was that monumentality by its very nature expressed the fascism of the governments that favored it, or reverted to the older Beaux-Arts forms of the nineteenth and early twentieth centuries. The Eameses' goal was to create spaces that facilitated a new kind of public life. While their contemporaries had devised new civic spaces from which popular culture was omitted, they proposed that the media of mass culture could serve a civic purpose.[28] In the "Jefferson National Expansion Memorial" entry, as in the 194X City Hall, cultural programming was the lynchpin and architecture the enabler of a civic society sustained by the arts—here even more clearly defined as popular culture by the inclusion of television and the omission of painting and sculpture. Leaving public opinion to decide on the center's programs and objectives was, once again, an expression of the Eameses' and Entenza's faith in the "people" to whom the center "reported," a notion repeated a stuttering eighteen times on the competition drawing.

Taking up the cause of mass culture was not necessarily a disinterested act. The center's facilities and personnel, the information it would disseminate, and the popular media it would use all foretold the evolution of the Eames Office and its products, making the Eameses' "Jefferson National Expansion Memorial" entry a projection of its authors' aspirations for themselves. As in the Living Memorial, so in the Eames Office: "great communicators" cooperated with "great thinkers" on presenting information (defined as a "completely fluid and never static truth") in all its forms. In both, the vital link between society and the truth was the group of "great communicators," capable of making a "true report to the people."[29] Since, according to the Eameses, the Living Memorial had become the "commemorative monument" and that monument was federally funded, it was essentially the Eames Office reconfigured as a branch of the federal government. The opportunity to put these ideas to the test, to use innovative technology to make a "true report to the people," would first come in their conversations with other nations.

Glimpses of the U.S.A.

In the City Hall for 194X, the arts were the catalyst for civic life and government to become a "cooperative enterprise." Four years later, in the "Jefferson National Expansion Memorial" competition entry, popular culture was the tool and the arena for public participation, and a government entity was no longer necessary. With postwar abundance assured, the Eameses' goal in the Jefferson memorial was not only to make "ENRICHING THINGS important, but IMPORTANT things more enriching."[30] With those principles in place, conversations between the "great communicators" and other nations could begin.

The USIA sponsored the Eameses' first cultural product for the federal government, an introductory film for the 1959 American National Exhibition in Moscow, a six-week-long exhibit that would give the Soviet Union and the United States the opportunity to address each other free of censorship or interference. The exhibition became famous for the Kitchen Debate, in which the Russian leader Nikita Khrushchev and Vice President Richard Nixon argued about their respective systems in front of an appliance-filled model kitchen (and made Nixon a viable candidate for the presidency). The USIA's objective for the exhibition was to project "a realistic and credible image of America."[31] The agency's use of the term "credible" implied its interest in presenting a truthful portrait of the pluralistic American identity and the varied, complex, and dynamic makeup of its constantly evolving culture.[32]

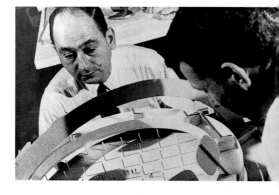

Charles Eames (right) and George Nelson viewing the model of the "bagel" film screen configuration for the 1959 American National Exhibition in Moscow

Soon after the bilateral agreement was executed, USIA Director of Design Jack Masey selected George Nelson as the exhibition's designer and R. Buckminster Fuller as the architect of its main structure, a geodesic dome. Throughout the complicated negotiations with the bureaucratic and disorganized USIA (which Nelson compared to the travails of the hero of Kafka's *The Castle*, while hoping for a different ending to his own "exciting nightmare"), two elements remained non-negotiable: the "full participation" of Charles and Ray Eames, and the need to convey the "single most important point...America [as] a changing society."[33] Even before they received an official contract, the Eameses joined Nelson and Masey in developing the basic scheme. Nelson saw the geodesic dome in which the Eameses' film would be shown as "a kind of information machine" (using the title of the Eameses' recent film on computers made for the Brussels World's Fair) empty of displays, while a second pavilion of glass would be full of consumer products. The Eameses' film would be "a way of compressing into a small volume the tremendous quantity of information we wanted to present," according to Nelson, and would serve as an introduction to the entire exhibition.[34]

Charles and Ray had first envisioned projecting enormous images of "landscape, people, flowers" on nine screens in what they dubbed a "bagel," or circular, configuration, surrounding viewers with images so that they would always feel they were missing some of the information. Nelson, however, was less enamored of what Charles called "the throwaway effect" of redundant information and the arrangement modeled on Disney's Circarama (a moving-image presentation first projected at the 1958 Brussels World's Fair). He preferred a tic-tac-toe-style grid of screens that allowed every piece of information (a "Milwaukee supermarket," a "Fort Lauderdale supermarket," and so on, explained Nelson) to be seen. The head of the USIA and creator of its policy of credibility, George V. Allen, accepted the multiple-screen solution because, as Nelson noted, it was the "one really effective way to establish credibility for a statement that the products on view were widely purchased by the American people."[35]

For the USIA and for Nelson, proving that the American consumer goods on display were not unique prototypes—as any equivalent object would have been in the U.S.S.R. and as Russians were sure to think— was a main objective to be served by the film's "projection of data." (For example, the multiple images of supermarkets would be drawn from visibly different regions that, when placed side by side, would present a map of American abundance and its wide diffusion.) Later in 1959 Charles described the design process. Accepting the goal of credibility and the idea that multiplicity would convince the Russians that the objects displayed were common, the Eameses had taken the picture magazines *Life* and *Look* as models for their film because of their "international acceptance" by readers in many cultures. However, the kind of human-interest photography and panoramas of generic American life typically gathered by those magazines did not mesh with the Eameses' aim of telling the "usual...truthfully." Missing, for example, were scenes of intimacy, of families and couples bidding each other good night, of the emotional side of everyday life that the Eameses considered the "usual." Charles and Ray supplemented photographs culled from the files

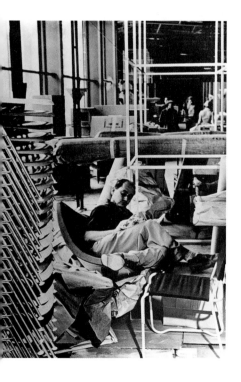

George Nelson with a stack of Eames fiberglass chairs during the installation of the American National Exhibition

of *Life* and *Look* with photographs specially made for the film in order to tell what they believed was a more truthful story. [36]

Contractually required to "give comprehension of, and credibility to, the factual story of present day U.S.A.," the Eameses' film was expected to depict a "typical American work day" in seven areas of the United States for nine minutes and "a typical weekend day" for three minutes on seven twenty-by-thirty-foot screens. [37] The seven-screen film translated the eleven themes established for the entire exhibition by the USIA almost verbatim into a simple linear narrative of a typical American workday and weekend. The first two themes, America's Land and People and America Lives, became the first section of the film. The third theme, America Works, became the second section, with the ninth theme, America Travels, appended to it. Skipping the next two themes, the Eameses passed directly to the sixth, America Learns, and the seventh, America Explores Man and Universe, illustrated by public elementary education of children, institutes of higher learning, and the laboratories of industry. These served as the preface to the two skipped themes, America Produces and America Consumes (which the USIA defined as "marketing, kitchens"). The remaining themes, America Creates and America Plays, became the typical weekend and a distinctly metropolitan night. Originally planned but omitted from the film was the final theme, Community Life, which would have been illustrated by PTA meetings, choir practices, and other communal gatherings.[38]

Like the Kitchen Debate, the film belonged to the culture of the cold war. As intended, it resembled the *Life* and *Look* photo essays on American life of the 1950s. In those magazines, historian Eric Sandeen has argued, documentary photography served an age in which conformity masked anxiety and in which individuals' identities and civil rights were "contained." These compendia of images echoed the advertising with which they were interspersed, ultimately stressing the fruits of abundance and the benefits of consumerism. In *Life* magazine's photographs, scholars have seen the way in which an image of America was constructed, defining Americans as white middle-class members of a nuclear family, minorities as the source of social problems, and women as homemakers and mothers. In the same magazines, analyses of American culture and of "the American mind" established categories like high-, middle-, and lowbrow, thereby controlling and containing lifestyles and homogenizing taste. ("Highbrows," for instance, sat in Eames chairs, according to *Life*.) Cultural and religious differences were celebrated, the better to characterize the exceptionalness of America, an entity that was stronger for having unified (and, according to revisionist scholars today, subjugated) cultural and class differences.[39]

However much it owed to the structure and content of *Life* and *Look*, the Eameses' seven-screen film depicted a country unlike the magazines' America. If suburbs predominate in the Eameses' film, they coexist with cities that have lost neither their cultural centrality, their economic vitality, nor their diversity. Types of suburban developments are shown systematically, but in plan, from the air, as if to admit their cookie-cutter similarity. Urban housing and skyscrapers, however, merit both distant skyline and close-up views of what the script called "their faces," all photographed with taxonomic precision and loving attention. In an inversion of California's stereotypical image, Los Angelenos commute to their downtown and visit its nightspots. Scenes of urban night life equate

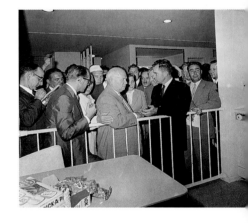

The Kitchen Debate between Soviet Prime Minister Nikita Khrushchev and American Vice President Richard Nixon at the American National Exhibition, Moscow, on July 25, 1959

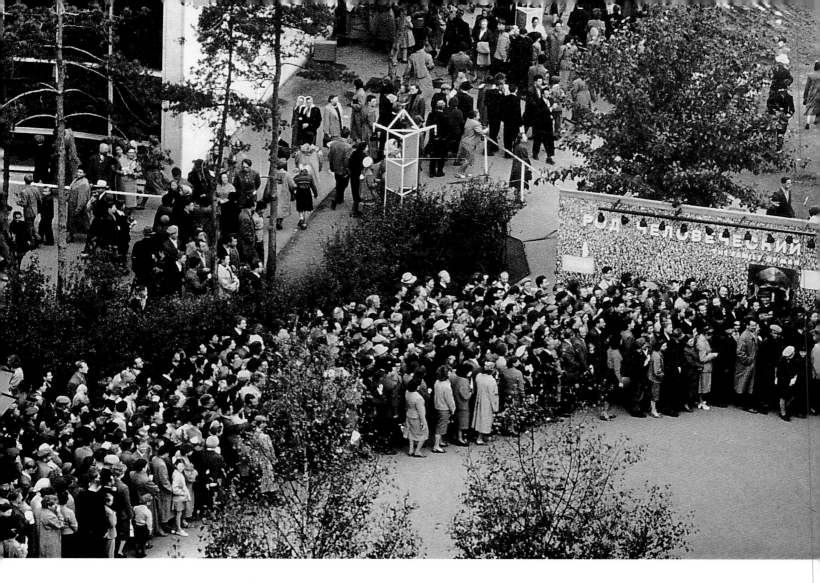

Crowds attending the American
National Exhibition, Moscow,
July 1959

L.A.'s urban "disorder" and movie marquees with New York's urban grid
and Broadway theaters. Automobiles proliferate, but public
transportation remains a necessity, to be used for commuting by "adults,"
comprising both men and, the film shows, women. Food is prepared
exclusively by women armed with a battery of kitchen appliances. Meals,
however, are ethnically diverse (represented by tortillas) and eaten in a
variety of settings and from a range of vessels, dispelling any impression
of uniformity. The film makes explicit the differences in clothing, posture,
and table manners of those who drank from upended milk bottles and
those who take wine with dinner and coffee in demitasse cups. Leisure
activities range from the classless (picnicking) to the quintessentially
middle class (golf) to the distinctly upper class (yacht racing). In this
explicitly biracial society, African Americans are found in the expected
places and roles—in Southern churches, on the baseball diamond, and as
jazz performers—but also in unexpected ones—on tennis courts, on
beaches, in the garb of city workers, and, demonstrating recent
innovations in race relations, as the subject of a Broadway play.

As intended, the Eameses' film equated commodity capitalism with
the American democracy, the multiplicity of screens proving the
multiplicity of things as the new medium became the exhibition's overall
message. In addition to seventy of the promised supermarkets, there
were seventy industrial plants, forty-two dams and irrigation systems,
and thirty-five different types of places of worship.[40] Besides tableware
and cars, however, the "things" given the greatest attention were raw

materials, not consumer goods: a steel ingot manufactured from start to finish in breathtaking moving footage.

Although the USIA's conventional definition of high culture—architecture, painting, sculpture, music—was given its due, the barrage of images from popular culture—chorus lines and crowded stadia, ballparks and racetracks—was greater. Similarly, scenes illustrating the government's notion of popular culture defined in terms of consumer objects—sports equipment, playgrounds, photography, radio, television[41]—were counterbalanced by images of popular amusements—fairs, circuses, fireworks, and amusement parks—and leisure activities like kite flying, soapbox derbies, and playing at swimming holes. Though religion was not on the list of the USIA's approved subjects, houses of worship were depicted, as well as rites of all faiths, including those of white and black Protestants, Asian Americans, Native Americans, Muslims, as well as the more prominent minorities, Catholics and Jews. They include as well the religious practices that the picture magazines avoided. The scenes of the Torah scrolls being read were probably a provocative sight for a Russian audience. Finally, the film made a point of embracing a part of culture unimagined by the USIA—the pleasures of the body, the mild eroticism of a grown-up's leisurely weekend bath, and the more explicit eroticism of a young couple's good night embrace.

The Eameses went beyond standard cultural values to create an extraordinary collage of differences in lifestyles and cultural practices. Furthermore, their film explicitly avowed those differences. To be sure, the Eameses' Americans lived in nuclear families and in relative comfort. The subject of segregation was passed over, poverty hidden, and politics—even the political campaigns and election days that made the U.S.A. a functioning democracy—avoided, the latter on the advice of the USIA, which thought it too provocative. However, to be American was to be heterogeneous, distinguished by regional identity, ethnic origin, and class. Motivated perhaps by their liberal political beliefs, the Eameses used their rationalists' habit of organizing information taxonomically and their artists' appreciation of undetected similarities to reconfigure the picture-magazine image of America as more pluralist and diverse than was usually allowed. In their survey of American society, the Eameses had stumbled upon the unspoken subject of class difference. In this film conceived for Russians, they made their "report to the people" truthful.

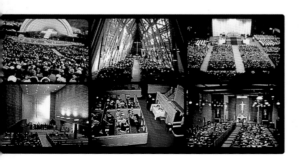

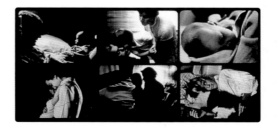

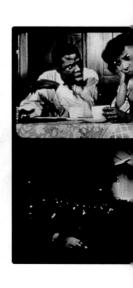

The seven-screen film was shown sixteen times a day to all of the estimated three million Russians who passed through the dome. Russian visitors ranked it as their fifth favorite exhibit, after the cars, color television, Disney Circarama, and the photography exhibit devoted to the human condition, *The Family of Man*.[42] American observers reported that most Russians thought it moved much too fast to comprehend.[43] However, affect, not comprehension, was the desired result, and apparently it was achieved. "So thoroughly did the Eameses communicate with the loving side of the human structure of American life, that everyone [sic] of the packed Russian audience could be seen at the end with eyes full of tears of [sic] the kinship of human beings," wrote Buckminster Fuller in 1973. "Watching [the]...multiple thing for the first time" made the cynical Peter Blake "nearly [cry] because it was so damned great!" As Charles had observed in 1959, it was the film's "very human thing," especially the food and around-the-house scenes, that caused couples to embrace, even before seven Marilyn Monroes had winked (in a scene borrowed from *Some Like It Hot*) and the final shot of forget-me-nots had caused them to mumble its overt message of everlasting love: "*nezabudki*."[44]

The film was, as one contemporary described it, "almost by definition...superficial and more than a little propagandistic."[45] Yet to criticize it today for its "familiar message of unified diversity, the democracy of information and the subordination of the individual voice to a common culture," as Sandeen did, is to ignore its subtleties and qualified achievements for a federally sponsored film of that time and place. To dismiss its final image—the offering of wildflowers—as "a greeting card that opened to a sentimental message" is to misunderstand the gesture.[46] For the offering of flowers is a universal, even transhistorical, cultural gesture of welcome, making a point about human behavior much like that made by *The Family of Man*.[47] If the use of wildflowers was sentimental, this was the signature of Ray's "woman's touch" and her faith in shared human values and the centrality of human beings, also a message close to that of *The Family of Man*. Ray's frequent inclusion of symbols of femininity and sentiment in products later designed for corporations and the government secretly made them a little less male, a little more accessible and human. If, in the 1950s, a pluralistic

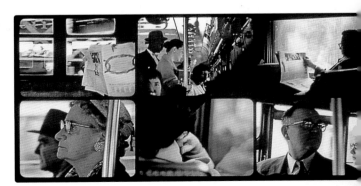

Frames from the film
Glimpses of the U.S.A. (1959)

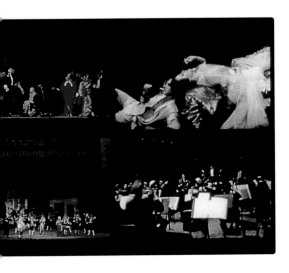

society was expected to sing in one voice, the pluralistic society depicted by the Eameses was made up of a choir of jazz singers, with a place for the solo riff and occasional creative notes of dissonance.

How did the Eameses manage to make their image of America the one that was purveyed in Moscow? The short answer is that the Eameses did not actually show the exhibition footage to Nelson, Masey, and the USIA's Sovietologists until the eve of the exhibition's opening day, in flagrant violation of the contract's stipulations. Successfully avoiding government-imposed contractual deadlines, the Eameses also evaded the required government oversight. This had proven a "happy condition," Charles later told a California audience, with the client busy in Washington and not knowing or caring what was happening in Southern California. He advised them that it was a "very excellent way to keep it. We are going to try and do it that way."[48] In this way, they created the "detachment" for which they were famed, intentionally making the appearance of ideological innocence part of their constructed persona, much like Charles's signature bow-ties and Ray's hair bows. Profiting from the chaotic conditions surrounding preparation of the exhibition,[49] the Eameses had discovered that distance could be artificially sustained despite meetings in Washington and Los Angeles. Distance created an independence that might have looked like detachment but actually provided the cover for their politics and ideology.

The Eameses also found that artistic autonomy was a wedge as well as a shield. Under its protection they were able to project their view of the United States, imbued with their Depression-era populism, into the USIA's documentary on supermarkets, sports equipment, and cars. The Eameses' first "conversation with other nations" on behalf of the United States was a conversation about their America in the "language of the people," in the medium of popular culture.

The World of Franklin and Jefferson

While the Moscow conversation was hardly a dialogue, participatory democracy was the subject as well as the political goal of the conversation in *The World of Franklin and Jefferson*. Conceived by the USIA to celebrate the Bicentennial of the American Revolution and funded by IBM during its American tour, *The World of Franklin and Jefferson* was the most complex project undertaken by the Eames Office; it eventually comprised three films (including the Eameses' longest one), seven different exhibitions in seven venues and five languages, and an exhibition catalogue. With forty thousand words and an extensive timeline, it was not only their largest exhibition, but it was also the one that offered the opportunity to create the forum to report to the people, the occasion that the Eameses had sought since 1943.

However, the media techniques of the 1950s and the manifesto-like propositions of government as a "cooperative enterprise" and its chosen communicators (the Eameses) as true reporters to the people took on a different resonance in the 1970s. Much to the Eameses' and their corporate and government sponsors' distress, this wide-ranging show, which the Eameses considered their crowning assignment, was panned. *New York Times* art critic Hilton Kramer proclaimed in horror in his review, "What Is This Stuff Doing at the Met?" when the exhibition opened at the Metropolitan Museum of Art in New York. His defense of the museum as a bastion of "pure art," sullied by the exhibition's "stuff," was echoed by

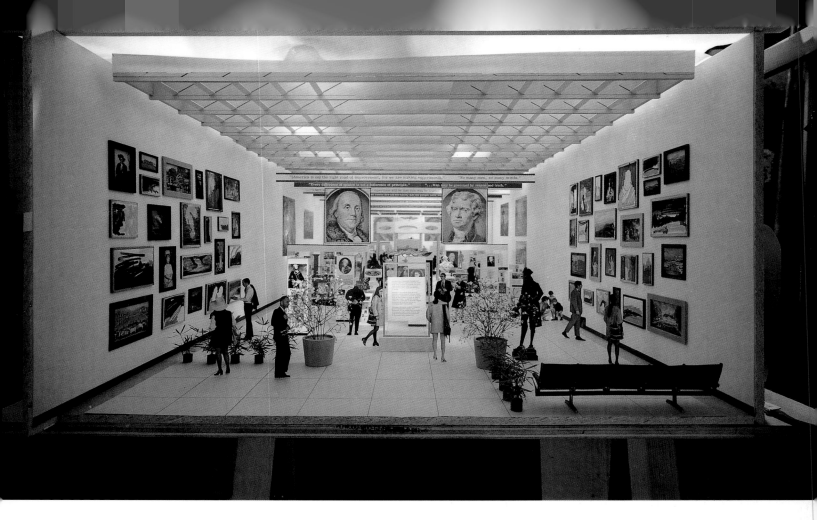

Model of the proposed exhibition plan featured in the film *Franklin and Jefferson (Proposal Film): Authors of Independence and Architects of the American Experiment* (1973)

critics in other cities. *The World of Franklin and Jefferson* was labeled the "Bison-tennial Bazaar." Kramer also criticized the exhibition both for being in "IBM's corporate taste—if that's what it can be called"—and for presenting images comparable to illustrations in *American Heritage*, a popular and patriotic history magazine.[50] The "stuff"—Charles's perfectly photographed architectural details, Ray's wildflowers, and, especially, the stuffed bison that Charles loved—became targets for a barrage of barbs.[51]

In a country made acutely aware of the government's management of information in the Vietnam War and Watergate, the exhibition's government and corporate sponsorship, populist interpretation of the Revolution, and upbeat message about American westward expansion all aroused suspicion. While the same mood made one museum-goer write to *The New York Times* that the exhibition gave her "something to be proud of, for a change," even among its admirers there was criticism of its wordiness and its large number of objects. The exhibition was, in the words of a Los Angeles visitor, "visually pleasing—but too much, jumbled—run together."[52] For the first time, the public was having trouble receiving the message transmitted by the "great communicators." Worse, the Eameses were blamed for their *lack* of detachment and for an excess of ideology—in short, for the natural overlap between them and the United States government. Jack Masey, interlocutor for the USIA, reported on their response when they read the Kramer review: they were devastated.[53]

Reading the catalogue and viewing the three films today, one might agree with a visitor who concluded that there were "too many things....a mish-mash" and with another who scolded them for their "inadequate

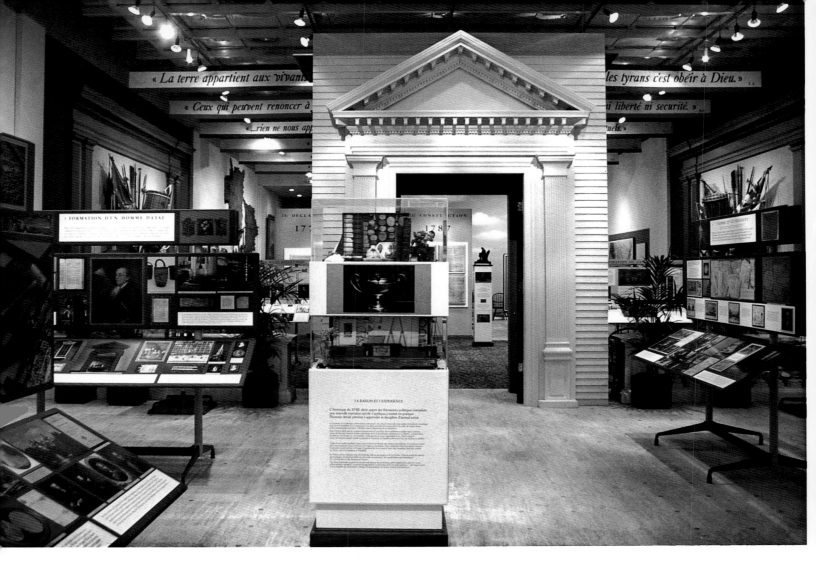

representation of slavery" and overly pious attitude toward Jefferson.[54] Had the USIA's ideology overtaken the Eamses' capacity to connect with the public, their love of the "popular" part of popular culture, and their belief in truth, or had they fallen victim to their own now outmoded liberal beliefs?

In 1970 the head of the Paris post of the USIA (called the USIS outside of the United States) conceived a show on Jefferson as the "counterpoint" to a recent Soviet Union–sponsored exhibition on Lenin. Recast as the USIA's exhibition for the 1976 Bicentennial of the American Revolution, the project was offered to the Eames Office in 1971 and a film about the proposed exhibition was commissioned immediately. In 1972 the Eameses were hired to do preliminary design work on the show itself, and the next year Charles suggested that Franklin share the focus with Jefferson. After the American Revolution Bicentennial Commission took over the project in July 1973 (with the USIA remaining in charge of logistics at its venues in Paris, Warsaw, London, and Mexico City), the partnership with IBM and the Metropolitan Museum of Art was forged by Masey. The support of IBM, which eventually came to half a million dollars, made it possible to bring the exhibition to the United States.[55]

The USIA had established goals for the Bicentennial that stressed "human values, not technological triumphs"; not material progress "but human and political meaning." It would transcend territorial imperatives and "commemorate something more than national splendor." When the Eameses proposed adding Franklin to the show, one official had visions of

Installation at the Grand Palais, Paris, of the exhibition *The World of Franklin and Jefferson* (January 11–March 10, 1975)

a "scientific, or more particularly, a technological phantom" haunting and destroying the political message. Others feared that a roomful of "kites and keys" illustrating Franklin's scientific inventiveness would make their exhibition look like one of IBM's. Nevertheless, the USIA and the Bicentennial Commission granted the Eameses the usual free hand since "that is why Eames [was] proposed in the first place."[56]

Although the Eameses employed many eminent experts in the histories of art, science, and the Revolution as consultants, along with several researchers and writers, the overall historical interpretation and exhibition structure were established by Charles. The WPA's support of art and culture, considered by Charles to have been "the last real lusty American celebration," was his ideal for the Bicentennial. These 1930s programs had grown out of "the proper ingredients—adversity and urgent need" of the Depression.[57] Charles laid out the format and themes of *Franklin and Jefferson* and made the argument for pairing the two men. For Eames they represented the Revolution, and for many reasons. Together their lives spanned 120 years of the country's development, including the Revolution's "pivotal years" when the two lives "overlapped." Their social origins represented "extreme contrasts"— Franklin from the northern urban artisan class, Jefferson from the southern plantation-owning elite. And for both, the written word (that is, communication) was primary in their work.[58]

Eames originally envisioned an organization in five parts: Friends and Acquaintances, Map of the Colonies, The Two Men, The Documents, and Epilogue. (Eventually, the Map of the Colonies was dropped and the show was organized in four parts: Friends and Acquaintances, Contrast and Continuity, Three Documents, and Jefferson and the West.) These sections were accompanied by one of the Eameses' signature timelines. The physical structures—the Atrium, Pavilion, and Rotunda—copied the plan of their counterparts in Jefferson's University of Virginia exactly. In the Atrium, an open space defined by the timeline and a wall of naive portraits of "ordinary" individuals of the period, a number of small monument-like structures covered with photographs and text panels represented the "special people" whose "web of relations" constituted the intellectual and political climate in which Franklin and Jefferson had worked. For the two protagonists, "politics and science were two different sides of the same coin," a unity exemplified by Franklin's experimentation and diplomacy and Jefferson's confidence in the "natural order" and "natural rights of man." A doorway inspired by colonial meeting houses identified the Pavilion, which housed three documents—the Declaration of Independence, the Constitution, and the Bill of Rights. After a section dealing with the reconciliation of the two quarreling ex-revolutionaries and presidents, John Adams and Jefferson, the visitor encountered the Epilogue, devoted to the Lewis and Clark Expedition and the Louisiana Purchase. Eames believed Jefferson's vision for the wilderness was the "moral ending" of the Revolution, and so he concluded the exhibition with these events. A circular space in the Paris exhibition site allowed Charles to place the materials borrowed from French collections in a suitably Jeffersonian domed rotunda.

These ideas were also made into a film, *Franklin and Jefferson (Proposal Film): Authors of Independence and Architects of the American Experiment* (1973). Using the diagram of the Jefferson and Franklin universe as a conceptual map, in the film the Eameses underlined the

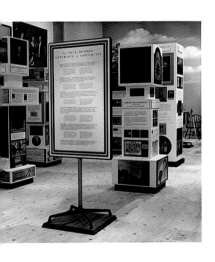

Paris installation of *The World of Franklin and Jefferson*

connections between Franklin and Jefferson, their "friends and acquaintances" among the European Enlightenment and learned colonial elite, and other Revolutionary patriots. The international learned elite were brought together by the need for communication and an interest in science, the patriots by a struggle with the wilderness. European learning was joined to American experimentation, Franklin's science to his diplomacy, Jefferson's architecture to his politics, and the thirteen colonies to each other. Similarly, the "social experiment" of the American Revolution found its "logical extension" in the Louisiana Purchase.[59] Both were bold experiments—the West, like the new continent, was a *tabula rasa*. Information gathering, experimentation, inventiveness, self-reliance, and reason were the qualities that made the country and were tested by the West.[60]

As it followed decades of popular and critical acclaim for the Eameses' cultural products, the widely perceived failure of *The World of Franklin and Jefferson* wants explaining. Sam Carson, an architect working for the office as coordinator of production, had warned Charles and Ray that the plan was chaotic, the graphics disorganized, the text "ordinary and dull," the photography overabundant, and the exhibition generally lacking in the "continuity, clarity and...order" necessary for understanding Franklin and Jefferson. A search for perfection that required eighty hours to choose a color for an edge no one would see struck Carson as a typical occurrence, and one that "bordered on absurdity." Another staff member recalls examining the model, "and it was beautiful, but [she] couldn't find Jefferson and Franklin."[61]

The exhibition's shortcomings resulted from the didactic and moral ambitions with which it had been imbued by Charles. The ultimate objective of the show, Charles told an audience, was to lead to "serious thinking about the possibility of greater continuity in our own lives."[62] Charles had laced *The World of Franklin and Jefferson* with a moral imperative of his own devising, one intended to serve as a restorative tonic for what he perceived as citizens' flight from responsibility and the incapacity of leaders to establish continuity between private and public spheres, as Jefferson and Franklin had. For the Eameses, the exhibition represented an opportunity to redirect America away from the narcissistic excesses of "self-love" and its retreat from reason in the 1970s. Spurred by their social vision, Charles and Ray designed the show as a critique of the counterculture's emphasis on the self at the expense of the common interest, on emotions at the price of reason—in short, on Thoreau rather than Franklin.[63] For the Eameses, the solution lay in Jefferson's vision of the wilderness.

To create their new agenda for citizenship and civic consciousness, the Eameses planned "new covetables," interactive computer educational tools. These Charles described as "concepts and processes which if shared will not diminish in value, will not lead to satiation, and which have to be 'wanted' enough to pay the price—the hard work and discipline necessary to arrive at the perception and understanding of the process inherent in the form of the problem." Charles and Ray believed that this new moral and political direction could not come from existing teaching institutions but would need to be built from "found objects," which they defined as "things seen in a fresh way." A "new set of 'covetables,'" instruments allowing the "mastery of ideas and processes," would lead to "a new appreciation of the aesthetic rewards implicit in the ordinary business of life." By providing new access to found objects, the covetables would return Americans to reason and the desire for knowledge and away from narcissism and television-induced passivity. The Franklin and Jefferson film was, Charles claimed, "an important step in that direction." In 1976 the Eameses were pursuing their objectives through commissions for projected on-site information centers for the Library of Congress and for the Metropolitan Museum of Art's Annenberg Center and through Eames Office designs for prototypical interactive videodisc games. Both were encompassed in Charles's new vision of a communication system in which the Internet, World Wide Web, and the Information Superhighway were prefigured. In the future, information stored in video libraries, transmitted over cable, and beamed in by satellite would, Charles told an interviewer, be instantly available in "regional information centers."[64]

The medium and the message—the technique and the content—of *Franklin and Jefferson (Proposal Film)* illustrated the Eameses' vision of information access through the new set of covetables. As the camera moved in one continuous traveling shot along the timeline, individual images pasted onto its printed narrative were transformed into screens for viewing sequences of related visual materials. The combination of the linear, horizontal, textual matrix and the windows opening up onto virtual vertical stacks of visual and printed information presaged today's videodisc and CD-ROM technology. In the Eameses' view, Jefferson and Franklin demonstrated, by the example of their own lives, not only the possibility of improving the quality of life through the exploration of knowledge, but also knowledge's ability to resist the arbitrary imposition of power.

It was no accident that *The World of Franklin and Jefferson* resembled a sermon built of words and "stuff." The exhibition's overdoses came neither from the USIA, nor the Bicentennial Commission, nor from IBM but, according to Jack Masey, from Charles. For Charles, political beliefs and the objects on view were interchangeable. One "never knew with Eames, what was ideology, what was stuff," Masey suggested.[65] Explicitly equating themselves with Franklin—as Charles implied in many interviews, while Ray wore a specially tailored Franklin coat—the Eameses seemed to be asking that the exhibition and its films be read as autobiography, as they had done with earlier government projects. The Eameses saw themselves, like Franklin and Jefferson, as great communicators and problem solvers. Totally involving the Eames Office in the preparation of the project for five years, they inspired others in the office to emulate Franklin and Jefferson or, at least, to own a piece of their heritage. The exhibition cases were filled with eighteenth-century artifacts belonging to Charles, Ray, and their employees and friends.[66] If Charles and Ray were Franklin, and Charles was the architect Jefferson, then their fellow modernists and the scientists whose friendship they enjoyed were the "Friends and Acquaintances" and the Eames Office staff were the self-reliant, pragmatic American people.[67]

Drawing on their own experience of the New Deal's cult of Jefferson and their own westward migration, the Eameses used their life and careers to rewrite the plot of the American Revolution. Charles's view of Manifest Destiny recalled his school lessons in which Missouri appeared as Jefferson's child. Reassessment of modernism was also part of their story. The Eameses modified their modernist belief in collective action

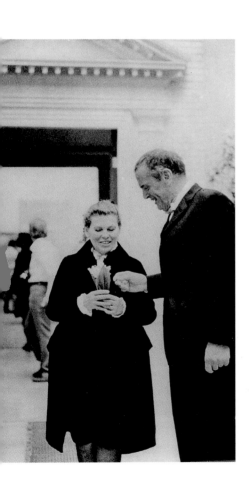

Ray and Charles at the opening of
The World of Franklin and Jefferson
at the National Museum, Warsaw,
May 1975

and the public sphere, making the coveting of knowledge a desideratum for civic society, and imagining video games as the means of satisfying that desire. Just as Charles had placed a media center in the City Hall for 194X and a television studio in the Jefferson Memorial, he now foresaw a virtual public sphere, the still-to-be-invented cyberspace.

One astute observer of the Bicentennial, historian Michael Kammen, praised *The World of Franklin and Jefferson* for its salute to folk culture and its objects, pointing out that it avoided the contradiction inherent in other exhibitions where the message of collective action was illustrated by objects from "high culture." He found its depiction of the "trial-and-error reality of Revolutionary America" convincing. [68] Furthermore, the Eameses' vision was not idiosyncratic but corresponded with a widely shared desire for America to be reconstituted by the Bicentennial. Their vision of greater continuity provided a restorative after the ambiguity and guilt of Watergate, one that returned Americans, as Kammen observed, to their "essential roots,...primordial values,...[and a] cleansed sense of national self."[69]

Conclusion: Revolution, World War, Cold War

By drawing the Eameses' projects of 1959 and 1971–77 together with those of the 1940s, it is possible to chart the natural overlap among them. Masey, who oversaw both the seven-screen film and *The World of Franklin and Jefferson* for the federal government, considers the two USIA projects to be cut from the same cloth: "The Federal government was irrelevant...in Moscow, irrelevant in *Franklin and Jefferson*....[Eames] had total freedom in both cases....[The exhibition] is Charlie's vision of what happened...the same emotion was going into both."[70] For the government's ideologues, there was no need to impress ideology on an Eames design. The idea of an ideology-free Eames production is, like the notion of their isolation from the outside world, yet another myth.[71]

In the Eameses' government projects, the colonial revolutionary, the wartime patriot, and the postwar citizen, along with the more cautious celebrant of the Bicentennial, would all be enfranchised by their capacity for problem solving. Knowledge was brought to them by the new media of popular culture, whether in the form of Franklin's press, an Eames board of education, the information-dispensing Living Memorial, or videodiscs invented by the Eames Office. These beliefs were expressed in their ideal architectural designs as well as the "stuff" that Charles and Ray exhibited and the imagery used to represent the United States in their conversations with other nations. Although they were not critical of the power structure of American society, nor of capitalism, and they did not draw Americans' attention to oppression or celebrate transgression and the oppressed, neither were the Eameses the unsuspecting tools or compliant allies of their USIA employers. If ideology was there in abundance, it was one of their own making.

Imbuing modernism's faith in the art of everyday life with the hedonism of the popular culture despised by architectural modernists, the Eameses embedded their values and goals in their work for the federal government. For the Eameses, native ingenuity and inventiveness—the intrinsic cunning of the artist and tinkerer—and the advanced knowledge and rationalism of the scientific elites were complementary. "Bottom-up" creativity and the fun of popular culture were as valued as "top-down" professional know-how. Abundance—of nature and of capitalism's products—was the cornerstone of American democracy, allowing difference, at least in lifestyles and taste.

Overlapping the two diagrams for the *What Is Design?* and the *World of Franklin and Jefferson* exhibitions clarifies the notion of natural overlap. Just as the Eameses had made the connections between Franklin and Jefferson and their twenty-five correspondents and friends into the story of the American Revolution, so they had represented and understood postwar America as their personal history. They had naturally overlapped with the government and the country itself. This attitude took form in other products as well, at least metaphorically. In the 1940s the plywood splints for injured sailors were made from a mold of Charles's body. In a 1947 photograph Charles and Ray assumed the position of Vitruvian man—the Renaissance diagram of humanity's inherent perfection—their postures held in place by the legs of their chairs.[72] While this projection of themselves, like their equation of their biography with America's, may seem not only naive but incredibly self-centered, it corresponded with their liberal views and their carefully controlled experience of their country's history.

Like their American history, the Eameses' ideology was also a summary of their experiences. After all, they had moved from Depression-era poverty (for Charles) to international celebrity and from the Venice beachfront to embassies and, on occasion, the White House, without compromising their modernism and liberalism or abandoning their appreciation of ordinary, everyday things. Enjoying upper-class amenities—a chef, a Mercedes, and a Jaguar—they persisted in envisioning themselves as updated versions of Franklin: reasoning artisans at home in popular culture and creators of ideas and objects for consumers not too, too different from themselves.

I wish to acknowledge the help of Margaret McAleer, Donald Albrecht, and Phyllis Ross of the Library of Congress, who continually guided my research and commented perceptively on this manuscript. The information provided by Jack Masey in a lengthy interview on Nov. 22, 1996, was invaluable. Esley Hamilton, Stephen Leet, and Susan Brower shared their knowledge of St. Louis and American modernism. A period of study in the archives of Cranbrook Academy of Art and the advice of Mark Coir, the archivist there, deepened my understanding of the Eames-Saarinen friendship. Ongoing discussions of the postwar years with Deborah Fausch, Sarah Ksiazek, Mary McLeod, Eric Mumford, Joan Ockman, and Hashim Sarkis have informed this essay. Finally, without the loan by Lucia Eames and Eames Demetrios of the rough transfer tapes of *Glimpses of the U.S.A.* and other films not in general circulation, this essay would have taken a different course. Parallel research on the Jefferson National Expansion Memorial, funded by the Graham Foundation for Advanced Studies in the Fine Arts and the Missouri Historical Society, enriched the section on entry no. 154 to the memorial competition. The support of both institutions and the help of the indefatigable librarians and archivists at the Society and the National Park Service archives in St. Louis are also most gratefully acknowledged.

1. Charles Eames was one of five designers invited by the Musée des Arts Décoratifs to participate in an exhibition titled *Qu'est-ce que le <design>?* The Eames Office referred to the show by its English title, *What Is Design?* For Eames quotation, see Box 173, The Work of Charles and Ray Eames, Manuscript Division, Library of Congress, henceforth WCRE.
2. Box 173, WCRE.
3. Peter Blake, *No Place Like Utopia: Modern Architecture and the Company We Kept* (New York: Knopf, 1993), 230.
4. On the Eameses' liberalism, see Billy Wilder, interview with Alexander von Vegesack and Donald Albrecht, May 20, 1995, 22, *The Work of the Office of Charles and Ray Eames* exhibition, Library of Congress. Richard Donges, in a telephone interview on Jan. 11, 1996, confirmed that politics were not discussed in the office (henceforth Donges). Pat Kirkham categorizes them as liberals and nonaligned in her *Charles and Ray Eames: Designers of the Twentieth Century* (Cambridge, Mass.: The MIT Press, 1995), 291, 315, 372,

and passim. Martin Filler describes them as detached in "All about Eames," *New York Review of Books*, June 20, 1996, 43.

5. For the diagram, see "What Is Design?," Box 173, and for Franklin and Jefferson, see Box 184, WCRE.

6. Donges.

7. "In Recognition of Service," Awards and Appointments, Box 222, WCRE.

8. Eames Chronology, Box 222, and Advisory Committee on Science and Technology, Box 64, WCRE.

9. Diplomats include Ambassador Sargent Shriver and Henry R. Luce III in London; Charles Eames, letter to "Sarge" [Shriver], American Ambassador, Oct. 30, 1968, Box 96, WCRE, and Charles Eames, interview, St. Louis, Oct. 13, 1977, Charles Eames Oral History Project, 218, private collection, St. Louis (there is a copy of the oral history with a different pagination in Box 225, WCRE); Charles Eames, letter to "Hank" Luce, Mar. 1, 1968, Box 105, WCRE. Charles viewed as exceptionally important personal moments the embassy-sponsored receptions that accompanied the openings of *The World of Franklin and Jefferson*, according to information gathered by Donald Albrecht. Agencies include the Atomic Energy Commission, Box 7; Bureau of Indian Affairs, Box 47; National Archives, Boxes 28, 75; National Endowment for the Arts, Box 79; National Gallery of Art, Box 79; National Park Service, Box 80; National Science Foundation, Box 80, WCRE. Spokesmen like S. Dillon Ripley valued his friendship; Box 99, WCRE.

10. For USIA proposals for films and exhibits and requests for information on behalf of their posts, see Boxes 105, 106, WCRE.

11. Charles's celebrity status at the USIA is described by Jack Masey, interview with Hélène Lipstadt, Nov. 22, 1996. *The Information Machine*, the Eameses' contribution to the IBM pavilion at the 1958 Brussels World's Fair, received a certificate from the State Department, "In Recognition of Public Service." For *The World of Franklin and Jefferson* they received an Outstanding Service Award from the USIA and a Federal Design Council Award of Excellence; Eames Chronology, Box 222, WCRE. The Smithsonian Associates sponsored a number of Eames slide shows, among others, "Charles Eames in an Evening of Sight and Sound," Dec. 1967, and a memorial, "Homage to Charles Eames," after his death; Boxes 99, 80, WCRE.

12. Charles Eames, "City Hall [for 194X]," *Architectural Forum* 86 (May 1943), 88–90. The designers worked from a number of conditions imposed by the magazine, including the siting of City Hall at the end of Main Street, which features a pedestrian mall, and the creation of an outdoor social and cultural center on its plaza; "New Buildings for 194X in Relation to the Plan of a Hypothetical Town of 70,000," ibid., 70. See also John Neuhart, Marilyn Neuhart, and Ray Eames, *Eames Design: The Work of the Office of Charles and Ray Eames* (New York: Abrams, 1989), 37.

13. "City Hall," 89.

14. Eames and Entenza used the example of juvenile justice to illustrate the interaction of education and administration. The juvenile court is paired with a children's clinic, whose ameliorating powers are enhanced by the activities of the board of education; "City Hall," 89.

15. Travis C. McDonald, Jr., "Smithsonian Institution, Competition for a Gallery of Art, January 1939–June 1939," in James D. Kornwolf, ed., *Modernism in America, 1937–1941: A Catalogue and Exhibition of Four Architectural Competitions* (Williamsburg, Va.: Joseph and Margaret Muscarell Museum of Art, College of William and Mary, 1985), 177–95; Mina Marefat, "When Modern Was a Cause: The 1939 Smithsonian Art Gallery Competition," *Competitions* 1 (Fall 1991), 36–49.

16. It also recalls Eliel Saarinen, who uses the metaphor of the heart in his description of the community center of the future in his *The City, Its Growth, Its Decay, Its Future* (New York: Reinhold, 1943), 256–57.

17. Elizabeth Mock, *Built in U.S.A., 1932–1944* (New York: The Museum of Modern Art, 1944), 25.

18. The fountain, designed in 1939–40, is located in Aloe Plaza. Eames worked closely with Luther Ely Smith, the civic leader who brought this controversial project to fruition; Charles Eames, letter to Luther Ely Smith, received Dec. 5, 1938, Box 1, Folder 5, Luther Ely Smith Collection, Missouri Historical Society, St. Louis.

19. Photo RU 104-240, National Park Service, Jefferson National Expansion Memorial Archives, Jefferson National Expansion Association Records, uncatalogued, RU-104 (henceforth JNEM-RU-104); Neuhart, Neuhart, and Eames, 85.

20. George Howe, for the Jefferson National Expansion Memorial Association, *Architectural Competition for the Jefferson National Expansion Memorial Program* (St. Louis: Jefferson National Expansion Memorial Association, 1947), 23.

21. Charles Eames, interview with Marek Suchowiak, "Franklin's and Jefferson's Circle," from an unidentified USIA publication (Sept. 1975), 12, Box 235, WCRE.

22. Leopold Arnold, Kenneth A. Smith, W. H. Hayes, et al., letter to Rep. O[tha] Wearin, Mar. 30, 1937, U.S. Cong. House, Committee on the Library Hearing on Site of the Thomas

Jefferson Memorial, 75th Cong., 1st Session, H. J. Res. 337 (Washington, D.C.: GPO, 1937), 38.

23. All quotations are from entry no. 154. There were a "drafting room, auditorium, printing plant, reference library, study and rehearsal halls, design laboratories, experimental facilities, dining [illegible], living [quarters?]" as well.

24. Merrill D. Peterson, *The Jefferson Image in the American Mind* (New York: Oxford University Press, 1962), 377–448, and Hélène Lipstadt, "A Modern Monument: Architecture, Politics, Commemoration and the Jefferson National Expansion Competition—Report to the Graham Foundation" (1996), 9.

25. Since the Jefferson Memorial had been created in order to extract the long-desired rehabilitated riverfront from Franklin Delano Roosevelt's administration, and since many of the memorial's administrators thought that the primary purpose of memorialization was the construction of museums and reconstitution of historic buildings, the construction of a Living Memorial was highly unlikely. In the second phase of the competition, the Living Memorial was, in fact, omitted; see Lipstadt, 9–10.

26. Eames to Howe, Oct. 14, 1947, JNEM-RU-104.

27. On the monumentality debate before 1947, see Sigfried Giedion, "The Need for a New Monumentality," in Paul Zucker, ed., *New Architecture and City Planning: A Symposium* (New York: Philosophical Library, 1944), and the other essays in the section titled "The Problem of a New Monumentality," 547–604. Giedion contrasts the spectacles to be organized in the new "civic centers" with "football games and horse races"; "The Need for...," 568. In the same book, Louis Kahn imagines a community arts center in his civic center; "Monumentality," 585.

28. On issues of monumentality and mass culture, see Sarah Ksiazek, "Architectural Culture in the Fifties: Louis Kahn and the National Assembly in Dhaka," *Journal of the Society of Architectural Historians* 52 (Dec. 1993), 416–19.

29. Entry no. 154. The program requirement of a local institution related in function to the Living Memorial became a "board of education," which employed art for the reeducation of juveniles on "probation," a feature transferred from the City Hall project. The definition of "information" as flow anticipates Charles's use of Claude Shannon and Warren Weaver's groundbreaking 1949 publication, *The Mathematical Theory of Communication* (Urbana: University of Illinois, 1949).

30. Entry no. 154.

31. *Facts about the American National Exhibition in Moscow*, 2–3, Folder–Exhibits and Fairs, Moscow, no.1, USIA Archives, Washington, D.C.

32. On the USIA's policies in 1958, see Eric J. Sandeen, *Picturing an Exhibition: The Family of Man and 1950s America* (Albuquerque: University of New Mexico Press, 1995), 112–19.

33. George Nelson, letter to Charles Eames, Oct. 14, 1958, USIA Archives.

34. George Nelson log, quoted by Stanley Abercrombie in *George Nelson: The Design of Modern Design* (Cambridge, Mass.: The MIT Press, 1994), 163–64.

35. Charles Eames, letter to George Nelson, Dec. 13, 1958; Nelson, letter to Eames, Dec. 11, 1953, USIA Archives. Nelson log, quoted in Abercrombie, 165. The bagel's disappearance is regretted in "Draft of Text from Tape Recording of the Remarks of George Nelson and Charles Eames at the Southern California Chapter, AIA, Nov. 10, 1959, Ambassador Hotel, Los Angeles: What Happens When One Nation Tells Its Story to Another Nation," 13–19, *The Work of the Office of Charles and Ray Eames* exhibition, Library of Congress. Information on the Circarama is from the Walt Disney Co. Archive, Burbank, Calif.

36. The projection of data is discussed in "Roundtable Discussion with Journalists on Plans for the Moscow Exhibit," Jan. 8, 1959, Folder–Exhibits and Fairs, Moscow, no.1, USIA Archives. George Nelson describes the supermarkets in Nelson, letter to Charles Eames, Dec. 11, 1958, USIA Archives; Eames remarks in "Draft of Text," 15–17.

37. Harold W. McClellan, letter to Charles Eames, Feb. 11, 1959, Box 1, and "Current Plan for the Exhibition," Feb. 10, 1959, Box 2, Records of the U.S. Information Agency, Records Relating to the American International Exhibition, Moscow, 1957–59, National Archives, RG 306-88-2 (henceforth RG 306-88-2).

38. *Facts about the American National Exhibition*, 2–3; *Glimpses of the U.S.A.*, script, outlines, and camera record, Box 202, WCRE.

39. According to the "containment" interpretation of the cold war, containing the Soviets abroad paralleled and was reinforced by containment at home, through commodity capitalism, consumerism, suburbanization, routinization in the corporate structure and factory, in child-rearing practices and other social forces that reinforced discriminatory racial and gender roles. The implications of containment for photography are discussed in Sandeen, ch. 1; Eames chairs are identified as highbrow in 1949; ibid., 68. For *Life* and *Look* of the 1950s, see James Guimond, *American Photography and the American Dream* (Chapel Hill: University of North Carolina Press, 1991), 166–77.

40. Figures from Charles Eames, in "U.S. Exhibit Aims in Moscow Given," *The New York Times*, n.d., *The Work of the Office of Charles and Ray Eames* exhibition, Library of Congress.

41. *Facts about the American National Exhibition*, 3.

42. Shoup Voting Machine Tally, Aug. 9, 16, 22, 1959. The tally for Aug. 29, 1959, somewhat contradictorily put the exhibit in thirteenth place for the fourth and fifth weeks, while the tally of Aug. 22 had it in fourth place for the fourth week; Box 5, RG 306-88-2. No mention of the seven-screen presentation is made in the press clipping summaries in Folder Summaries, Box 6, RG 306-88-2, or in translations of visitors' remarks in "Favorable Comments on Exhibition" and "Unfavorable Comments on Exhibition," USIA Archives.

43. "Image of America at Issue in Soviet," *The New York Times*, Aug. 22, 1959, sec. 8, 1.

44. R. Buckminster Fuller, quoted by Holly Camp, *Newsweek*, Nov. 7, 1973; Blake, *No Place*, 242; and Blake, letter to Charles Eames, Nov. 21, 1969, describing it as one of the "great events in my life"; Box 6, WCRE. Eames, "Draft of Text," 18.

45. Frank Getlein, "Pictures at an Exhibition: Russians' Reaction to the U.S. Show in Moscow," *The New Republic*, Aug. 24, 1959, 13. The musical score was by Elmer Bernstein and included refrains from current music. Perhaps unintentionally, some of the music is reminiscent of Leonard Bernstein's "America," an intensely ironic song about the Puerto Rican immigrant experience.

46. Sandeen, 151. The film is attributed to the "office of Charles Eames" and to "Charles Eames," 151, 191.

47. Jack Goody, *The Culture of Flowers* (Cambridge, England: Cambridge University Press, 1993).

48. "Draft of Text," 16, 13. For contractual obligations, see clause 4, McClellan to Eames, Feb. 11, 1959, Box 1, RG 306-88-2; and Masey.

49. Information communicated by Phyllis Ross, based on her research in the archives of the USIA.

50. Hilton Kramer, "What Is This Stuff Doing at the Met?" *The New York Times*, Mar. 14, 1976, and Larry Rosing, "Bison-tennial Show: The Bazaar World of Franklin and Jefferson," *The New Art Examiner* (Chicago; Summer 1976).

51. On Charles and the bison he "loved" and which "came back to haunt him," see Masey. A summary of the press reception is in Kirkham, 292.

52. On visitors' reactions, see Joseph T. Enright, memorandum to Jack Masey, Mar. 31, 1976, with a sampling of the visitors' remarks, "Some Comments on *The World of Franklin and Jefferson*," Mar. 28, 1976, Box 135, Records of the U.S. Information Agency, The World of Franklin and Jefferson, RG 306 (henceforth "Some Comments"). For the letter to the *Times*, by Harriette Von Breton, see *The New York Times,* Apr. 4, 1976. "Jumbled together" was quoted by Rexford Stead, Los Angeles County Museum of Art, to Dolores Barchella, American Revolution Bicentennial Commission, Jan. 12, 1977, Box 136, National Archives, RG 452 (henceforth RG 452). The visitors' book was returned to the Metropolitan Museum of Art from the Los Angeles Museum of Art and is now lost; Betsy Baldwin, telephone communication with Hélène Lipstadt, Jan. 11, 1996, Archives of the Metropolitan Museum of Art, New York.

53. Masey.

54. "Some Comments."

55. William H. Blue, memorandum to Mrs. [Mildred] Marcy, USIA, July 6, 1971; Blue, memorandum to [?] Carroll, Nov. 9, 1971; Blue, memorandum to Mr. [Hugh A.] Hall, July 3, 1972; Blue, memorandum to Chair, American Revolution Bicentennial Commission, July 11, 1972; Charles H. Clarke, memorandum to Record, Feb. 12, 1973; Sherman Lloyd, letter to Hall, July 27, 1973, all in Box 137, Records of the American Bicentennial Administration, The Age of Franklin and Jefferson, 1973–75, RG 452. The fact that IBM had asked Charles to reflect on what its Bicentennial show might be as early as Apr. 1972 suggests that the cosponsorship was long in the offing; see Charles G. Francis, IBM, letter to Charles Eames, Apr. 24, 1972, Box 48, WCRE. Formal negotiations with IBM did not take place until Apr. 1974, one year after the exhibition was transferred from the USIA to the Bicentennial Commission. Masey devised the solution of having IBM donate the offered $500,000 to the Metropolitan Museum; Jack Masey, memorandum to Mr. [Eugene F.] Skora, Apr. 24, 1974. In 1976 IBM agreed to underwrite the cost of a brochure for free distribution to visitors; Masey, letter to Charles Hollister, Feb. 4, 1976, Box 136, RG 452. The official credit read, "The American Revolution Bicentennial Administration Exhibition was designed by the Office of Charles and Ray Eames, with the cooperation of the Metropolitan Museum of Art in New York through a grant from the IBM Corporation." The USIA was listed at the end of the credits as manager of the exhibition in Europe. Outside sponsorship was necessary, for, by law, the USIA is forbidden from operating in the United States. For the ensemble of projects, see Neuhart, Neuhart, and Eames, 417–29.

56. On goals, see "Bicentennial Commemoration and Perception Overseas," Box 192, WCRE. On phantom, see Charles H. Clarke, letter to Charles Eames, Feb. 20, 1973, Box 192, WCRE. On kites and keys, see David Paul, memorandum to Mrs. [Mildred] Marcy, Feb. 21, 1973, Box 192, WCRE. On reasons for hiring Eames, see William H. Blue, memorandum to Hugh A. Hall, Acting Director, American Revolution Bicentennial Commission, Feb. 12, 1973, Box 137, RG 452.

57. On the WPA, see unidentified Charles Eames lecture notes, June 21, 1976, Box 218, WCRE.

58. All quotations from the Franklin and Jefferson Timeline, Box 176, WCRE. In his interview of Jan. 10, 1996, Donges identified this as the original concept for the Grand Palais and confirmed the desired analogy with the Jefferson plan.

59. For this film, see the home video *The Films of Charles and Ray Eames* 3 (Santa Monica: Pyramid Media, 1992).

60. See the Franklin and Jefferson Timeline for the West as the "great laboratory of the American experiment." In Overall Exhibit Ideas, Jefferson is called the "first advocate of manifest destiny"; Box 176, WCRE. The equation of the West with communication is made explicit in the exhibit catalogue, where the Lewis and Clark Expedition is also said to establish "a precedent for national information-gathering projects"; *The World of Franklin and Jefferson* (Los Angeles: American Revolution Bicentennial Administration, 1976), 74.

61. Sam Carson, memorandum to Charles Eames, Aug. 19, 1974, and Barbara Diamond, memorandum to Charles Eames, n.d., Box 189, WCRE.

62. Charles Eames, "On Reducing Discontinuity," speech given at the American Academy of Arts and Sciences, Boston, Mass., 3, Box 217, WCRE.

63. Jehane Burns Kuhn, office researcher and one of the primary authors of the exhibition texts, made this critique of the counterculture clear by describing "Thoreau [as]...the real anti-Franklin," in "Proposal for Monolith on Minorities," Box 188, WCRE.

64. All quotations are from "On Reducing Discontinuity," 12. The "regional information centers" are described in "Dreams, Designs, Arts, Education—All Make the Eames Connection," Charles Eames, interview with Benjamin Forgey, *Washington Post*, n.d., 1977, clipping in Box 216, WCRE. On the Annenberg Center, see Forgey and Metropolitan Museum of Art Report, Box 69, WCRE. On the interactive videodisc games, *Art Game*, and *Merlin and the Time Mobile*, see Neuhart, Neuhart, and Eames, 444–45.

65. Masey.

66. "Total involvement" is the term Richard Donges used in his interview. They called themselves "tradesmen," an apparent reference to Franklin; see "On Reducing Discontinuity," 1. Hugh De Pree of Herman Miller remarked that Charles "thinks a great deal about Benjamin Franklin," Aug. 30, 1977, Charles Eames Oral History Project, 126. See photographs of Ray in Franklin-style coat in "Franklin's and Jefferson's Circle," 12, Box 235, WCRE. For objects owned by Eames and others, see "Inventory of Artifacts for Franklin-Jefferson Exhibit in CE Studio," Box 180, WCRE.

67. Margaret McAleer of the Manuscript Division, Library of Congress, was the first to recognize this equation of the Eames Office with the citizenry.

68. Michael Kammen, *A Season of Youth: The American Revolution and the Historical Imagination* (New York: Knopf, 1978), 93–94. Kammen was familiar with the exhibition, for his opinion of the Franklin-Jefferson contrast was solicited by David Paul of the USIA after the presentation of Feb. 1973; Kammen, letter to Paul, Mar. 5, 1973, and Paul, letter to Kammen, Nov. 27, 1973, Box 192, WCRE.

69. Kammen, 240.

70. Masey.

71. The claim that Charles was not an ideologue is made by John Neuhart and Marilyn Neuhart in *Eames House* (Berlin and London: Ernst & Sohn and Academy Editions, 1994), 11.

72. Neuhart, Neuhart, and Eames, 81.

APPRECIATIONS

*In order to assess the Eameses' legacy — both personal and professional —
a selection of friends, colleagues, and contemporary designers offers these appreciations.*

DON ALBINSON
former Eames Office staff member
furniture designer
East Greenville, Pennsylvania, August 1996

*Charles was interested in all areas of design, so
the projects we worked on were many and varied,
but most importantly, no project whether
furniture, architecture, exhibit, film, or toy was
ever started unless it really interested Charles.
As a result we worked on interesting problems,
and the completion of them was usually a very
rewarding experience for the people in the office.
Normal practice was to use workers on different
projects when manpower was needed. This made
possible a broad exposure to different areas of
design. Parke Meek probably summed up the
feelings of many when he said, "I looked forward
to work every morning."*

RALPH APPELBAUM
exhibition designer
founder of Ralph Appelbaum Associates Inc.
New York, September 1996

*When I was studying industrial design in the
1960s, the Eameses' influence really came from
their body of work as a whole. There was an
essential truthfulness about it—such as their
constant focus on forms that would be
enhanced, not betrayed, by the technology of
mass manufacture—that provided us with a
standard for what "organic" design could mean
in the machine age.*

*Later I came to share their interest in
designing the whole of an environment—
to create out of a subject an "architecture
of information," as I have come to think of it.
This, too, is organic, for it draws spatial
metaphors, materials, forms, and media choices
from the subject itself and orchestrates them
into a wholly communicative environment.*

DANIEL J. BOORSTIN
Librarian of Congress Emeritus
Washington, D.C., March 1996

*I remember Charles Eames for the elegance of
his person and the childlike freshness of his
view of everything. When I was director of the
Smithsonian's National Museum of History and
Technology, Eames designed an exhibit that
accompanied his film* Powers of Ten, *which
created numbers in a delightfully playful way
that none of us had ever seen before. He gave
numbers a surprising concreteness, as if they
were not concepts but toys. Ray was a
perfectionist, who always had something
to add to the picture.*

RALPH CAPLAN
design historian and critic
New York, November 1996

*"We have to take pleasure seriously," Charles
said. No one did that better than these two
master practitioners of play. Their designs are
unfailingly magical, precisely because they
are so deeply grounded in the joy of how
things work.*

Image of the Eames House from
the office's slide collection

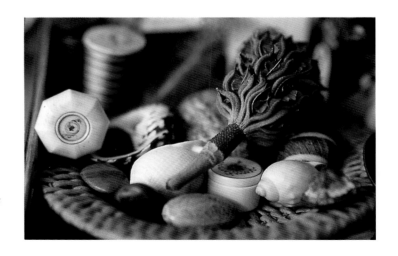

DON CHADWICK
designer
founder of Donald Chadwick & Associates
Santa Monica, California, July 1996

The legacy left through the work of Charles and Ray Eames will always challenge those of us who have advocated the integrity and refinement of structural forms arranged in serious yet lyrical compositions. The Eameses' experiments and explorations with materials and processes evolved into many of the classic furniture pieces of the twentieth century. Design has now embarked on the electronic express, with its world of virtual reality and gee-whiz imaging, where forms are seen and often not touched by the hands of their creator—which seems to run contrary to the very spirit and soul of the work of Charles and Ray Eames.

BARBARA FAHS CHARLES
former Eames Office staff member
exhibition and graphic designer
co-founder of Staples & Charles
Alexandria, Virginia, August 1996

The Eames Office introduced me to a magical world. A place where ideas and form commingled. A place where ideas shaped form and form reinforced ideas. Excellence and elegance were partners that could—and should—be applied to any challenge. Excellence was to be found in the shape of a lota or the words of history. An elegant scientific theory was as exciting—maybe more so—as an elegant design solution. And one could be used to convey the other. Nothing seemed too big or too small to investigate, understand, articulate, and share.

SIR NORMAN FOSTER
architect and designer
founder of Sir Norman Foster
and Partners Limited (London)
Pontracina, Italy, February 1996

The home Charles and Ray Eames created for themselves in Pacific Palisades changed the way generations of architects and designers would think and look—not only about the present and future, but also about the past. It certainly had that effect on me.

The Eames House was about clarity and whimsy—was complete yet open ended— serious but colorful—industrial and homely at the same time. Although it was permanent, you had the feeling that it could be packed away as easily as it seemed to have been assembled—but it did not look or feel temporary. There was the illusion of a do-it-yourself simplicity. I also remember thinking on one visit that it had a Japanese quality, that it evoked the spirit of an earlier tradition—even though I had never visited Japan at the time.

The building was inseparable from its contents, the furniture, toys, and memorabilia that inspired so many of the films, to which I still return with increasing appreciation.

Today I live with furniture designed by the Eameses and, like the films, I appreciate them even more with the passage of time. The lounge chair must be unique as a modern piece in the way that it combines luxurious comfort with the sculpture of modern technology. Some months back I used to haul this chair from a favorite spot in the living room to another one in the bedroom. It was always in the wrong spot at the wrong time. I finally gave in and bought another one. Like Charles Eames is supposed to have said, I take my pleasures seriously.

MILTON GLASER
graphic designer
founder of Milton Glaser, Inc.
New York, February 1996

*It is difficult to describe precisely what Ray and
Charles Eames meant to a generation growing
up in the fifties. I saw Charles once early in my
career, walking out of the legendary La Fonda del
Sol restaurant at Rockefeller Center, in his
signature tiny bow-tie and tweedy academic
sport jacket. He was a strikingly attractive man
who seemed very much at home in his skin. He
also seemed very "American" in a Gary Cooper
sort of way, especially for someone whose
parents had arrived here in the twenties fleeing
Transylvania. I didn't meet Ray until many years
later, after Charles had died. At that time she
reminded me of one of my Russian artists—
kind, wise, and easily teased into laughter.*

*Recently there has been an exhaustive
attempt to analyze what part of the work they
produced together could be broken down into
individual responsibilities. I consider this effort
to be thankless, if not perverse; my experiences
with the dynamics of partnership suggest that
the results are too interwoven to be pried apart
after the fact.*

*Ray and Charles were an inspiration for both
aspiring and practicing designers. The sense of
enormous optimism that pervades their work
suggests that design can transform the world
through the application of imagination and
intelligence. Their work was always thoughtful
but rarely became academic because of its
vitality, vibrant color, and sense of humor. The
projects were far-ranging—architecture,
exhibitions, furniture, objects, graphics, and film
all came within their purview, and all were
mastered with style and authority. Finally, what
encouraged us most was their commitment to
the belief that a design practice could have a
moral center.*

TIBOR KALMAN
designer and editor
New York, September 1996

*Charles and Ray changed everything. It was the
first time that designers infused everyday
objects with emotion. Suddenly common
objects were able to communicate feelings.
This because they were designed with feelings.
Charles and Ray were a good balance of
idiosyncrasy and rationality. It is hard to find
this emotion today as economics and the
unmanageability of inspiration force most
things to be merely logical. An Eames La Chaise
exudes as much feeling of life and wholeness
as a living, breathing thing. It is alive. It can be
lived with, seen every day, change and evolve,
and slowly reveal its beauty. Like a lover.
And it's a chair.*

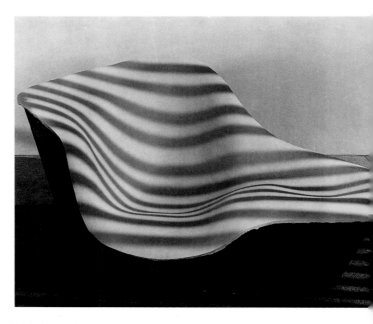

Mold for La Chaise with shadows, 1948

JACK MASEY
president of MetaForm, Inc.
former director of design
for the U.S. Information Agency
New York, August 1996

DATELINE: Moscow, U.S.S.R., July 23, 1959
*It was the night before the official opening of the
American National Exhibition in Moscow—the
first American exhibition ever shown in the
Soviet Union and the site of the famous Nixon-
Khrushchev Kitchen Debate. In a golden
anodized geodesic dome designed by Bucky
Fuller sat seven interlocked 35-mm projectors
aimed upward at seven giant twenty-by-
thirty-foot screens, each ready to receive
simultaneous film images. Together, these
images would tell the story of America at work
and at play. Into the dome burst Charles and Ray
Eames, who had just flown in from the States.
They were clutching seven cans of 35-mm film.*

*The Radio City Music Hall's top projectionist
was on loan to the exhibition. He lost no time
loading the projectors; and so, that evening,
in Sokolniki Park, we were able to have our first
full-scale testing of the multiscreen
presentation of "a day in the life of America."
Word spread in the park and a crowd began
gathering in the dome: there were Russian
construction workers, Finnish carpenters, and
American designers and exhibition staffers, all
eager to see what magic would appear on the
seven screens.*

*Soon the projectors were synchronized and
the multiscreen film got under way. The
combination of moving and still images,
accompanied by a powerful musical score by
Elmer Bernstein, was fantastic. Here were early
morning scenes of milk bottles outside front
doors across America; aerial views of deserts,
mountains, and plains; cloverleaf highways
jammed with automobiles; skyscrapers*
*glistening at night; and the final closing scene: a
bunch of forget-me-nots—the universal symbol
of friendship—depicted as a single image on the
central screen. The Russians whispered
"nezabudki" ("forget-me-nots") and there were
tears all around.*

*When the film ended there was silence.
Everyone was mesmerized by the show. None of
us had ever seen anything quite like it. Then the
audience burst into wild applause. Charles
acknowledged the ovation with a smile that
seemed to say: "Aw shucks. It was nothing..."*

RENZO PIANO
architect
founder of Renzo Piano Building Workshop
Genoa, September 1996

*Charles and Ray Eames have strongly influenced
my architectural development, in two ways.*

*First of all, in my approach to life and my
profession: their house in the Pacific Palisades
is what can be called the flag of "the liberation
movement"—liberation from the slavery of
rhetoric and style in architecture. A soft, almost
innocent way to violate the sacred canons.*

*Then comes the poetic aspect: the lightness
of the spaces, conceived either in a physical
or metaphysical way; their immateriality; the
transparency of their multiple planes; their
contact with nature; the textures of the materials
from which they were created; their frugality
and complexity—all this made with the
nonchalance of great people, of those who know
how to humbly accept the desanctifying idea
of "temporariness" in architecture.*

*This is what I have learned from them,
and I try to make good use of it.*

181

LISA LICITRA PONTI
daughter of architect Gio Ponti
managing editor and former
deputy editor of *Domus* magazine
Milan, April 1996

Humor creates the best links. Saul Steinberg's drawings of the plywood chairs have been our instant link with Charles Eames. And when we published, in 1951, an "invisible view" of his Case Study house through the fog, we had already entered the world of Charles and Ray with an "Eames eye."

Ray and Charles—two cameras, one eye. And beautiful Domus *pages as a result. "You can't prevent admiration from becoming a page," Gio Ponti used to say. We admired Charles's design through Charles's camera, captivated by his way of capturing detail. The two issues we dedicated to Ray and Charles in 1963 and 1965 were essentially* their eye on their own work—*this was the special thing—but year after year we could also show* their eye on other artists' work *(do you remember their views of the concave peopled interiors of Saarinen's TWA terminal?): Ray and Charles turned into* "Domus's eye" *on the world. This was a privilege.*

When thinking of Ray, Charles, Domus *magazine, I sometimes tell myself such a past will bless our future.*

PAUL RAND
graphic designer,
Weston, Connecticut, January 1996

They were quick to distinguish between needs and wants, between good and bad, beautiful and ugly, simple and complex, restrained and free, essential and frivolous, clear and obscure, honest and pretentious, interesting and boring. These are among the conflicting notions in the dialectics of Charles and Ray Eames, around which they fashioned their lives and their work.

To the question, "What is the future of design?," posed by a curator of the Musée des Arts Décoratifs in Paris, Eames's response was utter silence. To the question, "Who is the greatest designer of our time?," posed to me many times over the years by curious students, the visage of Charles Eames loomed large.

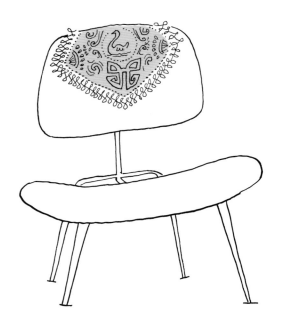

Plywood chair, drawn by Saul Steinberg, 1949

KEVIN ROCHE
architect
co-founder of Kevin Roche John Dinkeloo
and Associates
Hamden, Connecticut
excerpted from a piece originally written for
*Zodiak 11: 1994 AIA Los Angeles Centennial
Celebration Edition* (1994)

*A whole generation of architects and designers
wished they were Charles Eames. He epitomized
for them that modern equivalent of the
Renaissance man. In demeanor to the casual
acquaintance he was humble. He had a kind of
Jimmy Stewart "Aw shucks" reaction to any
praise. As those who knew him a little better
found out, sometimes to their chagrin, he was
a tough, hard-driving, unforgiving perfectionist
who had absolutely no patience with even the
slightest show of incompetence or carelessness
in executing any task. His lack of patience,
however, was usually clothed in an elaborate
and circumlocutory story which left the victim
unsure for some time if praise was in the offing
only to find a devastating chastisement like
a scorpion's tail tacked at the end of the story.*

*His considerable charm repaired all wounds
in short time, however, and his penetrating
intellect made him a fascinating companion.
He was without a doubt the most creative
and original designer in the twentieth century,
combining as he did the skills of inventor,
tinkerer, designer, architect, and filmmaker
together with those of scientist, researcher,
visionary, and creator — one who could make
those far leaps and improbable connections
of the true genius.*

ROBERT STAPLES
former Eames Office staff member
exhibition and graphic designer
co-founder of Staples & Charles
Alexandria, Virginia, August 1996

"What we need around here is a good furniture
designer." (CE [Charles Eames] to RS [Robert
Staples] after he became *the* furniture
designer in the office)

Eames Office A to Z
Albinson hires RS, 1957
Bubble machine for *Mathematica*
Computer Perspective
Design annex for 901
Edit live-action footage
Flat-bed animation
Grapefruit cans as GPRR
      (Griffith Park Railroad) oil drums
Herman Miller international house party
India—go for two weeks, stay twelve
"**J**ustify three places for house ladder."
      (RE [Ray Eames] to RS)
Killer frisbee
LA Showroom
Maria Poole's perfume bottles
"**N**eed new design for school seating."
      (CE to RS, NY hotel room)
Opening *Nehru* with labels in my tuxedo pocket
Photography and the City—Barbara Charles
Queen Elizabeth, Indira Gandhi, London
Roundhouse for *Toy Trains*
Segmented table base
Tandem Seating patent
Ultimatum—"Decision by 3pm, Charles, or...!"
      (RS to CE)
Variations—eight patterns for
      Aluminum Group antlers
World's Fair seating, IBM pavilion
Xylophone musical tower
"**Y**ou ask too many questions."
      ([Don] Albinson to RS)
Zonkers—sixteen years of sweeping floors
      and international opportunities

*Working with Charles and Ray was exhausting,
frustrating, rewarding, and as exciting an
education as one could have.*

PHILIPPE STARCK
architect and designer
Paris, February 1996

*Plus ma vie avance, plus ma maison se peuple
du travail de Charles Eames.
Naturellement, comme obligatoirement.
Tous ces objets me renvoient a moi-même et
me montrent à quel point je suis loin de cette
élégance issue de l'homme, de la nature,
de l'intelligence ét de l'économie.
Merci Ray.
Merci Charles.*

*As my life advances, more and more my house
becomes filled with the work of Charles Eames.
Naturally, and by necessity.
These objects cause me to pause and reflect
on how distant I am from this elegance born
of man, nature, intelligence, and economy.
Thank you, Ray.
Thank you, Charles.*

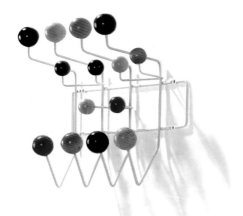

Hang-It-All, produced by Tigrett
Enterprises' Playhouse Division,
1953–61

DEBORAH SUSSMAN
former Eames Office staff member
graphic artist and interior designer
co-founder of Sussman/Prejza
Culver City, California, August 1996

Ray

India, December 1965. The Nehru *exhibit had
just been shipped to New York. I'd been in
Ahmedabad for months, the longest surviving
member of the Eames team. Seven days and
seven nights a week, interrupted only by
occasional fevers, our lives were submerged in
the exhilarating, often maddening process of
designing and building the exhibit. And in the
context of the embryonic National Institute of
Design. Ray had been there most of the time,
valiantly coping with the difficulties of life
in India, the powerful friends she and Charles
had made, the etiquette of stress and the
radical change of diet. She subsequently
became a vegetarian.*

*It was time for relief. Ray invited me to join
her for a sojourn in Rajasthan — but wouldn't
say where we would stay. We flew to Jaipur and
traveled to a dusty hilltop in nearby Udaipur.
Descending marble steps I began to hallucinate.
Or was it a mirage? There was an exquisite, white
palace in the middle of a lake. It had just been
converted into a hotel — and that was where we
were going! I think we were the only guests
(it was long before the Lake Palace Hotel was
discovered by the international travel
cognoscenti).*

*By day we explored the countryside. We were
the first women to have pink turbans made and
wound about our heads in the market. We had
our fortunes told, fought over the same necklace
as we left for Delhi. Our cameras hungrily
devoured the exotic, elegant people who
subsisted on next to nothing and moved like*

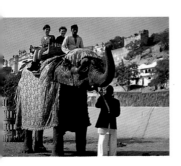

Deborah Sussman
and Ray in India, 1965

Balanchine dancers—and the connective tissue of their physical world, which expressed their culture in ways we could never have imagined.

At night we shivered in unheated rooms dining around a brazier, but our exhausted minds and bodies were soothed and renewed by the experience, and by the poetry of the Lake Palace Hotel.

This time with Ray was a gift. Her capacity for adventure paralleled mine and her acute observations sharpened my own. I loved her and will be eternally fascinated by her unique sensibility and her awesome internal strength.

Charles

It was 1960. Three years earlier I had left my job at the Eames Office with a Fulbright scholarship to study in Europe — and then to work and travel there. I was in New York when Charles invited me to come back. He described the ebullient climate at the office preparing the Mathematica exhibit. To our mutual surprise, I accepted. "I really didn't think it could happen," he said.

Charles and Ray had been parent figures to me ever since my summer internship, at twenty-two years old. We were a good fit, although it had taken me a while to deal with such an awesome notion. The office had grown considerably since my departure. What had been a family was now a community. It was full of intense young people engaged in gathering and organizing information and building two-and three-dimensional models, and the scale of everything had enlarged. People like Ray Redheffer, the body-building mathematician, were around. The walls were covered with compelling images from all conceivable scientific disciplines. The vibrant Eames organism buzzed day and night producing the Mathematica exhibit, and I quickly re-assimilated into the team, the pace of work, and the long hours.

There was a full-size mock-up of the history wall—forty feet long and thick with (too many) notes garnered from years of research. My first job was to edit the overwhelming amount of material attached to the wall in bits and pieces, taped or pinned to one another. As in all things, Charles made it clear that the material on the history wall was not to constitute a definitive or academic document, but rather a "felt" and personal selection. While Charles and I agreed on most issues concerning the design of the history wall, we hit a stone wall on the issue of typography. Charles wanted "his" typography. He insisted that all the text for biographies must appear in capital letters because it would be bigger and therefore more easily read than the classic lower-case roman text used in books for centuries. No argument would prevail, each rationale was negated by his scornful put-down, "That's just something you learned in school." Charles's allergy to "institutes of higher teaching," as he referred to them, would manifest itself from time to time. Even though he respected and supported certain schools, they were, after all, just schools. On the other hand, to be in the Eames Office was to learn by experience, to be taught a way of thinking, and, most important, to make your thoughts become realities. "Ideas are cheap," he always said.

The biographies were finally set in capital letters, as big as possible, all smashed together, with almost no space around them. And they are there today, still looking just as clumsy thirty-five years later. Yet, in spite of the naiveté of those graphics, Mathematica remains the benchmark exhibit against which all others are to be measured—and which continues to stimulate the visitor with ideas that matter, while dazzling the senses with "dynamic | interactive" demonstrations of truth about abstract concepts.

ROBERT VENTURI
architect
co-founder of Venturi, Scott Brown
and Associates, Inc.
Philadelphia, February 1997

I remember the first time I saw "the" Eames chair—I think it was 1948—at a student friend's house in Princeton, and I consider that moment one of the most revealing and inspiring in my life—a Modernist chair with truly organic-complex curves to accommodate comfort and aesthetics and engage the nature of the material.

I loved writing a while back that the Eameses in their house "reintroduced good Victorian clutter. Modern architecture wanted everything neat and clean and they came along and spread eclectic assemblages over an interior"—that created valid and vivid tension within our art—minimalist and now maximalist at the same time!

And then Denise Scott Brown and I loved designing the exhibition at the Whitney in 1985 called High Styles: Twentieth-Century American Design *so the Eames chair was at the top in a hierarchical arrangement of twentieth-century chairs, and we could show this to Ray Eames at the opening.*

Also what a nice prototypical example of spouses as partners, which Denise Scott Brown and I especially appreciate.

MASSIMO AND LELLA VIGNELLI
(signed by Massimo Vignelli)
designers and founders of Vignelli Associates
New York, February 1996

Charles and Ray Eames have been our idols ever since our days in architecture school in Venice. The universality of their work, the strength of their involvement, the range of their talent in every field of endeavor, and the notion of a husband-wife working team inspired Lella and me from the very beginning.

Their influence touched all of our work: in architecture, one of my first projects was a modular house, very much like their California home; in furniture design, we could not resist the temptation offered by their potato-chip chair and their storage units; in graphic design, their cards taught us to see the world in terms of textures, details, patterns; in exhibition design, their multiscreen projections gave us a new way of communicating information.

Their films, whose subjects ranged from toys to astronomy, opened our minds and projected the multiplicity of their interest and the depth of their involvement. Everything they did, everything they collected showed the intensity of their passions, from American-Indian artifacts to Indian crafts, from cast-iron objects to paleoindustrial toys, from the sublime to the kitsch. Yet, even while making such a significant contribution to design, their attitude and manners were incredibly understated: again, a great lesson.

By far the most influential American designers of this century, they opened our eyes to the meaning of design, they enriched our minds and engaged our souls. Champions of an America that was our dream, they stand out in our minds as immortal Giants of the Twentieth Century.

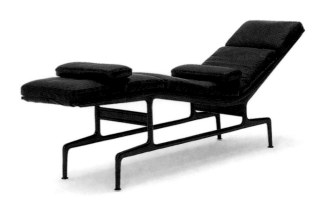

Billy Wilder–inspired chaise

BILLY WILDER

screenwriter and director
from an interview conducted
by Alexander von Vegesack
and Donald Albrecht
Los Angeles, May 1994

*Like the narrow couch. That, I would ask, could
you make me something that was very narrow,
because my office is not big, and then, and then,
I didn't hear a word, and then suddenly one
day they brought it to my office, with the men
from* Time *magazine...you know that's...but it's
very narrow. You know that couch. And the man
from* Time *magazine, he heard that it arrived
here...and he asks, "Well, what do you think?
What do you think of the new Eames thing?"
"I think," I said to him, I said, "It's absolutely
wonderful...if you have a girlfriend that is built
like a Giacometti."*

N.B. The first "narrow couch" was designed by the Eameses
specifically for Wilder, who wanted a chaise for brief
afternoon naps. Herman Miller started to manufacture the
chaise in 1968. Today it is also made by Vitra AG.

RICHARD SAUL WURMAN

information architect
Newport, Rhode Island, February 1996

*Shortly after Charlie died, I was asked along
with others to write a couple of paragraphs in
tribute. Now, more than one and a half decades
later and with my own life-perspective, I have
re-read these few words to see if his effect
on me maintains.*

*The memory of the pied-piper magic and of
his fairy-tale office certainly is still there. I
remember the intense delight throughout his
body as one day he pulled me toward a group of
aquaria, one of which contained an octopus that
he was completely convinced knew him. As he
approached the tank only he was personally
acknowledged by this graceful creature and I
believe to this day that it knew Charlie.*

*What isn't in my words reproduced below,
however, is another quality. A quality that I
ascribe to Piero della Francesca and Lou Kahn.
The quality of timelessness. Soft leather chairs,
molded plywood,* Franklin and Jefferson
timeline, and Mathematica. *They will mean the
same to my grandchildren and their great
grandchildren as they mean to me.*

*It feels special to have been in the presence
of somebody with such long tentacles
to curiosity.*

TRIBUTE WRITTEN ON THE OCCASION OF
CHARLES EAMES'S DEATH IN 1978

*If I were asked to design a twinkle, I would put
crow's feet around its eyes, award it the Nobel
Prize in Wonder, and name it* Charles Eames.

*If I were asked to design a cloud, I would
experiment with every possible configuration of
puffs of moisture, surround them all with
delightful marginalia, make a film of it that turns
five minutes into a day, and then a day into five
minutes, and title it* Charles Eames.

*If I were asked to appoint a Professor of
Curiosity or a Dean of Learning or President
of Imagination or Commissioner of Magic,
they would all be Charles Eames.*

*He was the truest student of seeing.
He allowed me to see those things I always saw
and never saw. He allowed me to distinguish
between learning and education and to
demand of the world around me that it become
self-revealing.*

*I can't believe that I won't have lunch in
his garden with him again.*

FILMOGRAPHY

The following filmography lists the films and multimedia presentations of the Office of Charles and Ray Eames from 1949 to 1988. The last two entries were produced by the office after the death of Charles and Ray, and relate directly to their work. The filmography was prepared by Eames Demetrios, media producer for *The Work of Charles and Ray Eames: A Legacy of Invention*, and is based on the archives of the Eames Office, which is committed to communicating, preserving, and extending the legacy and work of Charles and Ray Eames. Demetrios is also the head of the Eames Office Film Archive and Video Oral History Project. The archival research is ongoing and any updates to this list will be on-line at www.eamesoffice.com. The films marked with an asterisk are available on home video from the publisher, Pyramid Media, Santa Monica, California, www.pyramidmedia.com. Many of the films, including the seven-screen film presentation *Glimpses of the U.S.A.*, were screened in the exhibition. All films have sound, unless otherwise noted.

Raw Footage of House Construction
(1949; 25 min.; color)
Footage of the construction of the Eames House. Silent.

Traveling Boy
(1950; 11:45 min.; color)*
The Eameses' first film.
A mechanical boy leads a journey through a world of toys. Always classified as unfinished, although occasionally shown by Charles and Ray. Silent.

Blacktop: A Story of the Washing of a School Play Yard
(1952; 10:47 min.; color)*
Captures the forms and shapes created by the water and soap. This, the Eameses' second film, is the first one they considered completed.

Parade, Or Here They Come Down Our Street
(1952; 5:33 min.; color)*
A visit to a parade down the presumed main street of a world of toys, to the music of John Philip Sousa.

Bread
(1953; 6:02 min.; color)*
A visual essay on different qualities of "bread-ness." Made in conjunction with "Sample Lesson for a Hypothetical Course," Charles Eames and George Nelson's experiment in teaching.

Calligraphy
(1953; 8 min.; color)*
A film about different forms and qualities of calligraphy. Made in conjunction with "Sample Lesson for a Hypothetical Course," Charles Eames and George Nelson's experiment in teaching.

A Communications Primer
(1953; 22:14 min.; color)*
An introduction to the basics of communications theory. A first in many ways: the Eameses' first film scored by Elmer Bernstein, their first to deal with specific intellectual content, and the film that introduced their work to IBM.

S-73 (alternate title: *Sofa Compact*)
(1954; 10:40 min.; color)*
Traces the design and development of the collapsible Sofa Compact.

House: After Five Years of Living
(1955; 10:46 min.; color)*
A personal portrait of the Eames House, a classic of postwar American architecture that the Eameses designed and built in 1949 as part of the Case Study House Program.

Textiles and Ornamental Arts of India
(1955; 10:36 min.; color)
A record of the show designed by Alexander Girard and curated by him with Edgar Kaufmann, jr., at The Museum of Modern Art, New York.

Two Baroque Churches in Germany
(1955; 10:30 min.; color)*
Like the film *House*, an experiment in communicating the feel of architecture through the use of stills. The two churches are Vierzehnheiligen and Ottobeuren.

Lounge Chair
(1956; 2 min.; black and white)*
Made for the introduction of the Eames Lounge Chair, the film shows the chair's sped-up assembly.

Day of the Dead
(1957; 14:48 min.; color)*
A record of the Day of the Dead celebrations in Mexico.

Do-Nothing Machine
(1957 [edited 1991]; 2:09 min.; color)*
Eames footage of their remarkable Solar Do-Nothing Machine, made as a toy for Alcoa, offers a way to see it in action.

The Information Machine: Creative Man and the Data Processor
(1957; 10:01 min.; color)*
Made for the IBM pavilion at the Brussels World's Fair, the film attempts to place the electronic computer in the context of human development.

The Spirit of St. Louis (excerpt)
(released 1957; 6:30 min.; color)
Charles was the second unit director for this Billy Wilder film starring Jimmy Stewart as aviator Charles Lindbergh. The second unit was responsible for the aerial shots as well as the sequences showing the construction of the famous plane.

Toccata for Toy Trains
(1957; 13:28 min.; color)*
Vintage toy trains journey through a world of toy people, props, and scenery. On another level the film addresses the honest use of materials.

Tops (from "Stars of Jazz")
(1957; 3 min.; black and white)*
Made on a week's notice, the film,
which features black-and-white
scenes of tops, premiered
with an improvisational jazz score
on a local (Los Angeles)
television show.

De Gaulle Sketch
(1958; 2 min.; black and white)*
A spur-of-the-moment
encapsulation of the published
images of the 1958 de Gaulle crisis
in France (also broadcast in 1960).

The Expanding Airport
(1958; 9:25 min.; color)*
A film made for architect Eero
Saarinen's presentation of his
design for Dulles Airport, outside
Washington, D.C. Looks at the
history of airports as well as
the concept for Dulles.

*Herman Miller at the Brussels
    World's Fair*
(1958; 4:30 min.; color)*
A film showing Herman Miller
furniture in use at the Brussels
World's Fair.

Glimpses of the U.S.A.
(1959; 12:15 min.; color)
This seven-screen presentation at
the American National Exhibition in
Moscow was an attempt to credibly
convey the feel of American life to
the Russian visitors.

Kaleidoscope Shop
(1959; 3:46 min.; color)*
Asked to bring some footage of the
Eames Office in Venice, California,
to a lecture in London, Charles
honored both the request and his
privacy by shooting the images
through a kaleidoscope.

Time & Life Building International Lobby
(1959; 2:45 min.; color)
An unfinished film presentation
of an idea for the lobby of
the Time & Life Building in
New York City.

The Fabulous Fifties (alternate title)
(1960)
The Eameses made five films for the
CBS show "The Fabulous Fifties":
Comics of the Fifties, *Fifties Dead
Sequence*, *Fifties Music Sequence*,
Gift from the Sea, and *"Where did
you go?" "Out." "What did you do?"
"Nothing."*

Comics of the Fifties
(1960; 3:26 min.; black and white)
Recaps the 1950s by showing the
events that took place in comic strip
storylines during that time.
Fifties Dead Sequence
(1960; 4:40 min.; black and white)
Recaps the 1950s by showing the
people who died during that decade.
There is no verbal (audio or graphic)
identification of the dead, but the
film expresses a cumulative sense
of recognition and loss.
Fifties Music Sequence
(1960; 9:23 min.; black and white)
Recaps the 1950s by showing the
music of the decade. In some ways,
the first of a certain genre of
music video.
Gift from the Sea
(1960; 3:30 min.; black and white)
A presentation of Anne Morrow
Lindbergh's 1952 bestseller of
the same name. The images and
words suggest that "treasures"
washed up on the beach are gifts
from the sea.
*"Where did you go?" "Out." "What
did you do?" "Nothing."*
(1960; 4 min.; black and white)
A presentation of Robert Paul
Smith's 1950s children's book of
the same name. It is a story that
confirms the suspicions of every
parent who has had with his or her
child the dialogue captured by
the title.

Introduction to Feedback
(1960; 10:31 min.; color)*
An explanation of the concept
of feedback, which is present in
many "systems," from vaudeville
to the computer.

Kaleidoscope Jazz Chair
(1960; 6:28 min.; color)*
Further exploration and fun
with the kaleidoscope as well as
stop-motion of the multicolored
Eames stacking chairs.

ECS
(1961; 9:42 min.; color)*
A film presenting Eames Contract
Storage and the ideas behind it.

IBM Mathematica Peep Shows
(alternate title)
(1961)*
The Eameses made five "peep
shows" for the IBM *Mathematica*
exhibition: *Eratosthenes*, *something
about functions*, *Symmetry*,
Topology, and *2^n*.

Eratosthenes
(1961; 2:38 min.; color)*
About the Greek mathematician's
system for measuring the
circumference of the world, devised
two thousand years before Magellan
sailed around it.
something about functions
(1961; 2:11 min.; color)*
Introduces the important
mathematical concept of functions
by first showing some familiar
examples (the height of a burning
candle as a function of time)
and then demonstrating that
more complicated systems
also exhibit such invisible but
persuasive connections.
Symmetry
(1961; 2:39 min.; color)*
Introduces the concept of symmetry
and its various degrees. Suggests
that one way of quantifying an
object's symmetry is determining
how many different ways the object
could fit in a box shaped precisely to
its form (therefore a perfect sphere
could fit into a "sphere-box" in
an infinite number of ways, but a
curled-up dog could probably fit in
its box in just one way).

Topology
(1961; 1:59 min.; color)*
This short introduces a bit of the field of topology through the concept of closed curves.

2ⁿ: A Story of the Power of Numbers
(1961; 2:07 min.; color)*
Tells a story connected with the invention of chess that shows what happens when one doubles a number over and over again.

Before the Fair
(1962; 6:40 min.; color)*
Images of the building and construction of the 1962 Seattle World's Fair.

The Good Years (alternate title)
(1962)
"The Good Years" was the title of a CBS show about the era between 1900 and World War I. The Eameses contributed three vignettes: *Meet Me in St. Louis, Panic on Wall Street, San Francisco Fire.*

Meet Me in St. Louis
(1962; 2 min.; black and white)*
A bit of the flavor of the Louisiana Purchase Centennial Exposition of 1904.

Panic on Wall Street
(1962; 5 min.; black and white)*
The 1907 financial crisis that featured Teddy Roosevelt and J. P. Morgan as key players.

San Francisco Fire
(1962; 4:16 min.; black and white)*
An evocation of the 1906 San Francisco earthquake and fire.

The House of Science
(1962; 13 min.; color)
A six-screen presentation articulating a vision of the history of science as a human creative endeavor. Made for the 1962 Seattle World's Fair.

IBM Fair Presentation #1
(1962; 4:54 min.; color)*
A model in film form of the Eames Office proposal for IBM's pavilion at the New York World's Fair.

IBM Fair Presentation #2
(1963; 4:28 min.; color)*
A second model in film form of the Eames Office proposal for IBM's pavilion at the New York World's Fair.

The House of Science
(1964; 13:53 min.; color)*
A single-strand film version of the Seattle World's Fair presentation (see *The House of Science*, 1962), which articulated a vision of the history of science as a human creative endeavor. Though it was made to be projected on only one screen, up to six images are visible at one time, giving the flavor of the Eameses' multiscreen presentations.

Think
(1964; approx. 30 min.; color)
This twenty-two-screen presentation conveyed a sense that problem solving on a big scale is fundamentally similar to the approach used by the rest of us for everyday problems.

Truck Test
(ca. 1964; 2:50 min.; black and white)
A test of the technical notion behind *Powers of Ten* (first version, 1968; second version, 1977). Silent.

IBM at the Fair
(1965; 7:30 min.; color)*
Intended as a cinematic souvenir of the IBM pavilion at the New York World's Fair, this film uses time-lapse photography to convey the feeling of the pavilion being used by throngs of visitors.

IBM Puppet Shows (alternate title)
(1965)
The Eames Office made films of two of the mechanical puppet shows for the IBM pavilion at the New York World's Fair in 1964: *Computer Day at Midvale* and *Sherlock Holmes in the Singular Case of the Plural Green Mustache.*

Computer Day at Midvale
(1965; 4:17 min.; color)*
Addresses some commonly misused hyperbole concerning the computer.

Sherlock Holmes in the Singular Case of the Plural Green Mustache: Based on the Characters by Sir Arthur Conan Doyle in Which Sherlock Holmes Uses His Mastery of 2-Valued Logic to Solve a Baffling Problem
(1965; 4:21 min.; color)*
Sherlock Holmes uses Boolean logic to solve a case.

The Smithsonian Institution
(1965; 20:01 min.; black and white)
As close to a dramatic feature as the Eameses ever created, this film is a tribute commissioned for the two hundredth anniversary of the birth of James M. Smithsonian.

Westinghouse in Alphabetical Order
(1965; 12:10 min.; color)
A whimsical overview of the products of Westinghouse, arranged in alphabetical order.

Horizontes
(1966; 30 sec.; color)
Simply the titles for a series of films intended for Latin America. Silent.

The Leading Edge
(1966; 11:15 min.; color)
A film made for Boeing concerning the use of computers for systems management, including modeling and quality control, in the development of the supersonic transport and other projects.

View from the People Wall
(1966; 13 min.; color)*
Although it does not incorporate all twenty-two screens of the *Think* presentation, the nine screens included in this film convey much of the visual richness of the presentation, which aimed to help general audiences see that problem solving on a large scale (such as urban planning) is closely related to problem solving on a personal level.

IBM Museum
(1967; 10:05 min.; color)*
A proposal for a (never built) IBM museum of computers.

National Fisheries Center and Aquarium
(1967; 10:33 min.; color)*
A model in film form of the National Aquarium proposal the Eameses developed in the late 1960s.

Scheutz
(1967; 4:40 min.; color)*
A film produced for IBM that gives some of the feel of the Scheutz calculating engine, a mechanical antecedent of the electronic computer.

Babbage
(1968; 3:30 min.; color)*
About Charles Babbage's Difference Engine, another mechanical antecedent of the computer.

A Computer Glossary, Or Coming to Terms with the Data Processing Machine
(1968; 9:08 min.; color)*
A film made for IBM that uses an understanding of computer jargon in an effort to familiarize audiences not simply with the machine itself but with the concepts behind the computer as well.

The Lick Observatory, Mount Hamilton, California: A Brief Look at the Objects and People that Make Up Its Landscape
(1968; 8:24 min.; color)*
A film intended to give some of the feel of an astronomical observatory, particularly for those students who, given the nature of modern observational astronomy, may never have hands-on experience in one.

Rough Sketch of a Proposed Film Dealing with the Powers of Ten and the Relative Size of Things in the Universe
(1968; 8:01 min.; color)*
Starting at a picnic, the camera zooms to the edge of the universe; then the journey is reversed, ultimately reaching the nucleus of an atom. Literally a sketch and essentially black and white, this is the first full version of *Powers of Ten* (1977).

Image of the City
(1969; 15 min.; color)*
A record (of a sort) of the Eames exhibition *Photography and the City*, held at the Smithsonian Institution, but like all such endeavors of the office, the film represents a further refinement of the ideas in the show.

Mollusk
(1969; 2 min.; color)
Unfinished film about some of the denizens of the proposed National Fisheries Center and Aquarium. Silent.

Tops
(1969; 7:35 min.; color)*
Tops—many, many tops. In the words of a child who was asked to describe the story of the film, "Tops are born, they live, and then they die."

The Black Ships: The Story of Commodore Perry's Expedition to Japan Told with Japanese Pictures of the Time
(1970; 7:40 min.; color)*
When American Commodore Matthew Perry visited Japan in the 1850s, he and his crew were the first Westerners most Japanese had ever seen. These unfamiliar faces are depicted in Japanese prints of the time.

The Fiberglass Chairs: Something of How They Get the Way They Are
(1970; 8:39 min.; color)*
With a twelve-tone jazz score by Buddy Collette, this film looks at the design, production, and manufacture of the famous fiberglass chairs.

A Small Hydromedusan: Polyorchis Haplus
(1970; 2:50 min.; color)*
The movements of a tiny jellyfish.

Soft Pad
(1970; 4 min.; color)*
About the Soft Pad group of furniture; shot at the Eames House.

Clown Face
(1971; 16:27 min.; color)
A training film for Clown College of Ringling Brothers' Barnum and Bailey Circus.

Computer Landscape
(1971; 9:58 min.; color)*
A film created to give some of the feel of an industrial computer room to someone unfamiliar with such a place. Part of IBM's exhibition *A Computer Perspective*, complementing the historical artifacts.

Johnny Peer's Clown Face
(1971; 2 min.; color)
A brief excerpt from *Clown Face* that was used as part of the "symmetry" reel for Charles's lectures.

Alpha
(1972; 1:16 min.; color)*
About an important concept in algebra. The film could be viewed forward or backward.

Banana Leaf: Something about Transformations and Rediscovery
(1972; 1:29 min.; color)*
Once intended to be an *IBM Mathematica Peep Show*, this never-quite-completed film told the parable of the banana leaf, a lesson drawn from the Eameses' work in India.

Cable: The Immediate Future
(1972; 10:08 min.; color)
A film on the potential of
cable television.

Computer Perspective
(1972; 9:36 min.; color)*
A concise expression of IBM's
exhibition *A Computer Perspective*.

Design Q & A
(1972; 5:20 min.; color)*
One of the most condensed
statements about design ever
committed to film. Made as an
outgrowth of the Eames contribution
to the *Qu'est-ce que le <design>?*
(*What Is Design?*) exhibition at the
Louvre in Paris, it expresses quite
clearly the Eameses' notion of the
value of constraints.

Sumo Wrestler
(1972; 4 min.; color)
A spur-of-the-moment, unfinished
film capturing the ritual preparation
of the hair of a sumo wrestler
who happened to visit the
Eames Office. Silent.

SX-70
(1972; 10:47 min.; color)*
Presentation of the revolutionary
Polaroid Land camera and its
aesthetic potential that becomes
a meditation on the nature
of photography.

Copernicus
(1973; 9:30 min.; color)*
A film evoking the astronomer's
world and universe, made in honor of
the five hundredth anniversary of his
birth. Produced for the Smithsonian
Institution and sponsored by IBM.

Exponents: A Study in Generalization
(1973; 2:30 min.; color)*
About the concept of exponents.

*Franklin and Jefferson (Proposal Film):
Authors of Independence and
Architects of the American
Experiment*
(1973; 13:15 min.; color)*
With this film the Eameses
presented their proposal for
a Bicentennial exhibition.

*Two Laws of Algebra: Distribution and
Association*
(1973; 3:25 min.; color)*
The distributive and associative
theories are treated here.

Two Stones
(1973; 2:29 min.; color)
A video presentation of a puppet
show on Galilean physics.

Callot
(1974; 2:39 min.; color)*
The worlds within worlds of a tiny
commedia dell'arte engraving. This
film was shot in black and white but
printed onto color stock to give a
saturated look.

Kepler's Laws
(1974; 2:48 min.; color)*
Kepler's three laws of planetary
motion are presented here.
Made in connection with IBM's
exhibition *On the Shoulders
of Giants*.

Newton's Method of Fluxions
(1974; 3:25 min.; color)*
A brief vignette giving visual voice
to Newton's mathematic method for
calculus. Produced to accompany
IBM's exhibition on the scientist.

Metropolitan Overview
(1975; 9:21 min.; color)*
Presentation of a plan to introduce
visitors to and give them a cohesive
understanding of the Metropolitan
Museum of Art in New York City.

*Atlas: A Sketch of the Rise and Fall of
the Roman Empire*
(1976; 4:58 min.; color)*
To celebrate the two hundredth
anniversary of Edward Gibbon's
*The History of the Decline
and Fall of the Roman Empire*,
the Eames Office encapsulated
that history in a visually intuitive
way: a map of the empire
expands and contracts over
about a thousand years.

The Look of America, 1750–1800
(1976; 26:07 min.; color)*
An evocation of the life, style,
and feel of early America,
as seen through the prism of
extant buildings and artifacts
from colonial America.

Something about Photography
(1976; 8:32 min.; color)*
An essay featuring the Polaroid
SX-70 camera that gives voice to
the potentially rich and rewarding
aesthetic and philosophical role that
photography can have in one's life.

The World of Franklin and Jefferson
(1976; 28:20 min.; color)*
A synthesis of the themes
and qualities of the exhibition
The World of Franklin and Jefferson.
The show, organized for America's
Bicentennial, was probably the
largest individual project the Eames
Office worked on.

*The World of Franklin and Jefferson:
The Opening of an Exhibition*
(1976; 6:28 min.; color)*
A filmed record of the Paris
premiere, in January 1975, of the
exhibition *The World of Franklin and
Jefferson* gives some of the feel of
the installation.

Daumier: Paris and the Spectator
(1977; 18:52 min.; color)*
Based on a lecture on the graphic
work of Honoré Daumier.

Polavision
(1977; 10:30 min.; color)*
A presentation of the instant home movie system developed by Polaroid.

Powers of Ten: A Film Dealing with the Relative Size of Things in the Universe and the Effect of Adding Another Zero
(1977; 8:47 min.; color)*
Probably the best known of the Eameses' films, *Powers of Ten* refines and extends the journey of its 1968 predecessor by presenting it in color and in great scientific detail. Starting at a one-meter-square image of a picnic, the camera moves ten times farther away every ten seconds, reaching to the edge of the universe; then the journey is reversed, with the camera moving ten times closer each ten seconds, ultimately traveling to the interior of an atom.

Art Game
(1978; 12 min.; color)
A proposal for an interactive videodisc that the Eames Office created for IBM. This was a game centered on Impressionist and Post-Impressionist painters and their work. It was intended to have been integrated into a larger presentation.

Cézanne: The Late Work, with Quotations from His Letters and Reminiscences
(1978; 10:19 min.; color)
A record of an exhibition on Cézanne's late work, organized by The Museum of Modern Art, New York, and the Réunion des Musées Nationaux, Paris.

Degas in the Metropolitan
(1978; 10 min.; color)
Captures the Degas exhibition held at New York's Metropolitan Museum of Art.

Merlin and the Time Mobile
(1978; 3 min.; color)
A proposal for an interactive videodisc the Eames Office created for IBM, this film offers a glimpse of what would have been a time-travel game. It was intended to have been incorporated into a larger presentation.

Polavision Vignettes (alternate title)
(1978)
The Polavision system required that the user edit the two-and-one-half-minute-long film in the camera. The Eameses created six vignettes as examples of the rewards of working within these constraints: *Bicycles*, *Kites*, *Llisa Draws a Letter*, *Lucia Chase*, *Macbeth*, and *Masks*.

Bicycles
(1978; 2:33 min.; color)*
The glory of riding bicycles down by the beach.
Kites
(1978; 2:33 min.; color)*
The making of a kite.
Llisa Draws a Letter
(1978; 2:33 min.; color)*
Charles's granddaughter Llisa draws a letter at the Eames House.
Lucia Chase
(1978; 2:32 min.; color)*
Charles's granddaughter Lucia chases someone around the Eames house—a different visual take on the classic building.
Macbeth
(1978; 2:33 min.; color)*
A highly condensed version of Macbeth.
Masks
(1978; 2:33 min.; color)*
Play with masks.

Sonar One-Step
(1978; 8:12 min.; color)*
A presentation of Polaroid's automatic focusing SX-70 system.

A Report on the IBM Exhibition Center
(alternate title: *590 Report*)
(1979; 8:36 min.; color)*
Proposal for the use of the IBM exhibition space in New York.

Goods
(1981; 6:25 min.; color)*
An excerpt from the Charles Eliot Norton Lectures, which Charles delivered at Harvard University in 1970–71. Includes discussion of the "new covetables" and a look at one of the Eameses' famous three-screen slide shows. Made by Ray as a tribute to Charles after his death.

901: after 45 years of working
(1989; 28 min.; color)
Documents the Eames Office at 901 Washington Boulevard, Venice, California, using its closing as a prism through which to explore the Eameses' life and work. Filmed by Eames Demetrios. Distributed by Pyramid Media.

Powers of Ten™ Interactive
(1997; CD-ROM; 75 min. of video; 1,500 stills; 2,000 pages of text)
Uses the zoom from a picnic to the edge of the universe and back into a quark as the spine for an interactive essay on scale. Features six parallel journeys through space, time, the tools used to understand scale, people who have thought deeply about each power of ten, the Eames design process, and the patterns found at different levels of time and space. Written and designed by Eames Demetrios. Distributed by Pyramid Media.

SELECTED BIBLIOGRAPHY

Prepared by Phyllis Ross

Abercrombie, Stanley.
George Nelson: The Design of Modern Design. Cambridge, Mass.: The MIT Press, 1994.

Banham, Reyner.
Los Angeles: The Architecture of Four Ecologies. New York: Harper & Row, 1971.

Baroni, Daniele.
"La Forma e il suo doppio: L'Immagine—Charles Eames e la metodologia del progetto." *Ottagono*, June 1981: 78–85.

Blake, Peter.
No Place Like Utopia: Modern Architecture and the Company We Kept. New York: Knopf, 1993.

Canella, Guido.
"Struttura urbana e destrutturazione dell'architettura: La Competeneza del critico e quella del comune fruitore." *Zodiac*, Mar.–Aug. 1994: 4–11.

Caplan, Ralph.
By Design. New York: St. Martin's Press, 1982.

—. *The Design of Herman Miller: Pioneered by Eames, Girard, Nelson, Propst, Rohde*. New York: Whitney Library of Design, 1976.

—. "Experiencing Eames." *ID*, Jan.–Feb. 1990: 62–69.

—. "The Messages of Industry on the Screen." *Industrial Design*, Apr. 1960: 50–65.

Carpenter, Edward.
"Introduction: A Tribute to Charles Eames," in *Industrial Design 25th Annual Design Review*. New York: Whitney Library of Design, 1979.

Casciani, Stefano.
"Progettare il cinema." *Abitare*, May 1994: 235–41.

"Case Study House by Eames and Saarinen." *Arts & Architecture*, July 1950: 26–39.

"Case Study House for 1949 by Charles Eames." *Arts & Architecture*, Dec. 1949: 26–39.

"Case Study House for 1949 by Charles Eames." *Arts & Architecture*, Sept. 1949: 33.

"Case Study House for 1949: *the plan*." *Arts & Architecture*, May 1949: 38–39.

"Charles Eames, Creator in Plywood." *Interiors*, July 1946: 52–59.

"Charles Eames' Forward Looking Furniture." *Magazine of Art*, May 1946: 179–81.

"*Dallo studio di Eames*." *Domus*, May 1963: 26–40.

Danilov, Victor.
"Mathematica: Exhibition at the Museum of Science and Industry, Chicago." *Museum* (UNESCO), vol. 26, no. 2, 1974: 86–98.

De Pree, Hugh.
Business as Unusual. Zeeland, Mich.: Herman Miller, Inc., 1986.

"Design for Use." *Arts & Architecture*, Sept. 1944: 21–25, 38–40.

"A Designer's Home of His Own: Charles Eames Builds a House of Steel and Glass." *Life*, Sept. 11, 1950: 148–52.

Diehl, Digby.
"Charles Eames: Q & A," *Los Angeles Times WEST Magazine*, Oct. 8, 1972.

"Dormitory in a Nutshell: ECS." *Interiors*, Nov. 1961: 144–45,194.

Drexler, Arthur.
Charles Eames: Furniture from the Design Collection. New York: The Museum of Modern Art, 1973.

Eames, Charles.
"A Prediction: Less Self-Expression for the Designer." *Print*, Jan.–Feb. 1960: 77–79.

—. "City Hall." *Architectural Forum*, May 1943: 88–90.

—. "City Hall." *Arts & Architecture*, June 1943: 22–23.

—. "Design, Designer and Industry." *Magazine of Art*. Dec. 1951: 320–21.

—. "Design Today." *California Arts & Architecture*, Sept. 1941: 18–19.

—. "The Exploring Eye: Sun Mill." *Architectural Review*, Feb. 1959: 105–7.

—. "Language of Vision: The Nuts and Bolts." *Bulletin of the American Academy of Arts and Sciences*, Oct. 1974: 13–25.

—. "Organic Design." *California Arts & Architecture*, Dec. 1941: 16–17.

Eames, Charles, and Ray Eames.
"Eames Report" (also known as "India Report"). Los Angeles: Eames Office, 1958.

Eames, Charles, and John Entenza.
"Case Study Houses 8 and 9 by Charles Eames and Eero Saarinen, Architects." *Arts & Architecture*, Dec. 1945: 43–51.

—. "What Is a House?" *Arts & Architecture*, July 1944: 24–25, 32.

Eidelberg, Martin, ed.
Design 1935–1965: What Modern Was. New York: Abrams, 1991.

Friedman, Mildred, ed.
Nelson, Eames, Girard, Propst: The Design Process at Herman Miller, Design Quarterly 98/99. Minneapolis: Walker Art Center, 1975.

"Furniture Show Room by Charles Eames." *Arts & Architecture*, Oct. 1949: 26–29.

Gandy, Charles D., and Susan Zimmerman-Stidium. *Contemporary Classics: Furniture of the Masters*. New York: McGraw Hill, 1981.

Gingerich, Owen. "A Conversation with Charles Eames." *The American Scholar*, Summer 1977: 326–37.

Girard, A. H., and W. D. Laurie, Jr., eds. *For Modern Living*. Detroit: The Detroit Institute of Arts, 1949.

Goldstein, Barbara, Charles Lee, and Stephanos Polygoides. "The Eames House." *Arts & Architecture*, Feb. 1983: 20–25.

Greenberg, Cara. *Mid-Century Modern*. New York: Harmony Books, 1984.

Gueft, Olga. "The Castle Cabana of John Entenza, by Eames and Saarinen." *Interiors*, Dec. 1950: 92–99.

—. "Eames Chairs of Molded Metal Mesh." *Interiors*, Apr. 1952: 106–9.

—. "For Alcoa's Forecast Program Eames Creates a Sun Machine that Accomplishes: Nothing?" *Interiors*, Apr. 1958: 123, 182–83.

—. "Good Design Exhibit." *Interiors*, Mar. 1950: 85–97.

—. "Nehru and India: A Walk Through History." *Interiors*, Mar. 1965: 146–51.

—. "Steel on the Meadow." *Interiors*, Nov. 1950: 108–15.

—. "Three Chairs: Three Records of the Design Process." *Interiors*, Apr. 1958: 118–22.

Hamilton, Mina. "Films at the Fair II." *Industrial Design*, May 1964: 37–41.

Harris, Frank, and Weston Bonenberger, eds. *A Guide to Contemporary Architecture in Southern California*. Los Angeles: Watling & Company, 1951.

Harris, Neil, Robert J. Clark, David G. De Long, et al. *Design in America: The Cranbrook Vision, 1925–1950*. New York: Abrams in association with the Detroit Institute of Arts and The Metropolitan Museum of Art, 1987.

Herman Miller, Inc. *The Herman Miller Collection 1952: Furniture Designed by George Nelson and Charles Eames, with Occasional Pieces by Isamu Noguchi, Peter Hvidt, and O. M. Nielson* (with a new introduction by Ralph Caplan). New York: Acanthus Press, 1995.

Holroyd, Geoffrey. "Haus Eames." *Arch Plus*, Oct. 1989: 88–93.

"Il Teatro sospeso di Charles Eames." *Domus*, Mar. 1965: 25–27.

"Interior Design Data: Tandem Seating Evolution and Design, Charles Eames, Designer." *Progressive Architecture*, Nov. 1962: 140–44.

Jackson, Neil. "Metal Frame Houses of the Modern Movement in Los Angeles, Part 1." *Architectural History*, vol. 32, 1989: 152–72.

—. "Metal Frame Houses of the Modern Movement in Los Angeles, Part 2." *Architectural History*, vol. 33, 1990: 167–87.

—. "The Style that Nearly...." *Architectural Review*, vol. 193, June 1993: 68–73.

Jayakar, Pupul. "Charles Eames 1907–1978: A Personal Tribute." *Designfolio* (Ahmedabad), vol. 2, Jan. 1979: 1–6.

Johnson, Josephine. "Charles Eames." *Portfolio*, Spring 1950.

Kaufmann, Edgar, jr. "For Modern Living— An Exhibition." *Arts & Architecture*, Nov. 1949.

—. "Charles Eames and Chests." *ArtNews*, May 1950: 36–40.

—. *Prize Designs for Modern Furniture*. New York: The Museum of Modern Art, 1950.

Kenmochi, Isamu. "The Works of Charles and Ray Eames." *Graphic Design*, Oct. 1965: 39–46.

Kirkham, Pat. *Charles and Ray Eames: Designers of the Twentieth Century*. Cambridge, Mass.: The MIT Press, 1995.

—. "Introducing Ray Eames (1912–1988)." *Furniture History*, vol. 26, 1990: 132–41.

Lacy, Bill. "The Eames Legacy." *Los Angeles*, June 1989: 68–77.

"Life in a Chinese Kite: Standard Industrial Products Assembled in a Spacious Wonderland." *Architectural Forum*, Sept. 1950: 90–96.

McCoy, Esther. "An Affection for Objects." *Progressive Architecture*, Aug. 1973: 64–67.

—. *Case Study Houses 1945–1962*. Los Angeles: Hennessey & Ingalls, 1977.

—. "On Attaining a Certain Age: Eames House, Santa Monica, California." *Progressive Architecture*, Oct. 1977: 80–83.

McCullogh, Jane Fiske. "Some Thoughts about Eames." *Zodiac*, June 1961: 122–25.

McQuade, Walter. "Charles Eames Isn't Resting on His Chair." *Fortune*, Feb. 1975: 96–105, 144–45.

Miller, Judith Ransom. "Mathematica." *Industrial Design*, May 1961: 38–43.

Morrison, Philip, Phylis Morrison, and the Office of Charles and Ray Eames. *Powers of Ten: About the Relative Size of Things in the Universe*. Scientific American Library, vol. 1. San Francisco: W. H. Freeman and Company, 1982.

"*Negli aeroporti, il nuovo divano di Eames.*" *Domus*, Feb. 1963: 13–16.

Nelson, George.
Display. New York: Whitney Publications, 1953.

—. *Problems of Design*. New York: Whitney Publications, 1957.

Neuhart, John, and Marilyn Neuhart.
Connections: The Work of Charles and Ray Eames (essay by Ralph Caplan.) Los Angeles: UCLA Art Council, 1976.

—. *Eames House*. Berlin and London: Ernst & Sohn and Academy Editions, 1994.

Neuhart, John, Marilyn Neuhart, and Ray Eames. *Eames Design: The Work of the Office of Charles and Ray Eames*. New York: Abrams, 1989.

Noyes, Eliot.
"Charles Eames." *Arts & Architecture*, Sept. 1946: 26–44.

—. *Organic Design in Home Furnishings*. New York: The Museum of Modern Art, 1941.

"*Nuovo Eames.*" *Domus*, Jan. 1970: 25–27.

Office of Charles and Ray Eames.
Images of Early America. Zeeland, Mich.: Herman Miller, Inc., 1976.

—. *National Fisheries and Aquarium: A Report on the Program and Progress of the National Fisheries Center and Aquarium*. Washington, D.C.: The United States Department of the Interior, 1969.

—. *The World of Franklin and Jefferson*. Los Angeles: Eames Office, 1976.

—. Fleck, Glen, ed. *A Computer Perspective*. Cambridge, Mass.: Harvard University Press, 1973.

Ostergard, Derek E., ed.
Bentwood and Metal Furniture: 1850–1946. Seattle: University of Washington Press, 1987.

Phillips, Lisa, ed.
High Styles: Twentieth-Century American Design. New York: Summit Books and the Whitney Museum of American Art, 1985.

Pile, John F.
Modern Furniture. New York: John Wiley & Sons, Inc., 1979.

Roche, Kevin.
"Charles Eames." *Zodiac*, Mar.–Aug. 1994: 114–21.

Rubino, Luciano.
Ray & Charles Eames, il colletiro della fantasia. Rome: Edizioni Kappa, 1981.

Schrader, Paul.
"Poetry of Ideas: The Films of Charles Eames." *Film Quarterly*, Spring 1970: 2–19.

"A Science Film by Charles Eames." *Arts & Architecture*, July 1962: 22–23.

Scott, W., and C. Eames.
"A New Emergency Splint of Plyformed Wood." *U.S. Naval Bulletin*, Sept. 1943: 1423–28.

"Showroom: Los Angeles, California." *Progressive Architecture*, Aug. 1950: 47–50.

Smith, Elizabeth A.T., ed.
Blueprints for Modern Living: History and Legacy of the Case Study Houses. Cambridge, Mass.: The MIT Press, 1989.

Smithson, Peter, and Alison Smithson.
Architectural Design, special issue, "Eames Celebration," Sept. 1966: 432–71.

—. *Changing the Art of Inhabitation*. London: Artemis, 1994.

—. "Phenomenon in Parallel: Eames House, *Patio and Pavilion*." *Places*, vol. 7, Spring 1991: 19–23.

"Steel Shelf with a View." *Architectural Forum*, Sept. 1950: 97–99.

Steele, James.
Eames House: Charles and Ray Eames. London: Phaidon, 1994.

Talmey, Allene.
"Eames." *Vogue*, Aug. 15, 1959: 124–29, 144.

von Vegesack, Alexander, Peter Dunas, and Mathias Schwartz-Clauss, eds.
One Hundred Masterpieces from the Collection of the Vitra Design Museum. Weil am Rhein, Germany: Vitra Design Museum, 1996.

Wallance, Don.
Shaping America's Products. New York: Reinhold, 1956.

The Work of Charles and Ray Eames: Manuscript Division; Motion Picture, Broadcasting and Recorded Sound Division; and Prints and Photographs Division, Library of Congress, Washington, D.C.

Donald Albrecht is an architect, curator, and writer. He has organized exhibitions for the Getty Center in Los Angeles and Cooper-Hewitt, National Design Museum, Smithsonian Institution, in New York. He was a guest curator of the National Building Museum's exhibition "World War II and the American Dream: How Wartime Building Changed a Nation." He has written many articles and is the author of the book *Designing Dreams: Modern Architecture in the Movies*.

Beatriz Colomina is a professor or architecture at Princeton University. Her books include *Privacy and Publicity: Modern Architecture as Mass Media* and, as editor and contributing author, *Sexuality and Space*. She was a Samuel H. Kress Senior Fellow at the National Gallery of Art's center for Advanced Study in Visual Arts, Washington, D.C., in 1995–96.

Joseph Giovannini is an architectural designer, critic, and writer formerly with *The Los Angeles Herald Examiner* and *The New York Times*. He coauthored the book *Los Angeles at 25mph*, contributed an essay to the Walker Art Center's exhibition catalogue *Graphic Design in America*.

Alan Lightman is John E. Burchard Professor of science and writing and senior lecturer in physics at the Massachusetts Institute of Technology. His recent books include *Ancient Light: Our Changing View of the Universe*, *Einstein's Dreams*, *Good Benito*, and *Dance for Two*.

Hélène Lipstadt is a member of the faculty of the Institut de Recherche en Histoire de l'Architecture, Montreal. She has published and lectured widely on national competitions and on American postwar modernism.

Philip Morrison is a physicist, emeritus professor at the Massachusetts Institute of Technology, and the author of many books and articles. **Phylis Morrison** is a teacher and author. They collaborated with the Eameses on the film and book versions of *Powers of Ten* and wrote the book *The Ring of Truth*.

PHOTOGRAPH CREDITS

Every effort has been made to contact the copyright holders for the photographs in this book. Any omissions will be corrected in subsequent editions.

FROM THE EAMES OFFICE AND EAMES FAMILY

The following images were provided by the Eames Office and Eames family. Unless otherwise noted, each image is © 1997 Lucia Eames doing business as (dba) Eames Office. All frame enlargements are also copyrighted the date of the original film's creation. For further information, please contact Eames Office, Box 268, Venice, CA 90294.

23, 38–39, 105–7, 109–11 (images adapted from the poster "Powers of Ten," designed by and © 1997 Eames Office and commercially available), 118–25, 164–65, frame enlargements; 31, photographed by Tim Street-Porter; 48 (top 1, 2, 3), photographed by Eames Demetrios from the collection of Lucia Eames; 49 (top 5); 50 (1); 50 (2–3), from the collection of Eames Demetrios, photographed by and © 1997 Eames Demetrios; 64 (bottom) and 65; 112; 133; 134–35, photographed by Tim Street-Porter; 142 (top); 144 (bottom).

FROM THE LIBRARY OF CONGRESS, MANUSCRIPT DIVISION

The following material is part of the Library of Congress collection The Work of Charles and Ray Eames and is held in the Manuscript Division under the name The Papers of Charles and Ray Eames. Negative numbers of the Manuscript Division are listed. Intellectual property rights for most of the material in The Papers of Charles and Ray Eames is held and administered by Lucia Eames dba Eames Office. The images and content are used with the permission of Lucia Eames dba Eames Office as well as other copyright holders. The images may not be reproduced without permission from Lucia Eames dba Eames Office and other copyright holders. Unless otherwise noted, the images were photographed by Roger Foley.

27 (6), LC-MS-83006-27; 47, photographed by Jim Higgins, LC-MS-83006-28; 48 (bottom 1), LC-MS-83006-1; 48 (bottom 2), LC-MS-83006-1; 49 (bottom 4), LC-MS-83006-3; 57, LC-MS-83006-4; 100 (1), LC-MS-83006-5; 100 (4), with permission from Eaton, LC-MS-83006-6; 101 (1), LC-MS-83006-7; 101 (2), © Safeway International, LC-MS-83006-9; 101 (3), LC-MS-83006-8; 101 (4), LC-MS-83006-10; 101 (5), with permission and © Sackville Productions, Limited, LC-MS-83006-11; 102 (1), reprinted with permission, *T.V. Guide,* © 1965 News American Publications Inc., LC-MS-83006-12; 102 (2), LC-MS-83006-13; 102 (3), cover of Oct. 30, 1954, *Business Week,* reprinted by special permission, © 1954 McGraw Hill Company, LC-MS-83006-14; 103 (1), reprinted with permission, Heineken USA Incorporated, LC-MS-83006-15; 103 (2), cover of *Business Week*, Nov. 24, 1975, reprinted by special permission, © 1975 McGraw Hill Company, LC-MS-83006-16; 103 (3), courtesy *Vogue,* © The Condé Nast Publications, LC-MS-83006-17; 103 (4), reprinted with permission, Hughes Electronic Corporation, LC-MS-83006-18; 129 (top), courtesy *Architectural Design,* LC-MS-83006-19; 138, courtesy and © 1950 BPI Communications Inc., LC-MS-83006-20; 145 (top), LC-MS-83006-21; 145 (bottom), courtesy Arts & Architecture Press, Dec. 1945, LC-MS-83006-22; 146 (top), courtesy *Vogue,* ©The Condé Nast Publications; 152, LC-MS-83006-23; 153, LC-MS-83006-24; 155, © 1943 BPI Communications Inc., LC-MS-83006-25; 157, © 1943 BPI Communications Inc., LC-MS-83006-26; 171, Oversized #4 Publicity 1975, reproduced from *Poland,* Nov. 1975.

FROM THE LIBRARY OF CONGRESS, PRINTS AND PHOTOGRAPHS DIVISION

The following material is part of the Library of Congress collection The Work of Charles and Ray Eames and is held in the Prints and Photographs Division. Negative numbers of the Prints and Photographs Division are listed. Intellectual property rights for most of the material in the Prints and Photographs portion of The Work of Charles and Ray Eames is held and administered by Lucia Eames dba Eames Office. The images and content are used here with the permission of

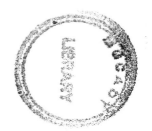